EDDIE JORDAN
The Biography

Timothy Collings

First published in Great Britain in 2002 by
Virgin Books
Thames Wharf Studios
Rainville Road
London W6 9HA

A catalogue record for the book is available from the British
Library.

ISBN 1 85227 968 0

Photographs © Empics
Typeset by TW Typesetting, Plymouth, Devon

Printed and bound in Great Britain by
Mackays of Chatham PLC

CONTENTS

ACKNOWLEDGEMENTS

As all those who know Eddie Jordan will confirm, there are a million stories that deserve to be published and a million that one dare not consider re-telling about this extraordinary human being. I am grateful, therefore, to a vast number of people for their generous cooperation, guidance, help and advice, or more, in the research, writing and editing of this book. It began with the working title 'Tripping the Light Fantastic' and that, I think, summed him up well. To translate the image of this man from a thousand and more memories into a cohesive account of his life has required patience and imagination and would not have been possible without the kindness of so many people and organisations. All of the following, in no particular order, have played a part, some by recalling hilarious anecdotes, some by giving telling insights or honest appraisals, others by sparing the time for interviews or by correcting the facts when the story began to wander away from the path of accuracy and truth or by supplying precious information that has not been available in the public domain: Eddie Jordan (courtesy, time and genuine help), Marie Jordan (generous time and great encouragement), Miki Jordan (insightful memories and kindness), Eileen Jordan (straight and colourful answers and an extraordinary sense of purpose), Des Large (memories), Ann Large, Martin McCarthy, Martin Donnelly, Johnny Herbert, Martin Brundle, Nigel Mansell, Jean Alesi, John Watson, Roberto Moreno, Michael Schumacher, Andrea de Cesaris, Bertrand Gachot, Dave Pennefather, Gary Anderson, John Walton, Trevor Foster, Mark Gallagher, Tim Edwards, Helen Temple, Paul Jordan, Ivan Capelli, Stefan Johansson, Mike Greasley, Sue Greasley, David Marren, Giselle Davies, Louise Goodman, David Kennedy, the staff of Jordan Grand Prix, the people of Dublin, Bernie Ecclestone, Alan Henry (books and articles everywhere), Gerry Donaldson (Grand Prix People), *Autosport* magazine (the weekly news pulse of the Formula One business), *Motor Sport*, *F1 Racing*, *F1 News*, *Formula 1* magazine, *Eurobusiness*, various websites including GrandPrix.com, AtlasF1.com, Reuters, the Press Association and others, Tom Walkinshaw, Jacques Deschenaux (Grand Prix Guide), the *Concise Oxford Dictionary* and many other newspapers and magazines as referred to in the text of the book,

Paul Stoddart, Bobby Rahal, Jonathan Legard, Stuart Sykes (keeping an eye on the text from Down Under), Bob Constanduros, Eric Silmermann, Herbie Blash, Alan Baldwin, Frank Burke and the staff at Synge Street C.B. School in Dublin, Maurice Hamilton (and his books *Against the Odds* and *Race Without End*), Eddie Irvine (and his book *Green Races Red*), David Tremayne (and his book *Jordan*), Pete McCarthy (*McCarthy's Bar*), Edna O'Brien (*Mother Ireland*), Michael Aspel (and *This is Your Life*), Anglia Television, my many colleagues and friends in the media corps, particularly the Irish boys, the *Spectator*, the cuttings library and staff at *The Irish Times* in Dublin, Jonathan Taylor at Virgin Books, for supporting the idea and for notable patience and Daniel Balado, for turning hurried and late copy into a readable yarn. Special thanks to the team at Collings Sport, including Will Gray, Gary Emmerson and Lorraine Varney, in particular. Very special thanks to the amazing Ian Phillips for being such a wise owl and for coping so kindly and serenely with my endless flow of inaccuracies for correction and also for supporting the idea and making things run smoothly. Finally, thanks to my wife Ruth and children Josh and Kitty for their tolerance in an A levels year at home. Some, I am sure, have been forgotten. To those, I apologise, while acknowledging also the work of the photographers who have recorded Eddie's life from Dublin to Silverstone and all posts between these last many years.

1. BARCELONA

His team had been created out of his own inspiration and energy. He had been born with more spirit and creativity than the average man and had refined this with the wit and wisdom of Dublin, distilled it with his experience of the banking and trading world and poured it all into a project seasoned observers predicted would be an abject failure. He had risked his life's rewards, a house and a business – all his money, all his material wealth – in order to create Jordan Grand Prix in 1991, and he had survived. One critic who predicted failure should have eaten his words, but being a Frenchman he may not have had the stomach for it without a trail of garlic sauce or olive oil. Jordan had gone on from there, had battled through debt and threats of winding-up orders, had seen his drivers sent to prison and whisked away by other teams, had survived scandalous allegations and frustrating years of mid-field muddle to claim a famous maiden victory and establish his team among the forerunners in a business that was, it seemed, bursting with money. As the 1990s drew to a close, Jordan and Formula One had seemed to be in good shape.

It was a warm spring morning on the Costa Brava. A slight breeze rustled the leaves and the sun rose gently in a clear blue sky. For anyone with a liking of the Mediterranean and its surrounding climes and countries, it was one of those days when life is worth living, but in the city of Barcelona, capital of Catalunya, there was an air of mild depression. FC Barcelona, arguably the world's biggest football club, had only the night before last been defeated in a Champions League semi-final first-leg match by their bitterest rivals, Real Madrid. The atmosphere of that white-hot contest and its aftermath was still reverberating through the bars, cafés and restaurants of the old city. On the Ramblas, under the shade of the trees, near the Plaza Real, scraps of torn posters, discarded flags and old newspapers shifted across the flagstones.

Down in the old harbour, away from the splendour of the new Olympic port, an impressive yacht called *The Snapper* was moored. It was waiting for important guests. The boat belonged to Eddie Jordan; it was home away from home for him whenever commitments allowed. In the previous week, his mother and his sister had been on board, enjoying the balmy sunshine. Now, after a stressful few days, Eddie was due to fly into Spain in readiness for the forthcoming Spanish Grand Prix, to be held high in the western hinterland of the sprawling city at the Circuit de Catalunya, a modern purpose-built 'facility' for motor racing, a place with all the soul of a grey breeze-block lavatory left behind by a retreating army.

Eddie was planning to entertain some friends, including the former French tennis player Henri Leconte, on the boat, he and his wife Marie hoping to find a few hours' relaxation and enjoyment during what promised to be a busy, tense and potentially difficult weekend. For months, Eddie had been fighting a rearguard action, warning many people that rising costs and falling revenues were threatening the fabric of the sport and putting into doubt the future not only of his own Formula One motor racing team, Jordan Grand Prix, but many others too. He had issued a notice on 23 April, just three days before the start of the Spanish Grand Prix meeting and only a few hours before Real Madrid dismantled Barcelona's defence, revealing that fifteen per cent of his team's workforce was being made redundant. This was as stressful for him as it was for those whose lives were being devastated by the news. Some of the staff being released were his friends, part of the 'family' he had built up in the eleven years since he had launched Jordan Grand Prix. It had been a tough decision.

The city around him, sobering up now after an excess of high expectations, at least offered warmth and an easy ambience. The tennis circus was in town, too, the Barcelona Open taking place that weekend alongside the Grand Prix as part of what should have been an exceptional sporting extravaganza for the Catalan people. Tuesday, after all, had been St Jordi's (St George's) Day, a public holiday designated in honour of the patron saint of Catalunya. The most high-profile motif of the fiesta was the many cartoons produced showing St Jordi spearing the Real Madrid dragon; in the Nou Camp stadium, however, it had not worked out that way. The dragon had won, and now, as his boat bobbed gently in the harbour and the sun rose again, Eddie Jordan was wondering just what lay ahead for him.

His team had been created out of his own inspiration and energy. He had been born with more spirit and creativity than the average man and had refined this with the wit and wisdom of Dublin, distilled it with his experience of the banking and trading world and poured it all into a project seasoned observers predicted would be an abject failure. He had risked his life's rewards, a house and a business – all his money, all his material wealth – in order to create Jordan Grand Prix in 1991, and he had survived. One critic who predicted failure should have eaten his words, but being a Frenchman he may not have had the stomach for it without a trail of garlic sauce or olive oil. Jordan had gone on from there, had battled through debt and threats of winding-up orders, had seen his drivers sent to prison and whisked away by other teams, had survived scandalous allegations and frustrating years of mid-field muddle to claim a famous maiden victory and establish his team among the forerunners in a business that was, it seemed, bursting with money. As the 1990s drew to a close, Jordan and Formula One had seemed to be in good shape.

But that was all before the first hints of recession in early 2001, when the dot.com bubble burst, when American industry began to disguise unpalatable results in accountants' reports, when life began to taste sour and the big automotive manufacturers moved in to Formula One sniffing a killing. And then – unexpectedly, shockingly, devastatingly – came 11 September and an act of terrorism that stunned the world. It was a warning to all that nothing could be taken for granted any more. The lives lost in the rubble of 'Ground Zero' were sacrificed for something, and everyone was beholden to find out what, and to react to it. The world needed to review many of its habits, not least the presumption in Formula One that more money would always come along next season.

The lessons to be learnt were not lost on Eddie Jordan. He talked frequently of the problems caused in Formula One by the richest teams spending more and more money on testing, research and development in order to gain milliseconds of advantage while their poorer rivals scratched around to stay solvent. Jordan wanted his team, one of the few not supported by a major manufacturer with a seemingly unrestricted budget, to have the ability to compete on the circuit and make a race of it at every Grand Prix, but there were no regulations to control the amount of testing, no rules to stop teams investing hundreds of millions of dollars in engineering and technology and blown engines in pursuit of more power, and no limits on a team's gross expenditure. It was an unregulated free-for-all, a business masquerading as a sport, and it had reached the stage where everyone knew that only an act of God or a miraculous climate change could prevent one of six cars, perhaps fewer, winning all the races. The rest were there to make up the numbers, literally.

As a free spirit, as a competitor, this was anathema to Jordan. But as a businessman, a man given the role of owner and custodian of his own team in which he had sold a significant shareholding to an investment company, he knew he had to consider security and viability above sport or competition. To safeguard his and the team's interests, therefore, it was necessary to abandon the idea of chasing victories or championships and to settle for a place among the also-rans with a hope, sometimes stimulated by conditions, that there would be days on which the outsiders could capitalise on circumstances and seize a glorious and unexpected victory for the small guys. All of this, and more, had worked away at the core of his mind for weeks and months. It meant tough decisions. It meant redundancies. It meant lost jobs and families hit by reduced levels of income. It meant the Jordan team had to give up thinking it belonged among the big boys and accept it was a small, aggressive, adventurous maverick. But this, he reasoned to himself, did not mean abandoning as well the image the team had built up as the most welcoming, amusing and engaging of them all, a family feel appreciated by everyone, a sense of fun that always attracted cameras and notebooks. No, Jordan would be returning to its roots, confirming its family origins. It was a reduction, not an end, and a reaffirmation of the original principles that had carried Jordan into Formula One in the first place in 1991.

The next day, Friday, 26 April 2002, was like nearly every other in the north-eastern corner of Spain in the months when summer is approaching. It was beautiful, the sun rising smoothly, the sky an azure screen untouched by clouds. It was a warm morning, too, not so warm as to be uncomfortable, but certainly no day to be squeezed among nearly a hundred perspiring reporters inside the hospitality area at the DHL Jordan Honda motor home. But there we were, enjoying the hospitality of the Irish boss and his team and being served a full English – perhaps one should say Irish – breakfast. We were also waiting expectantly for something else to follow the bacon and eggs, toast and tea.

As usual, Eddie Jordan did not let us down. It was, after all, a notable day in the paddock at the Circuit de Catalunya for the man who had built one of the most exciting and best-liked

Formula One outfits. It was the day Eddie, under fire from all sides for various reasons, explained why he had decided to cut the number of staff he employed, reduce the size and scale of his beloved eleven-year-old team and trim his lofty ambitions. It was the day, too, when he admitted he could not go on pretending his maverick outfit could challenge the established giants, backed by multinational manufacturers, and, as in his dreams, beat them, unless he was lucky or given similar financial backing. It was the day, for some, that a small part of the Jordan dream died. For others, it was the day the team returned to reality, cast aside the perceived glamour and glitz of Formula One and decided to revert to being a plain ordinary racing team. It was the day, too, when Eddie explained why he had decided to go back to work to keep alive an ambition for which he had sacrificed so much of his life in a chequered and extraordinary career that had seen him break the bones in his legs in racing accidents, lose close friends in others, take enormous risks and win the loyalty of people with more common sense than to allow themselves to fall in love with the sorcery of a honey-tongued Dubliner.

Jordan, after all, was known to be both the king of the deal and a rascal, a man as likely to talk about trading conkers during his schooldays as to squeeze an extra percentage out of a sponsor in the multi-million-pound business of Formula One. For years, Eddie had been the hot story in the sport as the last true privateer, the last independent entrant to have built and maintained his own team. He was respected for that, and loved, too, for his colourful and flamboyant style, his ability and willingness to take a risk. He had risen from nowhere, through racing, through driver management and through building his own team, to become a household brand name in Ireland and beyond. His name was enough to sell anything in yellow (because of the colour of the team's cars) in the late 1990s, when he hired the former world champion Damon Hill, put together a truly competitive budget with backing from the tobacco giant Benson and Hedges and won his first Grand Prix. His and his team's fans would have jumped ditches, climbed hedges and paid most of their salary to join him in his personal victorious heaven after that maiden victory at Spa Francorchamps in August 1998, when Hill led his Jordan team-mate Ralf

Schumacher across the line at the end of an unforgettably dramatic race.

But his luck had not stuck. After two more wins in 1999, it had ebbed away, and as money was gradually drained from Formula One, as the televisual strength of the sport was challenged by the dominance of football, and as the global economy began to shrink, he felt the pain in his pockets. He had sold, in 1998 to the investment house Warburg Pincus, a 45 per cent stake in his team, a substantial holding for a substantial amount of money (he was reported to have banked more than £40 million), and he came under fire from some for lining his own nest at the expense of his team. Performance on the track was of only secondary importance to his comforts away from it, said the critics. These were the typical conspiracy theories that burst into life from time to time in Formula One. Jordan, like all team owners, was vulnerable to them, whether they were true or false.

Eddie Jordan had, of course, been around the block. He was not a team owner with no idea of how life worked away from the paddock. He had traded on the streets of Dublin, he had sold carpet off-cuts in the market and smoked salmon of an indeterminate age to football and rugby supporters. He had worked behind the counter of the Bank of Ireland, and after work in the bank's car park he had sold second-hand cars to the customers he had talked to during the day. He had invested everything he had in his own racing career, his own management business and his team. He has spent hundreds of millions of pounds, most of it other people's money, but he has taken the responsibility. His team almost went under in 1991, his first year in Formula One, and suffered again in 1992 as it toiled to recover. He had to 'borrow' funds from Formula One supremo Bernie Ecclestone (by taking an advance on the following season's television fees). He paid it all back. He had been a winner and a loser, but all the way through he had been a racer, a man who added a frisson of real excitement and a sense of fun to the often dour business of motor racing.

'We've been through some horrific times, but we came through them,' he would reflect, when looking back on the early 1990s. His recovery and his sense of loyalty to his own men, his emotional responses to the way his team had grown up and shared everything, maintained the bond and the family feeling. But the sale of a shareholding that had appeared to make life easier for him had put pressure on his performance as the company's figurehead, and on the staff to deliver in the big league. Jordan had worried about that new era, when his team became a business that had an investor instead of one that was wholly owned by himself and Marie, his wife. But, as he admitted, Warburg Pincus had trusted him implicitly to get on with the running of the team, and he had quickly overcome those worries.

The problem, however, for Eddie Jordan was that trust and responsibility came with expectations and he had to deliver performances to match them. As it became more difficult, in 2000 and 2001, to rekindle the most magical moments, so also the world economy began to slide towards recession. And then came the day when the World Trade Center in New York was attacked by terrorists who had hijacked aeroplanes and flown them into the buildings. The impact was global, negative and frightening. Formula One, like the rest of the world, felt the reverberations. Prospective sponsors and investors turned away. The rate card for the business, the value of space on the cars in terms of sales for advertising or sponsorship purposes, began to fall. Income dropped. Costs, however, continued to rise, particularly if your team was attempting to compete with the likes of Ferrari, McLaren and Williams, each supported by a major automotive company (Fiat, Mercedes-Benz and BMW respectively).

Jordan rang the warning bell in late 2001. Others joined him. Teams grouped together in Formula One to call for cuts in running costs to enable the sport to flourish as an open competition again. Some team chiefs warned that they would be out of business by the end of the year unless something drastic were done. The days when Eddie Jordan had felt carefree, successful and lucky enough to bet £2,000 on his own driver, Heinz-Harald Frentzen, at 14–1, to beat Mika Hakkinen and win the Italian Grand Prix, as he did in 1999 at Monza to collect a tidy £28,000 in winnings, seemed long gone. So, too, did the days when he felt free enough to buy shares in Glasgow Celtic Football Club, or to make more appearances on television (as it seemed) than in his office. The relaxed feeling of the good days was long gone, as if it had ever been anything other than a passing mirage. Eddie, everyone knew, had his comfortable, sprawling family home in Oxford, his flat in London and his holiday place in Spain where he also kept his one real luxury, his Sunseeker Manhattan yacht.

In 1999, he had said he had big plans to develop the Jordan marque. 'I want to enlarge Jordan as a brand, and the deal with Warburg has allowed that to happen,' he said. 'Now we can get on with new ideas. Maybe we can create another company. We can add value to the brand. There's a real opportunity for major growth into different markets. I don't want it to be like Ferrari. I want to take Jordan out of racing, or at least not to be restricted by it. Designer companies, yes, clothing, eyewear, finding the new niche. The brand is strong already, and at a couple of races this year our merchandising outsold Ferrari. That is something. Jordan also has a young following. I think young motor racing fans were looking for something different, and Jordan fills that need.'

To those who knew Eddie Jordan, it was heart-warming to see such an honest, self-made success story. He had taken Ireland into Formula One and he had launched his own brand so well that he and it were now recognised all over the world. He had also proved himself adept at not only finding and making a deal, but also in identifying and developing future Formula One stars. He had introduced Jean Alesi, Michael Schumacher, Eddie Irvine and Rubens Barrichello to the sport long before he had seen his name climbing the *Sunday Times* Rich List. Yet he could recall the decade before when Marie, a fine sportswoman who had played basketball for Ireland, had been taking in lodgers to make ends meet for the Jordan family. He knew what that memory meant. He had been there and done it, and had worked hard to become independent and successful, a man of property, cars, boats and planes. So, that Friday morning, as the sun rose over the stretch of concrete and asphalt on which the Formula One teams park their motor homes, he knew what had to be said.

The DHL Jordan Honda motor home, according to long-held tradition, hosted the British media on the Friday morning of a Grand Prix meeting. Rarely did the routine suffer any interruptions, as Eddie Jordan moved sometimes serenely, normally noisily, among the reporters, catching up with the gossip and dishing out, in his own inimitable way, a few choice pearls of advice. Like most Irishmen, he knew how to talk, how to make his point and how to win an argument. Laughter was the currency, sport the language. The food and drink were there to oil the works and keep both sides happy. It was different, however, this time. In the hours before opening practice began at the Circuit de Catalunya, the dining area was packed. Every seat was taken, every vantage point used. It was standing room only. And the journalists had brought with them their notebooks, tape recorders, cameras and film crews. This was going to be a working breakfast, not an off-the-record briefing or an hour of fun.

Jordan, breaking with his regular habit, did not circulate, but instead answered questions from a standing position and explained why his team had had to make serious staff cuts that week and why Formula One, as a whole, had to face some unpleasant truths. Holding court, Jordan twitched with nervous energy as he talked. He often began sentences that had no clear final destination. He gave answers to questions that missed the point. But throughout this impassioned plea for greater understanding and more help in preserving not only his racing team but also the series in which he raced he was thoroughly genuine. His team, he said, did not carry debt, nor did it wish to do so. It was, he said, a result of enforced discipline, necessary because Jordan Grand Prix is, essentially, an entrepreneurial outfit, a team that lives from year to year on its ability, its performance and its promises to deliver. It was also a result of his own experiences in building Jordan Grand Prix from modest beginnings as a Formula Three outfit operating out of a small building at Silverstone into one of the world's most famous Formula One teams.

This time, it was timely, important and worthwhile to listen to the man with more words than most discussing his favourite subjects – money and the business of Formula One motor racing. In essence, of course, Eddie wanted to make certain that his message was conveyed, that his team was prudently managed and that the future, with Honda as partners, remained secure (in fact, he was to switch from Honda to Ford, a move welcomed by his workforce, by late summer). In all of that, he succeeded, but not without reservations appearing among some of his most cynical listeners, men who believed every bus in the world was there to run them over. He did not want people to think he was in trouble, acting in panic, or running scared. So, as the temperature rose, as the heaving mass breathed in slowly and nodded in agreement with his points, he talked on.

He said that staff cuts of fifteen per cent of the workforce, or 45 people, executed partly in November 2001, in a first phase, and then completed in April 2002, had been effected to reduce the costs for 2003, not 2002. In real terms, this meant even deeper cost cuts, since many of the engineers leaving would, had they stayed, have triggered further costs in research and development – perhaps, some said, as much as three times their cost in salaries. He explained his reasoning and he explained his feelings. For the record, too, it was stated that Jordan was in the middle year of a three-year contract with Honda, and that stories suggesting that the Japanese manufacturers were contemplating anything other than remaining fully committed to the partnership were so wide of the mark they were off the Jordan radar. One team source suggested that the Jordan budget for 2002 was the equal of any it had had in the past, confirmation indeed that the team was executing sensible plans for the future rather than panic measures to hide a current problem. As Jordan talked, making the most of the loyalty felt among the media for his friendly and open team, there was a sea of nodding heads, scribbling hands and wide-eyed concern.

Jordan talked of money and he talked of power. It was clear, from what he said, that both the BAR and Jordan camps felt that the power delivered by the Honda engines was not enough. Things had to change. Performance is all in F1. It dictates the results, the amount of media coverage, the value of the marketing tool the sport has become, the size of the sponsors' cheques and the ease with which they are secured. All of this was in the minds of those who listened as Jordan's lilting words washed over the crowd in the motor home. It was a morning for headlines. This was a big story, and everyone knew it as they sat and listened. Few team owners, if any, in Formula One routinely invited the media to breakfast, but none supplied breakfast and a big story on the same morning.

But all of this was, perhaps, a little much for breakfast. In Barcelona, after all, the hours are Catalan (some may say Spanish, but the locals would not agree). This meant late nights, dinners ending after midnight, bleary eyes in the morning and a more compliant and stodgy group of reporters assembled in the paddock when required for action. And, in the early-summer heat that brought temperatures of up to 30°C to Barcelona, few media men or women were running around for exercise.

EJ was sharp, however. The sound-bites were irresistible, the message consistent and dramatic. Admitting that the recession worldwide had cut into his and other teams' ability to compete with the increasingly heavily backed outfits at the front of the grid, he said, 'I will demonstrate a fighting spirit by the end of the year to prove Jordan is back with a purpose for sustained success.' He made it clear, too, that he would never, if at all possible, 'want to sell out to a manufacturer'. 'Everyone tells me that they [Honda] want to do a runner, but if they feel they want to do that, I don't know that,' he assured us. 'They have another year to run in 2003. We are planning ahead. I believe that what has been done [the redundancies] will ensure Jordan breaks even this year. You cannot continue to make losses.' The departures included such men as long-time friend, loyal servant and joint managing director Trevor Foster, the respected engineers Tim Holloway and David Brown, and John Putt, the chief operating officer. 'It has been difficult for me. These are people who we love, who we still love. They have been part of the family.'

As he talked, sharing his feelings as openly as ever, it was clear that Jordan had had to dig deep to effect his cost-cutting plan. He was wary, however, of allowing talk of any kind of crisis in Formula One. 'This sport, F1, is the envy of the world and we should not talk it down,' he said. 'But we have a blip. A big blip. And we have to make sure it is around in the future . . . At the moment, what we are doing is washing money down the toilet, for no reason.' He said he wanted to see major cuts, planned properly and introduced in a programme of changes designed to show that the business side of the sport is under control. 'I consider myself to be a proven businessman,' he said. 'I believe in making a profit. I want to stay in business as an entrepreneur. I will stay in business.'

It was richly ironic that, for the first time in this particular year at a Grand Prix, the most significant visitor to the paddock was a Frenchman. Not Henri Leconte, the famous tennis player with a taste for champagne, now part of the seniors' tour, who was staying with the Jordan family on their boat in the old harbour. No, the significant man was Alain Prost. The four-times champion, once so famous and recognisable that he could barely walk unmolested around a Formula One paddock, quietly slipped into the circuit and took up a guest's position with Ferrari. The diminutive former driver, of course, was at the head of the Prost Grand Prix team that had collapsed earlier in the year, an experience for which he had been vilified in France and humiliated across the world. How ironic, then, that Jordan, unaware of Prost's appearance in the paddock, said, 'It's a big sorrow for me that Alain Prost is not here . . . I don't want to follow him down that path . . . but we are not in that position. I want to make sure that we break even this year and have an even better chance in the future. I felt the team was going away from me. The only thing I could do was grab it by the throat and say, "I'm not going to put up with this."'

It was strong, emotive and rhetorical stuff. This was a man with a passion talking about his team. His words threw up questions about Formula One, and about Jordan. Is this a sport about passion, or a business about pragmatism? Is it only for a defined elite of well-heeled, fabulously wealthy men backed by limitless supplies of supporting finance from car manufacturers?

'We tried too much, we tried to build and grow the business in the way that others have done it,' Eddie admitted. 'In the last few years, we thought we were in the top three and belonged there and needed to have the kind of resources and staffing levels McLaren have got. But we are not a corporation, are we? Jordan is a family outfit, a racing team. We are one of the old independents. And I worry for the future of the independents, the privateers, and the colour and the future of the sport.'

More irony, of course, materialised that Sunday, when the three big teams filled the podium yet again, privateer teams, using customer engines, following them home. Some, too, the day before when Jean Alesi, a former Jordan driver who had retired the previous year, was seen in the paddock. And then on the Monday evening, back in Britain, another dose as the motor racing world learnt of the sad death at the age of 84 of one of the greatest privateer entrants of them all in the golden era, Rob Walker, just eight months after Ken Tyrrell, another entrepreneurial team owner held in high regard across the F1 community, passed away.

The sport-business about which Jordan was talking in emotive, anguished terms was one Walker, and to a lesser extent Tyrrell, would hardly have recognised. 'They want to own a significant percentage of the company that controls F1's commercial rights,' Jordan explained when asked about the car manufacturers' ambitions, 'and they have threatened to set up a breakaway championship in 2008 if they do not get it. But I have a fear of a fully manufacturer-backed championship. I have never seen a manufacturer-backed championship that is really successful in the long term. They come in for three or four years and then go out again. For them to get the most out of it, that is the right thing for them. But we have to make sure both can co-exist without one being pushed over the precipice into insolvency. We entrepreneur teams have had a good time for a long time. It is difficult to beat the manufacturers, but we privateer teams have been the most successful in the fifty years of F1.'

Jordan had struggled in the early days of the 2002 season, and their troubles continued in Barcelona when both cars were reloaded on the transporters before the race was run, both having had to retire in the opening dozen laps. Jordan's team sat at the foot of the championship without a point, and with only one other pointless team above them – BAR, similarly powered by Honda. Yet only three years earlier, in 1999, Jordan had been challenging for the championship, his German driver Heinz-Harald Frentzen leading the way. Frentzen, a proven race winner, was sacked, unceremoniously, by Jordan in mid-2001. It was one of that summer's most controversial moves.

The 'necessary cuts' in the week before the Spanish race were painful; the blood-letting was also a concession by Eddie Jordan and his team that they had gone down the wrong road. Jordan had started to copy the big boys, he had brought in 'star' engineers and designers, imported big names, built up the workforce, and the team had lost its original identity. It is said that Honda offered to buy Jordan out in April 1998, but Jordan refused. In Spain, he showed no signs of regretting that decision. He remained defiant. An Irishman fighting for his principles, a man hurt by an honest realisation that he had taken his eye off his business.

'I believe what has been done will ensure Jordan will break even this year,' he said. 'You cannot continue to make losses in this business. We need to be leaner and sharper. We will maintain a workforce of just over 200 in a revised structure to return Jordan to a more flexible, open style of organisation. That is Jordan returning to its roots. Jordan has always been at its best when lean and efficient. Once you sense complacency creeping in, or costs become exorbitant, a prudent business needs to take action. These are the changes that will generate a more efficient structure at a time when our focus is on the performance and reliability of our cars, and that is what is most important.

'And to suggest,' he emphasised, 'that Honda is part of my thinking behind all of this is completely wrong. I did not once, never once, consider Honda in this whole thing. This is about Jordan Grand Prix. The team. Jordan is not under pressure, or on any beauty parade . . .' This last colourful remark was a reference to suggestions that Honda might eschew his team in favour of joining up with BAR if they selected to race with only one team in future instead of sharing their energy between two. It was obvious that Eddie meant it. When Giancarlo Fisichella, his lead driver, came to the circuit, he knew nothing of the eruption and had not been briefed in advance. The Jordan explosion was just that, a genuine move by a team owner to ward off a problem and secure his and his team's future. 'We have to make changes, Jordan has to make changes. I am sure as hell going to make sure we survive. We had less than a third of the people that we have now and we won three races with them. What does that mean? It means we've got to change and adapt and get on with it. Now we've got to start again. We need to go out and win some points.'

On that Friday morning in Barcelona, over a full British breakfast, EJ confirmed he was back in control, hands on, busy and loud. 'Beware' was the message broadcast to his rivals and any circling jackals. The team that invented the 'lean, mean and green machine' had announced it was on the way back with some menace. The race result that weekend in Barcelona had to be ignored. It was the last of the old days. Of course, as Jordan said, it would take time to cure the problems. It would take time for the new structure to replace the old, for the slower reaction time inherent in departmental teams to be overtaken by the more direct and fast approach. And mistakes should be expected. But with Gary Anderson, the Ulsterman who had been part of the Jordan scene at the start, back in the heart of the garage and running things, EJ himself cajoling everyone within earshot and chasing sponsors around the globe, and a team that believed in the future ready to race hard and live for the moment, the old Jordan was brought back to life.

The Barcelona presentation was pure Jordan. The theatre was unforgettable, the sincerity disarming. The whole operation swept the audience along like a small boat crossing the Liffey in Dublin on a stormy tidal day, or a man in an Irish pub falling into beguiled love with the atmosphere of his hostelry and the city. It was a typical Jordan move, a public relations coup par excellence. He turned a redundancy announcement into a heroic statement of intent and laced it with a warning to the sport that financial difficulties lay ahead for everyone unless the changes he advocated were adopted. Bold, outspoken, lyrical and sensible, Jordan grabbed the attention of his sweaty audience and the public. His speech meant more to most than anything else that day. It was Jordan bravado at its best, achieving its aims in a way that had always been his and that had ensured an Irish imprint across Formula One for a decade. The headlines that followed made him one of the pit-lane heroes again. A man who had rediscovered his roots in a business notorious for burning money had answered the clarion call of common sense. His experiences in banking, in building his own business and in making a fortune were back in use.

'It has been a difficult start to the season for us,' he had concluded, 'but we are now regrouping for an even more vigorous assault on the remaining 13 Grands Prix. I would like to thank all our personnel for their hard work and continued commitment.' Eddie had considered his own position, he had weighed up all his options, he had revealed a little defeatism briefly to Marie, but he had come back all guns blazing to try to survive and triumph again. He had too much to lose and everything to gain, as always, in dancing in the moonlight and swinging to the beat. And he knew, deep down, that he was too young to give up strutting his stuff just yet. The fighting Irishman was ready for another bout.

But, as Eddie returned to Barcelona that evening to relax for five minutes, host a drinks party with team personnel and sponsors and then a dinner party, he had no idea what it would lead to – an upturn in his team's fortunes or a controversial battle for future control of the sport? Still, for that weekend at least widespread coverage was guaranteed, ensuring that the Jordan name was back, if only briefly, among the big boys. And that, in essence, is all the man himself ever wanted from the start, when he began dreaming of his own team, of his future in sport and of his life beyond the watery fringes of Ireland.

2. DUBLIN

A minute in Eddie Jordan's company and it is easy to understand his heritage of wit, his Irishness, his Dublin roots. It is where he is from, all right. The noise and energy he produces make amplifiers redundant; his positive exuberance and optimism can light up a gloomy room in a dark field miles from nowhere with no call for electricity. He has always been like this, and this field of personal energy comes from his birth, his source, his mother, his Ireland, his Dublin, his joy of life and his confidence to go out and scoop it up in his arms and dance with it every day. His joy and his rhythm are derived from being in tune with life around him and the music in his head. Even at the worst of times, Jordan can raise a smile. Even at the best of times, he can share a self-deprecatory joke with anyone and bring the most pompous occasion down to earth. His richest and most important Formula One sponsors have suffered this indignity. He is the Dubliner, after all, who knows the musicians, who plays the drums and exudes the sounds of his birthplace and his childhood and his schooldays.

'Countries are either mothers or fathers, and engender the emotional bristle secretly reserved for either sire,' wrote Edna O'Brien in her superb memoir *Mother Ireland*. 'Ireland has always been a woman, a womb, a cave, a cow, a Rosaleen, a sow, a bride, a harlot, and, of course, the gaunt Hag of Beare.' Her words stir feelings for Ireland that help explain the background that created Eddie Jordan, a man who loves his country and her women – his mother, his wife and his daughters.

Dublin is the capital of Ireland. In any season, it is a city of magic and music, literature and love, a place of passionate life and poetry and mysticism. It has energy and invention, imagination and humour. It is a city of writers such as Jonathan Swift, Oscar Wilde, W.B. Yeats, George Bernard Shaw, Samuel Beckett, Oliver St John Gogarty, Liam O'Flaherty, J.P. Donleavy, Roddy Doyle, Molly Keane, O'Brien, Clare Boylan, Maeve Binchy, Brendan Behan, Patrick Kavanagh, Bram Stoker and, above all, James Joyce, whose *Ulysses* and *Finnegan's Wake*, fired by brilliant imagination and stream-of-consciousness narrative, were books that carried the English language into new intellectual territories. Statues of Joyce, these other dazzling artists and more are all around the city, lending to Dublin the grace and air of a place where words are highly valued, more so than anywhere else. *Ulysses* follows Joyce's characters around Dublin for a single day – 16 June 1904, the day Joyce met Nora Barnacle – and it ends with one of the most famous chapters in the history of literature, a discourse by Molly Bloom expressed in eight vast and unpunctuated paragraphs. Much of it was originally considered to be pornographic. The book was for a long time banned, and was not published in Britain until 1937 by which time the tradition of great Irish writers and artists of passion was so strong it was an irresistible part of British and European life.

To visit Dublin is to visit the birthplace of Joyce, Yeats, Shaw, Donleavy, Wilde, Swift – and Eddie Jordan. EJ, of course, would not call himself a writer, but he is a lover of words and music and he is a real Dubliner, a graduate of the university of life and a man who enjoys a chat, a joke and a smile as much as anyone bred on the banks of the Liffey. Born on 30 March 1948 at the Wentworth Nursing Home, Edmund Patrick Jordan belonged to the city and to its heart, and he has taken it with him as his inspiration to the world beyond the Irish Sea. The district of his birth is known as Ranelagh and is within reach of Rathmines, the Leinster Cricket Club and Synge Street, where he later went to school, but more significantly where Shaw was born. The house of Shaw's birth still stands, in exhibition, re-decorated to 1838 fashions of décor. To the east, in the southern part of this great entertaining city of pubs, bars, eating houses, dance halls and entertainments, lies Balls-bridge (once a centre for calico printing), Dodder Bridge (where EJ bought a small house after leaving home in his twenties) and Lansdowne Road (the venue for Ireland's rugby union internationals where Eddie sold smoked salmon on the pavements to inebriated supporters). Further south lie the Wicklow Mountains, Blackrock, Dalkey, Killiney, Enniskerry and Bray, where Eddie spent much time as a child with the relatives and family relations of his father Patrick, an accountant with the local electricity board, his mother Eileen and his older sister Helen. Bray was away from the bustle of the city, away down to the coast.

As a child, growing up at the first family home in Beechwood Avenue, Eddie was a sickly boy. He took his time in growing to full strength and learnt to make do using means other than physical. He was determined and resourceful, he loved dancing and girls, and he exhibited all these qualities frequently. But the Ireland and the Dublin he grew up in then was not the place that sits there today enjoying the relative prosperity introduced by European grants, the euro and the trading that has come with the nation's decision to open its doors to the world beyond the British.

Where now there are salons dedicated to cappuccino there once were glorious celebrations of Guinness, the black beer that has been as emblematic of Ireland as the harp.

Ireland, as O'Brien and many others have said, has always been 'Godridden', as filled with religion as it is with magic and wizardry, influenced by the Druids as much as by the music and mirth that fills the pubs and dance halls of the city of Molly Malone. 'You are Irish,' wrote O'Brien, again, 'you say lightly, and allocated to you are the tendencies to be wild, wanton, drunk, superstitious, unreliable, backward, toadying and prone to fits, whereas you know that in fact a whole entourage of ghosts resides in you, ghosts with whom the inner rapport is as frequent, as perplexing, as defiant as with any of the living. To meet one's kinsmen is to unleash a whole sea of unexpected emotionalism.' All this borrowing of words from others is to help stir up a feeling for the Ireland in which Eddie Jordan was born and grew up. It was an island of imagination that encouraged dreams of escape, or rebirths as O'Brien described them, but it was a place, too, that always brought people home, lost Irishmen looking for their source, third- and fourth-generation descendants or long-ago-gone-away Americans returning to find their forebears. Ireland, in short, was and is no ordinary place filled with pragmatic or gloomy people, but a party-loving land of magic and hangovers and wistfulness and wonderful dreams and ambitions.

Pete McCarthy, whose best-selling book *McCarthy's Bar* concerns itself with 'a journey of discovery in Ireland', writes of childhood and agricultural smells, the rural bliss of natural dairy products, potatoes, plain living, raspberry-jam sandwiches made with sliced white bread, home entertainments, beer and pies, tea and scones, hard outdoor physical work, drinking and partying and enjoyment and reeling in the 'craic' and old-fashioned courtship and God-fearing religion and love and metal baths. It is an Ireland of another time and age, but it is an Ireland closer to the place where Jordan grew up. In his sickly childhood (a description offered by his mother that, according to his unreliable memory, is not too accurate) there were no televisions and no computers, no electronic games and no late-night shops, but there were people and families and girls with lovely dancing Irish eyes, and there was always warmth and humour and love and togetherness. And the humour was often a touch bawdy or saucy. In *Mother Ireland*, O'Brien recalls that 'Urine stories were sauciest, especially the one about the parish priest who, suspecting that his housekeeper was helping herself to his sherry, decided to dilute it with urine, and after weeks of this and still the level in the decanter flagrantly going down, he tackled her about it and she said, "Oh, Father, I put a drop in your soup every day."'

A minute in Eddie Jordan's company and it is easy to understand his heritage of wit, his Irishness, his Dublin roots. It is where he is from, all right. The noise and energy he produces make amplifiers redundant; his positive exuberance and optimism can light up a gloomy room in a dark field miles from nowhere with no call for electricity. He has always been like this, and this field of personal energy comes from his birth, his source, his mother, his Ireland, his Dublin, his joy of life and his confidence to go out and scoop it up in his arms and dance with it every day. His joy and his rhythm are derived from being in tune with life around him and the music in his head. Even at the worst of times, Jordan can raise a smile. Even at the best of times, he can share a self-deprecatory joke with anyone and bring the most pompous occasion down to earth. His richest and most important Formula One sponsors have suffered this indignity. He is the Dubliner, after all, who knows the musicians, who plays the drums and exudes the sounds of his birthplace and his childhood and his schooldays.

He has also the determination of a human being that began its fight for survival when it was only a tiny child. 'Well, he was a very ill baby, to be sure,' confirmed his mother Eileen, a formidable woman in anyone's estimation, a woman who at 85 years old is still playing golf once a week, driving herself to the club, enjoying a round, taking a glass of wine for good health and then driving home without anyone's help. 'He was only a few years old and he was back to the weight he was born at, so I mean he had a very poor beginning. It was a big worry. He had a disease called Pink's Disease which meant that his liver was not functioning properly, and that took a long time to get working. But, other than that, he grew on. At five years of age, he had pulled up out of the disease, he started school and he did rightly.'

It is hard to imagine that the strong, healthy, wealthy and happy man who owns the Jordan Grand Prix team in middle age had started life as a sickly child, nursed closely by his mother, watched over by his older sister and fretted about by his father. But it is true, and it is one of the reasons Eddie went to school at the local Milltown National School on the southern fringes of Dublin until he was eleven, when he was transferred to the famous Christian Brothers School (CBS) in Synge Street, Dublin. 'He went to the national school because it was near me,' said Eileen. 'But he was a determined little child. Always. In fact, too much so. He was fond of the girls and he was fond of dancing and very fond of music. A difficult handful, a difficult boy.' At school, she said, he was not an academic star; instead, he preferred to concentrate on other pursuits including sport, his social life and his budding career as a businessman. She laughed when talking of Eddie's schooldays. 'What was he like at school? Mediocre. Good enough. He was good at maths, wasn't good at English, quite good at Spanish, although he left it then and he wouldn't know two words of Spanish now. But he was quite good then. What else? Sport? Always, yes. He was always very competitive and he was very good at sport. He started doing golf and was very good at that. He liked to be in the teams. He was in the teams for football and for hurling and all that type of thing. He was quite good.'

It is little wonder that Eddie Jordan has the gift of the gab, a love of music, an enthusiasm for sport, a wheeler-dealer's brain and the loving loyalty of a typical Irish family man. His life has been one long nurturing session for such a scenario, punctuated by trips into magical experiences and some tough learning fields. The CBS is where he learnt to adapt and survive in life. At first, he thought he wanted to be a priest, then a dentist, then a banker or accountant. Finally, he became a racing driver and one of Ireland's greatest entrepreneurs. He found his escape and rebirth, but never lost his love of his roots.

The CBS is a high building surrounded by schoolyards in a cramped old residential area of Dublin, a good ten minutes' walk south from St Stephen's Green and beyond Camden Street, where Jordan was later to work in the Bank of Ireland. It is surrounded by busy streets crammed with shops, pubs, bistros, cafés, building works, roadworks, wind-blown crisp packets, boys, girls, cars and the eternal chaos of the city. On the day of my visit, the upstairs reception at the school was also busy. A boy arrived with a bleeding nose and waited in a queue along with others who were in need of a writing implement. They had neither a pen nor a pencil and needed one or the other. 'I've been robbed, Miss,' complained one pen-less pupil. 'I've no pen now.' 'Oh, now, you've never lost your pen, have you?' came the soothing reply as a second-hand Biro was handed over in trade for the blarney. So, I thought as I sat in that hard-benched reception area, so this is where it all began. The birthplace of the art of persuasion, the mother of invention and rogue grins and charm. The place might have been a little run-down, but it had a toughness that belied its interior of security, warmth and calmness. There were few signs, notices or plaques, and the modern uniform appeared to be trainers and ski-jackets, but there was a happy air around the place.

The school was founded in 1864 and, according to the prospectus, is a place of great tradition renowned for its academic, cultural and sporting excellence. 'Our school values its genuine Christian spirit which is manifested in the respect shown to each member of the school community, whether management, staff, teacher, pupil, parent or past pupil. This is reflected in our school structures which are based on democratic values.' The list of famous past pupils tells much about the qualities of the school. It features many politicians, journalists, sportsmen, actors and musicians, and reflects the richness of experience in Jordan's own life: former leader of the Fine Gael party and president Liam Cosgrave; former Minister for Finance Richie Ryan; former Fianna Fáil minister Dr Michael Woods; Sean Moore, a former Lord Mayor of Dublin; the great television broadcaster Eamon Andrews; Irish international footballer Don Givens; swimmers Liam Bolan, Brian Battielle and Mark Battielle; the athlete and actor Jim Norton; Donal Donnelly, an actor; Michael Donnelly, a Lord Mayor of Dublin; Fr Tom Burke, who started the Young Scientist of the Year scheme in 1963; Cornelius Ryan, who wrote *The Longest Day*; actors Milo O'Shea and Noel Purcell; singer John McNally; actor Owen Roe; and more in modern times. It was also a religious school, and it is no wonder that Jordan was touched by the idea that he might have a calling to work as a priest. 'The aim of the religious education given by the school is to develop the whole person and impart Catholic values which will be a foundation for a full and happy life,' the prospectus explained. 'Students are given the opportunity to deepen their faith and to respect the beliefs of those of different persuasions. A new oratory provides opportunities for class Masses and other liturgical exercises. The school welcomes and facilitates pupils of other faiths.'

There is no doubt that Eddie Jordan was a fully integrated member of this school, submerged in all its beliefs and values. The way in which he seems to have used those values in the institution of business practices within his team reflects the importance of his schooldays to him in every facet of his life. But he was not a model pupil. He was too independent for that. He had his own ideas, his own outlook, a feature developed in him during his childhood before he arrived at CBS. In his early years as a young scholar, he sat next to Frank Burke, who years later returned to CBS and remains as a teacher. 'I think we met for the first time in 1956,' Burke recalled. 'Together in school. We were in the same classes together in primary school and then for one year in secondary. We were split up then after the first year. I remember him coming to school and back on the train.' He also remembered Jordan as an unexceptional scholar, but as a boy with obvious social and sporting skills. 'Well, we were all kind of middle of the road. I was probably about division two and he was division three, if you think about four divisions. We probably didn't work hard enough because of our interest in sport. But Eddie always had entrepreneurial skills. Undoubtedly. He was always wheeling and dealing. He used to sell a comic to me, *Roy of the Rovers*; he would buy it and then sell it on again at half price, but he would have read it too. It wouldn't have surprised me if he had gone into marketing, put it that way. It was not unusual for me to see him going into the bank, and he was always a great sports aficionado.'

The teenaged Eddie Jordan developed a taste for both the good life and the good things in life. He liked to have his clothes prepared as fashionably as possible, and he maintained an image.

He also enjoyed going out, with girls and to big sports events. But Burke recalled only one social occasion when they were together. 'The only time Eddie and I socialised was when we went to the Theatre Royal one afternoon. We didn't really live in the same area. We saw a film followed by a show and that was the first time that I met his mother. She dropped him off outside. He was really a class-mate to me more than anything.

'His father worked for the ESB [Electricity Supply Board], as far as I can remember. And I think I heard something about him playing for Shamrock Rovers. I don't think he was in the first team, but his father was definitely interested in sport. He took Eddie along to watch the Gaelic football at Croke Park, and when he was involved at Shamrock Rovers he would of course have been into soccer. I am certain Eddie went out to sport regularly and I think that is one of the great common denominators he has with his wife Marie now.

'Our school was very famous for sport. I don't think it is as good now as it once was, but then a lot of academic standards are not as good now. But at the time when Eddie and I were at school there, it was always in the top ten in the country. We had all sorts there from ministers' sons to working-class children. The quality of the education was excellent and you just had to look at the roll of the past pupils to see it was absolutely top-class. We were all ambitious, and we had no fear or any trepidation about the bigger world. Eddie was involved in everything and anything that was going on. Somebody started a football team, I remember, that was all pretty cloak-and-dagger stuff, and I think Eddie was involved in that. We weren't allowed to enter the team under the school name. It was a league, and he would have chanced his arm. He would always come to the fore if anything was going on. But Eddie never drew any attention, or any notoriety, to himself. He was always well behaved. The discipline was very tough. Very tough. There was no quarter given. There would be at times about five or six hundred applications there for 150 places, and in one case there were seven hundred. So the school was creaming off the *crème de la crème* of the students so you just didn't draw any attention to yourself. Most of the students came from south of the Liffey, but they came from all quarters really, thanks to the railway line.'

Jordan's own recollections of his schooldays with the Christian Brothers are of strictly disciplined activities. He remembered his childhood in Dublin 6, a postal district on the fringes of the city where he, his sister and his parents lived in a comfortable semi-detached four-bedroom house at the end of a cul-de-sac, and his days down at Bray, twelve miles away on the coast, where his many relatives had homes and he passed many summer days. His was an orthodox middle-class childhood, once he had beaten the threat of Pink's Disease, but it was not a wealthy one. 'What she said ruled,' said Jordan, reflecting on his mother's role in his childhood. 'My father was on a salary, but they didn't go out a lot. I can remember my father and my mother going to a banquet or a posh dinner maybe only four or five times while I lived at home. Those things just didn't happen. We weren't poor, but we had to be very careful. Ireland was a relatively poor country when I was growing up, but somehow that helps to make you much closer as a family.'

He and his family did not have a television when he was growing up, and it is this that encouraged his intuitive musical ability, his individuality and character. Those that had the dreaded boxes through which America transmitted its advertising messages were the first to succumb to changes which have since swept around the world and turned the most individual of countries into popcorn colonies. Instead of television and affluence, the Jordan family was interested in Ireland and Irish things. Ireland was a land rich in culture and tradition with a strong emphasis placed on folklore, poetry and music, and all these things struck a chord with the young Jordan. Life centred around home, the local football team and the pub; without televisions and computers, each family made its own entertainment. 'Even when I was in my mid-teens, we still didn't have a television at home,' he said. 'I remember having to walk a mile or so down the road to a relative who had a television set to watch a European Cup final. It's important to remember that we had to amuse ourselves mostly in those days.

'My memory of Christmas Day was not the dinner. It was two things: the excitement over the presents and the fact that, after dinner, every single member of the family had to stand up and do their party piece. My mother would do an unbelievable jig with everyone clapping out the beat! And that's when I learnt to play the spoons. They were a very inexpensive way of making music. Everyone did his or her own thing – singing, playing an instrument, dancing or just telling a story. It did your confidence the power of good, and it explains why such a small country can produce such a phenomenal amount of talent. It all derives from those cold days and evenings in the days before television, when there was no money about.'

Jordan's skill with the spoons developed into a love of music and an ability to play the drums. 'As a teenager,' he said, 'I was desperately confused because I wanted to play in a band, but I didn't have any equipment. That's why I played in what was known as an "interval band" because I could use the vacated equipment. That was how I started playing the drums.' Some in the music business say he was a good enough drummer to have considered turning professional; some in the motor racing business wish that he had. Either way, his love of both, derived from his early life in Dublin, has given him a full life into which he has packed music, theatre, entertainment, business, golf, skiing and fun. He revels in a bit of the 'craic' (an Irish word that means fun delivered through a mixture of jokes, insults, banter and wild behaviour) and can be relied upon in the Formula One paddock to provide the best hospitality and the loudest parties. But, as his formidable mother Eileen has pointed out, there is a harder and competitive edge to this man, too. He will scrap for his fair share of rewards in life and he does not like to be cheated out of what he thinks is rightfully his, though he has had to undergo a few tough experiences in order to learn this.

'I can become quite violent at times,' he admitted. 'I had a terrible temper when I was young and I've since learnt to keep it under control. But it's always there in the background, although it takes a huge amount to bring it to the surface. When that happens, it's not something I'm particularly proud of. I'm like a lot of Irish people in that I am probably at my most dangerous when my back is against the wall. People talk about the "fighting" Irish, a term that really comes from the time when the boys would be like warriors on the building sites, working hard all day, getting out of their heads in the pub and then fighting all the way home. But those images are not so prevalent now. The same basic trait of bloody-minded determination remains. There's nothing wrong with that, provided you have some fun along the way. That's something I learnt as a boy, and it has stood me in good stead ever since.

'I try very hard to treat everyone the same, and that means that everyone will get the same amount of abuse. I don't know whether it is my Irishness or what, but if I was English I certainly wouldn't be able to swear as much as I do. People hear me talking to sponsors and they wonder how I get away with it. They think the relationship will be over in no time at all. But the fact is that if you're not verbally abused, then you're not appreciated!' Anyone who knows Eddie Jordan will know that is true, but it is also true that he appreciates the company of more people than any other team owner in Formula One. His very Irishness, instilled during his childhood, shines through from within every day.

His father, Paddy, was a very different kind of person, however, and preferred a quiet life. He enjoyed a relaxing pint at the pub, avoided fuss and took deep satisfaction from sport. 'He was a very soft man,' Eddie recalled with affection. 'He was a quiet and stable kind of person. I am different. I take after my mother.'

Eileen Jordan has always been a ball of energy, a whirlwind and an achiever. Even in her dotage, as a lady in her mid-eighties, she remains formidable. She can look after herself, thank you very much. And she will not suffer fools. She is polite, when required, but only briefly. To obtain an interview with her for this book required three months of patient diplomacy and long-suffering hopeful waiting, but in the end it proved worth the waiting. If anyone wondered how Eddie Jordan learnt to talk with such force, colour and energy, Eileen is the answer.

In the Jordan family, she was the one pushing and driving for more and more in life, though with a sense of proportion. She worked until the late 1970s, she always cared about appearances, she had aspirations and enjoyed a good life. She had the vision and the drive and the belief that she and any member of her family could achieve all they wanted. She also gave them total and unquestionable support, the kind of backing that can make a man believe he can do anything, turn his dreams into reality, build castles from the sand, turn a love of racing cars into a business that entered Formula One as one of the world's top Grand Prix teams. Yes, Eileen, thanks. Eddie knows it comes from your spirit, even if he did it himself.

Michael O'Carroll, an executive sports producer for the Irish station RTE and one of the best known men in Irish television, had a heart attack in 1979. He convalesced in the local hospital where, at the time, Eileen Jordan worked. 'She used to come and see me every day,' he told James Allen, for the *F1 Racing* magazine. 'She would bring me the paper and she would spend time telling me to put this experience behind me and get on with my life and so on. She really motivated me not to lie down after this setback. She is such a very powerful woman. And she adores Eddie. She always watches the races and she reads every article about him. She is a typical Irish mother. They're a bit like Italian mothers, always taking care of their boy, cooking all the meals, making sure they look smart and giving them everything they need to get on well in life.'

Though EJ prefers to deny this, or to shrug it aside as only partly true, he is in the habit of telephoning his mother every morning to stay in touch. The call is made from wherever he is, in whatever corner of the world. There are times when he misses a day, but it is not liked. It may only be the briefest of calls to say hello, but it matters. It is a call that holds the fabric of his life and his humanity together. 'He only rings to make certain that I'm still alive, and of course if I'm not then he can have my house!' she said, roaring with laughter at her own self-effacement. Eddie admitted that the idea is reasonably true and accurate (he prefers to use approximations for everything), but he responded with his own confirmation of these early-morning touchstones of family ritual: 'If, for some reason, I don't call her, the next time I call she'll give me the old "Ah, well, you're very busy" in that way all Irish mothers have.'

Eileen is the key to the Eddie Jordan success story. She has the fortitude, determination, humour and dry wit, not to mention energy, imagination and sheer joy of life, to fuel an army. Yet for many years after her son left home she found it difficult to reconcile herself to his ambitions and his decision to leave Ireland for England and a career in motor racing. Her own family history had been punctuated by much of the pain of conflict in Ireland's twentieth-century history, her father having been shot dead by the Black and Tans, a brutal regiment of the British army that had been sent to Ireland to control the uprisings after World War One. For Eddie, this meant the loss of a grandfather, and that single act also plays its role, in its own deep-rooted way, helping him drive himself to the levels he has achieved, and further. His mother's life is the bedrock of his own, her pains and wants are his, just as his near idyllic childhood days were given to him by the kindness and love of his family.

3. BRAY

'. . . It was a famous thing, this Monkey Pole, halfway up the Bray Head – a mountain. If you can visualise it, there was this mountain people used to walk up, there was a golf club there, and things like that, and you looked down at this beautiful-shaped beach. And, I remember, I fell in love with a girl from Leeds. I suppose I was thirteen. She was blonde and she used to write to me every day, and my mother used to go absolutely ape about it. And if she didn't write to me at least once a month, I would go absolutely mad myself. That, I think, was the first idea my mother had about losing me. Not losing me, but being sort of a bit wobbly. I always liked the girls and she knew it. Anyway, you had to be in with the lads from Bray.'

'I was born in Dublin,' Eddie said, 'but most people would prefer it to say I was born in Bray. My parents had just moved to Dublin. It was so fantastic because during holiday times there was a train at the bottom of the road and I used to get out to Bray for next to nothing. And what you have to understand about Bray, in those days, is that before Spain and places like that became so popular to visit, Bray was the place to go. Instead of people going to Skegness, or Plymouth, or Brighton, or Blackpool, or wherever, hordes and hordes of them came to Bray for their holidays. It was Ireland. It was cheaper, and it was tax-free.

'At this time in my life – I was about twelve or thirteen – I was getting a bit of a sense about girls and a few drinks. I remember my aunt used to have an account with the local grocer, and I would be sent down to collect the groceries, and unbeknown to her I'd change, like, a pound of butter, which used to come at regular intervals, into a flagon of cider, and in the afternoon you would go up to the Monkey Pole at Bray Head and it was just great . . . It was a famous thing, this Monkey Pole, halfway up the Bray Head – a mountain. If you can visualise it, there was this mountain people used to walk up, there was a golf club there, and things like that, and you looked down at this beautiful-shaped beach. And, I remember, I fell in love with a girl from Leeds. I suppose I was thirteen. She was blonde and she used to write to me every day, and my mother used to go absolutely ape about it. And if she didn't write to me at least once a month, I would go absolutely mad myself. That, I think, was the first idea my mother had about losing me. Not losing me, but being sort of a bit wobbly. I always liked the girls and she knew it. Anyway, you had to be in with the lads from Bray.'

And Eddie *was* in with the lads from Bray. He knew it. He knew how to enjoy the place and keep his mother sweet and how to travel back to Dublin on the trains and live the life of a lad who understood all about craic and how to make the best of it. He had the right name, and the right personality, for those long summer days on the coast, where the waters are warmed by the Gulf Stream, and freckled skin, exposed shoulders and sandy beaches made for blissful cider-fuelled afternoons. These were also the times when his personality was moulded, as he learnt to chat and wheel and deal, sup Guinness and compete in sport, spy an opportunity and do all he could to take it. These were the halcyon teenage days when Eddie's name and reputation were built and he grew up and imbibed life.

Jordan, if historical research can be relied upon, is one of the traditional names in Ireland and comes from Mayo. The Jordans of Mayo were predominantly of Norman descent, their source one Jordan D'Exeter, a man who acquired estates in Ireland following the Norman invasion in 1172 (even if the reliability of this research is in question, some link with the modern business style of E. Jordan Esq. suggests itself). In the book *The Intelligent Traveller's Guide to Historic Ireland* by Philip A. Crowl, there is a reference to the ruins of Ballylahan Castle, the seat of the Mayo Jordans, which stands alongside the junction of the N58 from Ballyvary to Ballina and the R321, linking Straide with Bohola. 'These scattered ruins are those of a thirteenth-century castle built by Jordan of Exeter,' the guide states. 'It was a polygonal courtyard castle with a twin-towered gatehouse, of which the remains of only one gatehouse remain to be seen.' The name is said to have originated with the knights of the Crusades who brought back bottles of water from the river Jordan and used it to baptise their children. In Irish, apparently, the name McSiurtain, or MacSuirtain, denotes one who is a descendant of Jordan. Whatever the truth of this, the name Jordan is certainly an old Irish name with strong historical connections that were good currency down in Bray among the summer-holiday girls passing long days on the beaches.

Eddie and his family may have no connections at all with the Jordans of Mayo, they may instead be connected to descendants of the English Jordans who arrived on the east coast, but in either case his name has a signal meaning in Ireland and is commonly regarded as Irish. Eddie shares his name with other famous Irishmen and women of achievement including the film director Neil Jordan, who was born in Sligo, and the Irish-born American playwright Kate Jordan. The Jordans also have a crest of arms, depicting a lion rampant between three crosses. Its motto, *percussus resurgio*, translates as 'when struck down, I rise again' and is entirely appropriate for Eddie Jordan, a man who may sometimes seem bowed, but is never beaten. Not in Bray, nor Dublin, nor Barcelona. Nor anywhere else in the world.

Jordan's summers in Bray and his schooldays in Dublin embroidered the rich weave of his heavily textured life. He mixed with anyone and everyone. As a child, as a little boy with an older sister, he was sheltered and nurtured and given the best chance in life. As a growing boy, he was exposed to a world in Dublin of fun and laughter and warmth and happiness that extended from his family and spilt out through the city in every direction. Ireland was a country where everyone talked to everyone else. Among Eddie's schoolmates was a man who became the chairman of the Anglo-Irish bank, among his friends were several who played golf well, and among his pals on the beaches of Bray were many who launched rock bands and helped Ireland send its talented musicians on to successful careers. 'To be honest,' he said, reflecting on these summers of bliss, 'it was down there that I have my first memory of ever playing the drums, as a fifteen-year-old. I could never afford the drums, so I used to play in a support band that came on at 8.30, in the interval between the acts, when no one turned up until 9.30 when the main band came on . . . So, I would get the chance to play the big band's drum kit for an hour and it was a thrash! I was in a band that went on to be called the Chosen Few.'

These teenage years were golden days for Jordan, but as he grew older he learnt about the more serious side of life, became more aware of the tragedy being played out in Ireland through the conflict always loosely described as 'the troubles'. While he played in the Chosen Few, his friend Des Large played in another band known as the Mugged Ones, or Mudwall – Eddie wasn't sure which. 'I think it was the second one. It was a very funny name, anyway. We were very, very, very upset when one of the best keyboard players, a guy called Fran O'Toole, who was sort of always around, and who was one of the lot of us, and who we all used to play with ... when he was killed we were all terribly upset.' The death of O'Toole, a fellow musician, a friend, an Irishman with a smile and no intent in life other than to make music and happiness, was a drastic rite of passage for Jordan. It brought home to him the harsh realities of the violence that had afflicted his Ireland for most of the twentieth century. 'He always played in a way that was almost identical to Georgie Fame,' Eddie recalled. 'This guy played all the blues, he was unbelievable, and at the height of the troubles he was the keyboard in a band called the Miami Showband. They got ambushed at the border, just over the border, into Northern Ireland. They got him to play, up north, and he was shot dead. I will never forget that because he was such a great guy and that was just so horrific. It was terrible.'

By the time of the shooting of O'Toole, Jordan was in his early twenties, had left home and was making a living for himself for the first time. Having abandoned his earlier designs on a life in service to God, he had instead moved on to the idea of following others in his family and going into dentistry. He had applied for and taken up a place at University College, Dublin, but had found the lure of pulling teeth as nothing compared to the lure of understanding money and banking. As a result, having given up dentistry, he had studied accountancy at the Dublin College of Commerce and was now working for the Bank of Ireland. His first posting was to the branch in Mullingar, in Westmeath, where he was based, during the week, for four years. At this stage in his life he had not yet met motor racing or Marie McCarthy, the girl who was later to be his wife. He was a single man, still learning his way around Dublin and learning, too, about the broader politics and geography of Ireland.

'It was strange at that time for me,' he recalled. 'I couldn't understand it at all. The conflict in Northern Ireland was strange to me because all during the 1970s – and this is during my first experience of working, in the bank – I remember doing relief work. (Large said he thought the band was called The Good Times.) That's what they called it if there was somebody on holiday and the branch he was in needed some help. It was good for me. I needed a bit more money, out and about, so I'd jump in the car and I'd be gone. It was great. I worked in one place called Keady. It was very close to Armagh. I suppose, having lived in the south all of my life, I was semi-cocooned. I just drove to Keady, got to the bank, worked, turned up the next morning, worked away, and then you would hear someone say, "See you on Monday." And I'd say, "But today is Thursday." "Yeah, but tomorrow is a day off." "And what's that for?" "It's the twelfth of July." And I had no idea what the twelfth of July was, what it meant. It was a bank holiday [the anniversary of the Battle of the Boyne]. It was a very big experience for me.

'Then, later, I went racing in the north and saw things, too. Some of my very, very best friends were there, and I saw and heard about some of the fights. Some of my racing friends, the best guys, were around then. All these guys like Derek Daly, Gary Gibson and the McGarriteys . . . it was phenomenal. In those days, you would drive up north early on a Saturday morning with your trailer, go through a border check, no problem, and then suddenly you're there with the troubles. I suppose in many respects I was quite fortunate because Marlboro gave me a chance and I was able to move on to the UK. But I suppose when Fran O'Toole was killed was the first time the troubles really hit me in the face. That was a horrible thing because there were people giving up their time to go and entertain people in the north of Ireland and they were innocent, being ambushed and shot at and murdered, irrespective of what side they were from. It was just horrible.'

For the young Eddie Jordan, these experiences formed a watershed in his life, an unexpected and unwanted rite of passage. 'I don't want to go too far into my politics, but on one side I was brought up to be a Republican. I believe in one country. There are circumstances, nevertheless, that have to be achieved before I could accept it properly, but I fully understand and respect the views of the people on the other side. And I understand people like Eddie Irvine [of Protestant stock] so much. We are close friends and we have been close friends for a long time. What makes me a little sad is that had I lived in Belfast near the Irvines I am not sure if we would have been able to be as close as we are.'

But before he lost his innocence in matters religious and political, Eddie was engulfed in the musical and social scene of Dublin at a time when it was emerging as one of the most creative capitals in Europe. As an outgoing, communicative and ambitious young man, he was in tune with his time, an era when the film business took off with Neil Jordan and the rock 'n' roll industry followed suit with Van Morrison, U2, Sinead O'Connor, Thin Lizzy, the Cranberries, the Corrs, the Waterboys and the rest. Eddie was into the sad and sentimental music of America's deep south before he widened his musical appreciation. 'I was seriously into the blues – Otis Redding, James Brown, that kind of thing. It was probably the greatest time to be into music and hanging out in clubs. Sure, there were the Rolling Stones and the Beatles, but there were a lot of cover bands doing that sort of thing and also stuff like the Beach Boys. So, it was all quite cool. We were trendy. The Chosen Few was a good band to be in. Trendy was black American music, soul, kind of rhythm and blues. It was a combination of the blues, B.B. King and Otis Redding. "Sitting on the Dock of the Bay". I don't know what you'd call it now.'

There is no doubt that Jordan's love of music was a powerful part of his life in Dublin, and still is. ' "They call me Mr Pitiful, that's my name",' he sang as he continued to relive his musical past. 'Ugh! Remember that? And Al Green! Wow. He was just so brilliant. It was just culture going on. And there was a guy called Done Devaney who was a saxophone player, and a bass player called Paul Ashford. Paul went out with Marie's sister; well, I am grateful to her for having some boyfriends. Later on, I saw him when I came to England for the first year. He sent me a message and invited me, when I was living in an absolute one-room place in Brackley, to a show. So we got into the car one night and we went into Northampton and the Fury Brothers were playing, Davey Arthur and the Fury Brothers. And they were all playing in the Crucible, or whatever it is in Northampton, and who was on bass? Paul Ashford! God, we had a laugh. What a night.'

It can't be stated enough that it was in those dreamy days in Bray and the musical nights in Dublin that all else was born. Eddie

Jordan the schoolboy was always encouraged to develop his talents, and he gave them every chance. 'I would say one thing beyond all doubt,' he said. 'If I was to be very analytical about Ireland, the thing I would give the most credit for beyond all else is that from immediately after the war, from about 1950 onwards, Irish governments traditionally have always invested heavily in education. I think you can see the state education is very, very good, to a high level. It has worked well for the country, and we have produced some really fantastic people. I was lucky to benefit from that system too.' Eddie's flirtation with the Irish education system paid off, right up to his brief months at University College, Dublin, where, of course, he found that though his grandfather and some uncles had been dentists, it was not the life for him. 'I knew I didn't want to be there, in UCD,' he said. 'I knew I shouldn't be there, so I ran away. I was only about eighteen. My mum was really so upset that I agreed to do a course, a commercial course – with about a thousand girls! I learnt how to type, do shorthand and all that sort of stuff. It was great. It was a wonderful thing.

'But if I was asked,' he continued, picking up the theme again, 'to say what was the most important thing that happened to Ireland to transform it from a lovely, quiet, beautiful place to visit in a cultural way to being a young, dynamic, adventurous, highly profitable country filled with people who were, if you like, conquering the world in terms of business and business ethics and dynamic business gurus, I would say it is the education system. Why come to England? What I don't understand is that when I was going to school, the teacher, the doctor, the lawyer and the Irish priest were all viewed as being in a similar position. And that does not happen now, certainly not in the UK. And it doesn't happen any more in most other countries in Europe. It has always been the case in Ireland that the teacher demanded unbelievable respect. In England, it is not an industry you are automatically attracted to because the payment level is, well, it is a bit like the poor nurses. Why not give the credit due to the education and the health and the nurses? Ireland has looked after health and education and it has prospered without doubt.'

It is typical of Jordan that a brief question about a chapter in his early life can prompt a heartfelt speech on the morals of his homeland and its system of government. He remains true to his boyhood and his adolescence. He may have grown up to become a successful businessman, but underneath, whatever suit he is wearing, he is a joyous, hustling Dubliner.

'I was always a hustler,' he admitted. 'I always felt it was my only passport to a better way of life. I always wanted to have, and I always had, a nice car. And I always liked the girls, of course, so you always had to have a nice car, too. They went hand in hand. I used to buy and sell cars all the time. I remember when I first met Marie – and she couldn't have been any more than eighteen at the time – I was in the middle of a deal selling some foreign students a Skoda. She used to help me too, selling other cars. These Arab guys came in, and there were not many Arabs around in those days, and they said they had seen a car in the paper and I had my own stock of cars. I was working for the Bank of Ireland at the time, in Camden Street. I would have a stock of maybe eight or ten cars. I kept them all in the bank car park. Well, not all. I had some in the bank car park, some in the driveway of the house I was living in, or where I was staying; there was one here and there, Marie had one, it was just always like that. We parked them up in all sorts of places. It wasn't like it was going up a back alley to buy a car from me, but in the winter it was always horrible and they would all be lined up for a week or more and the batteries would go dead on them all so you always had to park them on a hill. I made a point of always doing that, I promise you. I bought a flat in Dodder Bridge – it was a house, really, with one up and one down – and it was partly because it was good for parking cars. I used to rent places out, too.

'Anyway, I used to put an advert in the paper, in the *Evening Press*, and you used to have to ring the ad in by twelve o'clock on the Monday. And, of course, you had to put in a whole load of different phone numbers because of all the issues with dealers and so on. I did it for each car later on, but in the early days you would just call in and say, "Listen, there are ten cars there – just sling them in!" and you would then wait for the punters to call. It is a strange thing about Irish people. They wouldn't normally go to a garage. They would automatically think they were getting a better deal out of a private sale.'

Eileen, asked about her son's capacity for this kind of work, said she believed he began showing signs of turning a profit on a deal soon after he began work for the Bank of Ireland, and in particular when he began working for them down at Mullingar early in his career. 'I suppose his salary was poor enough in those days and he started wheeling and dealing then,' she explained. 'Number one, for me, as I noticed, was that he came home to us every weekend, and soon, rather than drive him straight back all the way to Mullingar, I would take him part of the way and Joe Dolan, that fellow who sings, who went that way every Sunday from his digs in Dublin, would pick up Eddie. I think Eddie realised, "Here, I must get a car of my own." So, there and then, I think he started to wheel and deal. And, then, of course, he got moved back to Dublin and that is when he began it more in earnest.

'He spent so much of his time out in the yard, in the car park, at the bank. I say he had a wonderful boss. She was a good girl, she was. She'd cover for him when he was out of the way, dealing in the yard and selling a car. Then he left home and went to a house up along the banks of the river Dodder. And he would always say to me, because he knew I could deal with things with his father, he would say, "Mum, come up here and I'll show you this." And so up I went to look at it, and it was a two-over-one job and, oh!, the paper was peeling from the walls. I said to Eddie, "This is not value for money." He said, "Mother, of course it is. It's standing, isn't it? And for £11,000, what will you get for that?" So he bought it, and he sold it about three years later for double the price!

'Yes, he could do that all right. Wheeling and dealing. He also went and bought a little house down in County Wicklow, and he called me and he said, "Come on down, Mum, to see this with the auctioneer in Wicklow." And we went down and we went out to view this house and I said, "Eddie, son, it is not in great order." And he said, "Mother, really, for the money it's marvellous. I don't give a damn. I am going to go back and I am buying that place." "Well," I said. "It's your money." So back we went to the auctioneers and he bought the house, and the next thing, of course, was that he had Mother down there fixing it up and painting it and all the rest and then we were letting it to someone. And it paid for itself. And then he sold it. I think he bought it for something like about £10,000 and he sold it for a lot more. It was a very good deal!'

Among Eddie's Dublin friends, some from early days, some from school, some from his jobs with the Bank of Ireland or his time studying accountancy in the city in his early twenties, some from his love of music and associations in the Dublin music industry, are a host of writers, journalists, musicians, actors, agents, businessmen, chefs and entertainers, sportsmen and sportswomen. He has acquired them as he has gone through life, each enjoying the larger-than-life and utterly unique personality of Eddie Jordan that is, even to an Irishman, enormously Irish. He has friends in every walk of life and is recognised in boardrooms in the City of London, at English Premier League football clubs, at famous racecourses, restaurants, bars, clubs, concert halls, theatres and, of course, race circuits. For Eddie is everyman, and can be at home anywhere. He can sink a pint of Guinness in a pub, delight in the taste of a favourite Thai curry, revel in the conditions on a breezy day as he takes his boat out sailing off the Spanish coast, and furrow his brow as he ponders the strategy that may win him a new sponsor or help his team win points at a Formula One Grand Prix.

And he learnt how to be everyman from his experiences in Bray and Dublin. Having left the Christian Brothers School in 1966, the summer when England won the World Cup, he spent a year at UCD before plunging into the world of finance and business in 1967, when he joined the Bank of Ireland. He proved a natural businessman with a head for figures and a full appreciation of the value of cash in hand, a decent balance at the bank and a deal on the horizon.

All through these times, in the years from the summer of 1966 to the summer of 1970 when another decisive event took place in his life, EJ was happy in his life of banking and studying and music and fun, weekends and summer days down on the beaches at Bray and nights in the clubs and bars. It is no surprise now that after all these years Jordan's friends include a large circle of people from the music business, that his guest list at Grands Prix includes men such as Chris Rea, Chris de Burgh and Nick Mason, and, probably more significantly, Dave Pennefather. They do not attend every racing weekend, they are not regulars, but they are fans and friends and they love the craic in the Jordan garage, the tension of the preparations and the racing as much as they enjoy their own high-pressure occupations.

Pennefather, a very good friend of Eddie and of the Jordan Grand Prix team, is one of the most respected and successful producers in the music business, a man credited with rescuing and re-launching Chris Rea's career just at a time when it seemed his unique talents were not appreciated enough for him to believe in continuing. Pennefather is arguably the most influential man in the Irish music business and has been a loyal and long-serving friend to Rea and Jordan, and the whole Irish gang.

'Dave is a friend of ours who has been very good to us,' Jordan explained. 'Hopefully, we have been good to him. He was the head of UCA in Dublin and he is now the head of Universal Music for the whole of Ireland. We would not be here without him and he is a great man. He knew a certain musician, a singer-songwriter, who had some very good songs, but had failed in the UK. He was quite big in Ireland. But his record deal came to an end, then Pennefather put his neck on the block. He went to look for money to pay for an album and he produced it, and the album was called *Shamrock Diaries* and it was absolutely sensational. He then went and sold it and it was fantastic and it re-launched the singer-songwriter's career. He was a nothing before that, but Pennefather did it. He hadn't got a pot to piss in! He was dead in England. He was, sure, a very talented musician, but he needed belief and help. That was the re-launching of our best mate, one of our many best mates, Chris Rea.'

Doing a good turn for a mate was and remains one of the most endearing and likeable traits in the Eddie Jordan personality. Even those who have been on the losing end of a clever Jordan deal would admit this. Like most who know him, however, they would readily agree that losing out in a deal to EJ is part and parcel of the Irish School of Life from which he has graduated and that it is never going to harm the personal relationship. In the end, as most people discover, the generous side of Jordan reappears sooner or later when the hard-headed businessman who learnt the ropes at the Bank of Ireland takes a rest. Not that he did much resting in his early days in Dublin, nor did he in his pomp as he built up and ran the Jordan Grand Prix team. To say he is a restless spirit with a short attention span and a low boredom threshold is to state the obvious. But this restlessness and high level of energy is what drove him around Dublin and ultimately beyond the Irish Sea.

In the city of his birth, he has long been a legend and his Formula One exploits have made him ever more famous. At the Bank of Ireland, in Camden Street, he is remembered with glee and giggles as a man who got away with every trick in the book, combining charm and genius to run his second-hand car business at the same time as working behind the counter as a bank clerk. Young students, or young Dublin workers, innocent girls often enough, would arrive in the bank, face EJ across the counter and ask for a loan to go out and buy a car. Brimming with excitement at the prospect of another deal for himself, Jordan would scribble down the details, discuss the proposed purchase, then hand the purchaser a note. 'Here you are, these are my numbers, please give me a call tonight as I may just have one of those cars for you,' he would say. By the evening, he would have found one of those very cars the customer was seeking and bought it, probably from a dealer; he would have it delivered to his doorstep, check it over and sell it on. This was the business that grew to become the firm he called Kerbside Autos.

In this period, too, he was busy flogging the smoked salmon (source unknown) to football and rugby fans on their way home from Lansdowne Road. When the police came along and warned him to go, he would pack up and leave, moving on around the corner to another vantage point where he would set up all over again. The visiting French rugby fans were his plum targets, for their keenness to enjoy only the best of food and cuisine and for the fact that they had usually had a drink or two and would hardly notice that the original sell-by dates had been rubbed out.

If this was his occupation for making extra money on Saturdays, he was just as busy on Sundays as well. He would take to the Dandelion Market and sell carpets – off-cuts, to be more accurate.

Like most self-made men, Jordan has built his empire out of toiling seven days a week himself. 'A pal of mine had a stall in the Dandelion Market and it was a place that was full of gypsies and tinkers, the kind of people we used to call "knackers", kind of street hawkers,' he explained. 'I would go down there early in the morning and unload the remnant carpets and off-cuts I'd picked up from the Dublin Carpet Mills. Particularly, coming up to Christmas, I'd do great business flogging carpets. I'd be in there shouting like the rest. "Get your pure wool Youghal carpets here!" It was great. Remember, too, that these were off-cuts and I knew nothing at all about carpets. But I'd be giving it all the old spin. "Now, then, Ma'am, you see these aren't your cheap old rubber-backed carpets. These are the ones with the proper hessian. You see, look at it and just rub it like this . . ." And so I went on and on. The old boy that owned the carpet mills was pleased, too. He was amused with me and with what I did. He ended up giving me the off-cuts for nothing. They were no use to him.' Later in his career, of course, as you might expect, Jordan was to return and ask the same man for sponsorship for his Formula Ford racing.

One of Eddie's best friends, a man who knew him well in the Dublin days and who has remained a close friend ever since, was Des Large. He understood him, shared his outlook and saw him work his magic. He knew Eddie was as Irish as they come, with a dose of good business savvy thrown in to make sure he was a man capable of turning a deal and delivering a decent profit. As Michael O'Carroll once said, in an interview with James Allen for *F1 Racing*, his very 'Irishness is in his imagination and his ability to make money. All that business selling the carpets and the salmon and so on, buying property and then renting it out, it is typical. He's a good manager of money, which he learnt in the bank, and he also has the ability to shake your hand and at the same time tell you to f*** off, which is a typically Irish form of diplomacy and is immensely attractive to people from other cultures.' This contradictory, unpredictable, elusive man was the one Large knew and loved. Together, they made a relatively formidable double act in Dublin, Eddie forever cutting a new swathe through the city. 'He is a completely non-conservative

Irishman,' said Large. 'He's outgoing and he doesn't stand on ceremony too much. He's not afraid to walk in anywhere and to present himself and his ideas to people. It doesn't matter who he is talking to – it works in all cultures. Americans, Japanese, South Africans . . . It's what I call his Irish neck, which never holds him back. What I love about him is that he's always in it for the craic.'

Amazingly, given the curious relationship between the English and the Irish, Jordan has been a success as an Irishman in England, too. He has used his Irish charm to work for him in both countries, but without compromise. He can wink at both sides at once. He is the ultimate knacker, a sorcerer who can sell anything to anyone with a smile on his lips as his brain calculates the profit. Yet it is worth recalling here, given that Eddie was to leave Dublin to make his fortune in England, how some of the Irish viewed, and still view, their relationship with the English.

In the *Spectator* of 25 May 2002, just as Roy Keane, Ireland's captain, was sent home from the World Cup finals in disgrace to be greeted by howls of shame and anguish among his countrymen, Martin Walton penned a piece on why the Irish still disliked the English. He blamed it on their feelings of inferiority. 'Ireland is portrayed as a land of lush greenery, infused with mystical powers,' Walton wrote, 'where jolly individuals are always welcoming, in spite of overwhelming odds, broken hearts, famine and the constant presence of hostile imperialists. For the Irish spirit to be defined, it must be in opposition to some malevolent force – and that force is just across the Irish Sea. The Irish are happy, in their attitudes and culture, to claim pole position as most oppressed nation in the British Isles, with England as the oppressor-in-chief. Irish popular history revels in the struggle of the romantic individual, who can never be bowed and will always live to fight another day, with the help of the little people, and a pint or two, and a spot of story-telling by the fireside. Even the fat cats of Ireland – the Desmonds, O'Learys, Smurfits, McManuses – are viewed as roguish chancers rather than what they really are: uber-capitalist manipulators of corrupt government, cronyism and blind EC largesse . . .'

But this, as anyone can rightfully point out, was the distorted view of an outside observer, hunting for an angle for his piece in order to achieve the bite and the twist to attract readers; a piece, too, about an Ireland of the turn of the century when the Celtic Tiger was roaring. It had no relation to the Ireland, or the Dublin, of Jordan's youth, let alone the Bray days of his sunny teenage summers. But then, it is important to understand, too, that the Celtic Tigers of the 1990s were men and women born in the middle of the twentieth century who learnt how to achieve their success when Dublin was a different kind of city.

'In the [Irish] banking sector, the brains drain away to London,' Walton continued, 'only to return with enough money to breed horses. Irish education standards are among the highest in the OECD (PISA Report, 2000) and reading-literacy levels are superior to those of England, yet English businesses benefit as the graduates emigrate. In sport, and on television, we find the same awkward mixture of envy and admiration. *EastEnders* and *Coronation Street* occupy top-five slots in the ratings, while the smash hits of the last year were *Popstars* and *Survivor*. Sunday pubs are full of shaven-headed TV fans wearing the finest man-made colours, not of Shelbourne or Bohemians, but of Liverpool or Manchester United. Yet the pre-, mid-and post-match songs revel in heroic victories over English force, or interminable catalogues of bloody defeat unjustly borne. No team is more loudly praised than the foreign team that defeats England. It was no surprise that the only sound in a Dublin hotel bar on the night of England's World Cup qualifying victory [in September 2001] was the roar greeting the one German goal.

'There is also a moral dimension. As inhabitants of a famously priest-ridden society, the Irish can always dismiss England as some latter-day Gomorrah. I was talking to a Kerryman friend about the recent abortion referendum and he rapidly ascended the Catholic high ground. "The outcome doesn't really matter," he concluded, with a sort of resigned contempt. "They can always go to England to get it sorted anyway."'

Eddie Jordan, of course, did go to England, though not for that reason. He had discovered a love of motor racing, and in it an opportunity for him to fulfil his business ambitions. But in his teens he had been more interested in other far distant thoughts, including a calling from God. It is, therefore, fascinating to realise that the forces and powers within Ireland that shaped it and brought about the Celtic Tiger boom, as seen by such visiting writers as Walton, were those that created EJ and his own Irish visions of a life that can be entirely fulfilled on both sides of the Irish Sea without any conflict. Jordan, like most Irishmen of his age and experience, has learnt to handle these things in a way that works for everyone, and some of this intuition of his must be due to his education and his deeper reflections at an early age.

'My parents would have been very happy for me to be a priest,' he admitted. 'It was a very big thing in my mind for the best part of a year when I was at school. When I was fifteen, I was sure in my own mind that I had a very serious calling from God to follow that kind of life. You've got to consider the atmosphere in which I was brought up. Most days, it would be unusual for us not to kneel down after tea and say the rosary, but then that was a very common thing to do in Catholic Ireland. And it will go on as it always has done. It was not regarded as anything unusual, not at all an authoritarian kind of upbringing. It was just the way things were done in my family.' Jordan confesses, too, that he was brought up in a family that was mentally attuned to the 'safe, secure job' syndrome, and that he began his life, once he had relieved himself of the unhappy tortures of dentistry, by launching himself as the epitome of that philosophy. 'I went for the job for life, in banking – do the institute exams, boost it up with an accountancy degree and make a career. It was the thing I had been into all the way through the school system, and I knew how to play golf, too . . .'

He certainly did know how to play golf. By the age of seventeen, Eddie could play off a handicap of four or five, it was said. Evidence to corroborate this has been difficult to find, but there seems to be a widespread belief that he was a highly promising golfer, even if Marie, his wife, had a game of such controlled excellence by the turn of the century that Jordan was often reluctant to be too involved in any kind of competitive outing with her. But instead of the priesthood, golf and banking, Jordan would, of course, turn to another career. He had first been exposed to motor racing, without becoming attracted to it powerfully, during his school years. He sometimes went to the

Dunboyne circuit, outside Dublin, and he was also aware of the famous TT motorcycle races held on the Isle of Man. He has recalled that the visits to Dunboyne were 'awesome and quite electrifying for me, when I was at school'. It is not certain that these adolescent memories played any real part in firing his ambitions in motor sport, but they may have laid some foundations. Strong ones, too.

4. LEOPARDSTOWN

These were the days when Eddie believed he would be a top-flight racing driver. He was so confident about this that he worked all hours to raise the necessary funds. 'I remember us driving down the dual-carriageway section of the Naas Road, after we had stayed at the Ormond Hotel in Dublin, on our way to Mondello Park,' recalled Martin Donnelly, the Belfast-born driver who was later to be managed by Jordan. 'In those days, everyone used to have Volkswagen pick-ups, and you could let the back end down and hold it horizontal with chains and there was enough room to transport a racing car. A lot of teams used them. Anyway, I remember my father saying, as he went by a parked pick-up at the side of the road, "That was Eddie Jordan, there, selling rugs at the side of the road!"' Donnelly remembered this anecdote with some glee, given the reputation Jordan later developed as one of Ireland's leading managers, dealers and entrepreneurs in motor racing.

Go south from Dublin, staying inland, away from the coast and Dublin Bay, and steering clear of the James Joyce Museum at Sandycove, away from the celebrity-inhabited village of Dalkey and the old picturesque settings of Killiney and Killiney Hill, and there is a racecourse, for horses, called Leopardstown. Apart from being a good place for a day out, a breath of the special air that sweeps off Killiney Bay and sweetens the atmosphere and a chance to lay a bet, it is also not a bad spot for meeting pretty girls. That is, of course, if you stay late. Late enough to call into the nightclub that is also known as Leopardstown, where Eddie Jordan met Marie McCarthy in 1977. She was eighteen, he was ten years her senior. She was already a well-known Irish sporting heroine, a member of the national basketball team, a girl who was clearly being groomed for the top. He was a man in a bow tie, with a beard, curly hair, flared trousers and ambitions to be a top-class racing driver.

Marie was there with her childhood sweetheart, Peter Lynch, a bass player in an interval band known to Eddie, enjoying a typical Dublin night out at a local discotheque where there was plenty of loud music and bright lights. 'Who's the broad?' asked Eddie, talking to his friend Lynch but staring at the tall blonde who was with him. It was the last time he needed to ask. Marie McCarthy was to make a mark on him, with her looks, her athleticism, her intelligence, her grace and poise; he would need no further reminder of her name. Turned around the other way, it was also true that Eddie Jordan was a man who made an impact, not just with his appearance, but also with his confidence, his experience and his optimistic zest. She knew she had met someone a little different, shall we say; not the average Dubliner. 'I thought he was, you know, a little unusual, a bit more interesting than usual,' said Marie. 'He was not thin then. He was a little bit on the fat side, really.'

He knew he had seen a woman he wanted to know much better. Marie was not only an international basketball player for Ireland, she also worked as a settler for a bookmaking firm by the name of Floods, a job that brought with it plenty of respect from the ordinary Irishman but not the same level of respectability she enjoyed when she moved to her next job, with the international accounting company Price Waterhouse, at around the time Jordan was posted by the Bank of Ireland to work in a branch directly underneath her offices in the city. Marie was not interested in motor racing – 'I went to Mondello Park [a race track] but I got bored and left after twenty minutes,' she admitted – but she was amused and intrigued by the way in which Eddie Jordan tackled his life. Still, it was going to take more than one brief preliminary meeting with him for her to be won over.

She remembered the first time she met him clearly. 'He turned up with his girlfriend and I met him there [in Leopardstown] for the first time that night,' she explained. 'Then we met another time, when he turned up on his own, without her one night. He'd already well checked me out by then! He was a very confident kind of person, even then. He earned himself a smack on our second date! He stopped outside the house and then he started the car up again and drove it around the corner. He deserved his smack when he got it, I'll tell you. He was 28 and I considered him then to be an absolute bachelor. Not totally unmarriable, but he had been on his own a long time and he was used to it. He was used to being his own man and doing what he wanted. I'd not really left home and I'd done very little travelling. Relatively speaking, I was quite a sheltered girl, but he had been around and about. He was well up and around. Absolutely. He knew a bit about the world.'

These were the days when Eddie was enjoying his life in Dublin as a single man and trying to establish himself as a racing driver. He had settled into his banking career, but had also discovered motor racing as the inspiration in his life. That had happened by chance when industrial action in the summer of 1970 left the banks virtually paralysed and Eddie with no option but to go elsewhere to earn some money. He decided that the best thing was to move somewhere else for a while to make sure he could survive comfortably, and nowhere was as attractive to him then as Jersey. He went to the Channel Island for the summer and took a job with the Jersey Electricity Company – a posting that had echoes of his father's work – while also working in the evenings in a bar. This was a case of choosing to combine business with pleasure, as Jersey during the tourist season was not only a lucrative place to work but also fun.

But it was not the money in Jersey or the girls or the weather that had the most striking effect on Jordan that summer, it was the action he found himself absorbed by when he stumbled on the kart racing circuit at Bouley Bay. He was hooked by it immediately, for it combined all the qualities of life that had fascinated him since childhood. This sport had speed, daring, danger, colour, noise and a sense of adventure. Soon after this, he became a regular at the kart track at St Brelades. Investing his own hard-earned cash, he set about teaching himself to drive and to race. At the end of the summer he returned to Dublin and bought a 100cc kart for himself. Fewer than eighteen months later, he was racing successfully and became the champion of Ireland, thus taking the first traditional step on the ladder towards Formula One. The only problem, so far as Eddie was concerned, was that by that stage he was already 24 years old; most people achieving this kind of success with similar ambitions were anything up to ten years younger. But with characteristic determination, he decided his relatively advanced age should be no deterrent and proceeded to race with even greater energy than the average man among such resolute and often gung-ho sportsmen.

Yet he had one regret: his commitment to racing would dramatically slash the time available for music. 'That was the only real drawback for me of getting into motor racing,' he admitted. 'I always loved the music scene in Dublin. One of the first places I took Marie when we started going out together was to hear Van Morrison play in Dublin. He would sing with his band every

Sunday in a place called Stella House. The gig was known as "The Teenies" and it ran from five until about 7.30 p.m., so you didn't have to tell your parents you had been to a dance – even though it must have been pretty obvious when you came home, lipstick and whatever else on your clothes. I really loved it, that music. It was just part of my life, just as it is for anyone living in Ireland. Music, poetry and folklore are interwoven in our history.

'I was really into Irish music. It was a culture in itself. Pub life revolved around Celtic music and I learnt to play the bodhran, which is a hand-held drum. It's not a very sophisticated instrument, but it actually takes a bit of doing to get your wrist to work the double-sided stick to hit both the up and the down beats. I first met Marie through my friendships in music, so that's another reason for my love of it all. We went to rock music dances and we had a great time. If there was a good band playing, you always got up and you danced. Irish tradition dictates that there is not much point in going out to hear some music if you are forced to sit down. So, you get up and you jump all over the place, and it is this freedom to enjoy myself with music that I knew I would miss most if I was going to be dedicating a lot of time to racing. But I knew I had to do it.'

He was, absolutely and certainly, not put off. He went on to race real cars, moving first to the Formula Ford Championship in Ireland, then, in a preliminary foray, to England where in a race at Mallory Park he suffered the first major accident of his racing career, breaking his left leg in several places and suffering other injuries that were considered sufficient to bring a halt to most ordinary people's ambitions. It certainly put an end to his jaunty hopes for 1975, but he returned, full of hope again, in 1976 to contest the Formula Atlantic Championship in Ireland. It was not quite the foregone conclusion he suggested, but in 1977, his physical strength and self-confidence fully restored, he had a highly successful year in the Irish Formula Atlantic series, using an old March formerly run by Formula One champion Alan Jones. One year later, in 1978, he won the title in a Chevron B29, justified his great faith in himself and, if anything, increased his own high expectations to such a level that it was inevitable, to his mind, that he would soon be rising to the ranks of the best

Formula One drivers. By the time he made that night-time excursion to Leopardstown, he was already thinking that a move to England was inevitable.

'When he first met me,' Marie recalled, 'I think it was the other girl who was the one with the money. But I think she soon got the heave-ho. When they were going motor racing and so on, before I was on the scene, she used to make them things like smoked salmon sandwiches, and I'm afraid I was only up to making bacon butties. She'd arrive in her smart clothes, or whatever, and I'd arrive in my jeans, and that was it. So there was a big gap, if you like. But we started going out seriously quite quickly and we worked pretty close to each other in those early days. He would pick me up from work and I used to go with him, and he was always trying to find ways to pay for his racing. He used to buy and sell cars. I was only just starting to learn to drive and I'd be helping him sell these cars on and then going to the races with him and so on. But, you know, he didn't spend all his money on cars and racing. He had a good social life as well, and we used to go out most nights. There were loads of nightclubs around and we used to go out with a lot of the other boys who were buying the cars and selling them on, and it was just great fun to be there then. It was all go at that time.

'At that stage, Eddie had his little house on Dodder Bridge, which is very well known. It was almost a one up and one down! Probably two up and two down, but that house was only about a mile and a half from my family home, so it was all very convenient. I was very happy to fit into things with him. I am always happy to get on with my own thing and not make demands. I am now, and I was then. I had my basketball and I was very happy, and it worked for us both. We just spent as much time together as we could. If I was not playing basketball, I would go with him to the races, and if he wasn't racing, he would come to see me play basketball.

'I didn't worry about him racing then. We just weren't bothered. We were having a good time and that was it. I didn't realise until he gave up racing how much pressure it put on both of us. It was only when he stopped, or around that time, that we saw how much we both worried. I worried for him and he worried for me.

Of course, when we got married and had children it worried me then as well. It was then I realised the strength of our relationship, really. I used to go to quite a few races with him and they were more like social events than anything else. We'd head off in the morning and we'd sing all the way home. There weren't the same laws then that we have now about drinking and driving, you know! We were probably doing well because Eddie was winning a few as well, which helped! It was not a bit like racing is now. And he would come down with my brother in law to watch us play basketball. We'd be in, I don't know, somewhere like Killiney and they'd come down. You might think that with us both doing so much, there would have been a bit of strain on our relationship, but it never seemed like that at all.'

Eddie and Marie were having a great time. Eddie was enjoying her company and he was free also to continue to enjoy his life with his male friends and his racing. This included a motor racing social life that had always embraced trips to meetings all over the place, as a participator or as a spectator. It should come as no surprise that Jordan loved to visit Silverstone and, given the opportunity, to take many friends with him to the famous old circuit in Northamptonshire. 'I remember, so vividly, my first visit to Silverstone,' he said. 'I was in my early twenties and I recall having the best view I've ever had. The cars were hurtling towards us at Copse Corner and we were at the very top of these huge advertising hoardings, towering over the spectator bank on the outside of the corner. Not many people were brave enough to climb up there, but it didn't seem to be a problem for a bunch of Irishmen! It was great. More often than not, we didn't have enough money to get in, so somehow we'd find a way through the perimeter fence. On a good year, though, a couple of us might have been able to afford the admission price, so we'd have a car park pass on our Transit van with the two up front buying their tickets. In the back would be our bedding and nothing else, but beneath all the cushions would be half of Dublin. Over the years, our escapades included all sorts of people, many of them now upright members of the racing community such as David Kennedy and Derek Daly [both former racing drivers who reached Formula One and who are now involved in the media].

'At the time,' Eddie continued, 'we were all young heroes racing Formula Fords at Mondello Park and such places. Formula Ford was savagely competitive, but we would all head together for Silverstone because that was the Mecca, the highlight of the motor racing year, the place to be. This was where we could go to watch the men we aspired to be when we grew up. Some hope! But some of us did it. Those were great days. When the activities of the day were all over and done with, we'd have a bit of the craic with the girls in the pubs around the area and then go back to the van in a fairly inebriated state. We'd return to the track the following morning for some more fresh air on top of the advertising hoarding. The security people would shout at us to come down, but "hoarding" was not a word we were familiar with so we'd stay put and pretend that we didn't know what they were talking about. Of course, in later years we'd have to pay to get in, but we never had a better perch than the one we had then at Copse Corner. The view was fantastic, and those were the days when the drivers were hard on the throttle all the way from Club Corner. We were just a small band of Irish Formula One worshippers; Silverstone was our annual pilgrimage and we loved it. Ireland wasn't as sophisticated as it is today and money was always tight, but we somehow managed the trip, borrowed a van and got away. It was great fun and it was a wonderful part of my life in those days.'

These trips, of course, did not include Marie (until much later) and were strictly men only. Marie would not have minded had she known. It was always her view that it was better to let Eddie have his own time and space. 'Yes, the age gap worked okay because, I suppose, I let him make all the decisions. That made it easier for us both! And he never got jealous about anything I went off to do. He liked making his own mind up about his things. We both understood the need to give each other plenty of space.

'I wasn't around when he had his first accident, and then there was another one when we were living in England. But I do remember, in 1980 – when I was pregnant with our first baby; it was due in early September – Eddie racing in a Formula Three race at Brands Hatch before the Grand Prix, I think, and he went off at about 130 or 140mph and crashed his car. In those days,

Eddie used to go off, and it was never taken too seriously. But that time somebody came to me and said, "It's okay, he's out and he's walking," and it was then that I suddenly thought, "Oh my God, he must have had a big one." I remember the shock on his face. But he hadn't qualified that time, so he borrowed another car, did three laps and he qualified. And he came in all proud, and all the press were after him and wanted to talk to him. He just went off into a caravan to take a rest and calm down.'

These were the days when Eddie believed he would be a top-flight racing driver. He was so confident about this that he worked all hours to raise the necessary funds. 'I remember us driving down the dual-carriageway section of the Naas Road, after we had stayed at the Ormond Hotel in Dublin, on our way to Mondello Park,' recalled Martin Donnelly, the Belfast-born driver who was later to be managed by Jordan. 'In those days, everyone used to have Volkswagen pick-ups, and you could let the back end down and hold it horizontal with chains and there was enough room to transport a racing car. A lot of teams used them. Anyway, I remember my father saying, as he went by a parked pick-up at the side of the road, "That was Eddie Jordan, there, selling rugs at the side of the road!"' Donnelly remembered this anecdote with some glee, given the reputation Jordan later developed as one of Ireland's leading managers, dealers and entrepreneurs in motor racing.

For EJ, of course, it was all part of getting to where he wanted to be. He wanted to be a success in business and on the race track, and he always understood that the two objectives were inter-twined. As Martin McCarthy, one of Jordan's unpaid team of mechanics and friends, recalled, Eddie appeared to spend four or five times his annual bank salary on motor racing in the early years when he developed an art for escaping from tight situations. He said, 'One of those that I remember very distinctly was when we were coming home from Mondello Park on Sunday night, racing to reach the pub. Of course, the car wasn't 100 per cent legal – the tax was a little out of date and so on! Well, the next minute, a policeman decided to wave us down. We sat in the car and Eddie got out and he started talking to the policeman for a few minutes. Eddie came back and we asked if we were in trouble. Are we going to jail? What's the score? he said "no, not at all . . . your man is coming round and he is taking the car on Tuesday!" He'd sold it . . . He'd sold the car to the policeman. As I said, he's a good man to escape from tight situations.' Yet, as an Irishman endowed with a particularly strong streak of romanticism and adventure, he also understood there was more to life than money and results. So, on 25 January 1979, at St Joseph's Church, in Terenure, he married Marie McCarthy and, full of self-belief, he decided to leave Ireland, for a while at least, and move to England.

'When we first married, we basically came straight over to England,' said Marie. 'Eddie was going to do a season. He had just won the Formula Atlantic season in Ireland and he then took six months' leave of absence [from the bank]. There was no way – though we'd already planned to get married anyway – I would have been able to come over then without being married. I was working for Price Waterhouse at the time. They were training me as a computer programmer, so I had to see that out for a month while Eddie went over.

'We got married in Dublin, in Terenure. Eddie played the drums, and it was the first time I knew that Eddie played the drums. I had no idea. I didn't know he could do that. I never knew he played golf either, but he played quite a bit at the time.' This was not secrecy, it was simply that the highly focused Jordan way of thinking did not include a briefing on his talents.

'When we were going out together,' Marie continued, 'he was always generous. Very generous. One of the things he did, which I will always remember, was when my sister, myself and another girl we used to play basketball with, we all went away to Greece on a cheap flight for two weeks. I was only eighteen, still, and they were about 23 or 24. They were women of the world and I was still a bit green around the gills. I had never really been away on my own before, but we had to go abroad and we somehow, for some reason, got our day wrong, turned up for the wrong flight and had to go home again.

'The next day, we turned up and it was about half eleven or twelve and we were just going off that night. We were sitting there, and it was about one o'clock in the morning because our flight had been delayed, having gone past security with our passports. The next minute, there's a call on the loudspeaker system for Marie McCarthy! Now, I was fairly shy, and everyone is sitting around, as they do, and nothing is happening. But there are two hundred people there, and for me to stand up in front of all these people in there was excruciating enough. So I ignored it. And then there was a second call, and my sister and my friend both said, "That's you, Marie, that's you, Marie!" By now there's a lot of commotion, so I had to get up and walk around. And who do I find? Who has got in past security, somehow? Eddie. Yes, Eddie! Coming out to say goodbye. And he told me afterwards – I think this was pretty early in our relationship – that he had come to tell me he had given the girl with the furs and the smoked salmon and so on her marching orders. So, well. I remember asking distinctly where he had been and he said he'd been out for dinner with his parents. Now, I hadn't met his parents at the time, and I should have known. You know, finishing supper with your parents at getting towards two o'clock is a bit late! But I was fairly impressed. He said he'd collect me when I got home. Well, when we did arrive home, he had all kinds of motor racing bits for me. He had asked the sponsors for old jackets for me, and whatever. That time and those events all remain in my mind. But if I had known he had just been out with his old girlfriend, you know, I might not have been so impressed!'

For Eddie Jordan, this was all in a day's work. He was so used to the idea of combining his lives and bringing the best out of everyone that in his inspirational, helter-skelter progress through each day and night, when every hour was used to the full, he did not consider too many negatives. Only as he grew older, wiser and more experienced as a result of occasions when others took advantage of him did he reflect more carefully in this way. Thankfully, however, he did so without losing any of the charm, honesty or infectiously normal nature that had carried him through in the first place.

'He used to sneak out of work, too, to meet me,' Marie continued. 'We used to go to the Hibernian for lunch on a Friday and he'd bring his *Autosport* magazine – as he still does – and he'd sit there. And he'd read it. He just used to like to have me there. Always. Not to talk to me. He was always surprising me like that.

Just turning up, or having something ready for you, when you didn't expect it, or something like that. Sometimes, he was several moves ahead. He is so difficult to predict in ways like that. He is difficult to second-guess. You don't always know what to expect.'

Clearly, for Marie, there was a time in her life when, by marrying Eddie Jordan, she decided to abandon all hope of a life in which the future was laid out like an organised plan, each season, year and decade coloured in and drawn up ready for life. In choosing this extraordinary, larger-than-life husband, she had committed herself to the unknown and the unpredictable.

'When we first came to England we lived in Brackley. We rented a house. We left everything else behind, with our friends. It was three bedrooms. Eddie started racing then and he ended up running the team, and I did some temping work at £1.25 per hour. I wouldn't take a permanent job. I didn't want to travel down to London. It wasn't for me. I was just twenty, and the idea of travelling all the way down to London from there was, for me, just incomprehensible. Perhaps I should have done it, but anyway, I didn't. I used to work in all the factories doing light assembly work, whatever was available, and then I could still go to the races at the weekends.

'I used to do the catering; it was either roast chicken or chilli con carne. And bacon butties, of course! Everyone seemed to enjoy it. The bacon butties always went down well. But if I had known then what I know now, about cholesterol, I wouldn't have been doing them. But that was our six months [in England]. At the end of that I did go home and then I think I worked with Des [Large], earning £60 a week. It was huge money then. And that was our only real income at that stage. It just about paid for food and things like that. And we had one car between us.

'I remember my twenty-first birthday. We arrived in February [1979] and my birthday was in March, and Eddie bought me a bike! So then we had two ways of getting around. I didn't worry. They were not easy times. He was older and he was wiser and I let him do all the decision-making about what we were doing. We had had quite a good income between us when we were in Ireland, and then we went to England and we had nothing, really. It was pretty difficult, and I found mixing with the people working in the factories was quite difficult, too. I was not really on the same wavelength as them and I didn't really have any friends, not to start with. We used to go around a lot with other racing drivers.'

By the modern-day standards of the Jordan household, sup-ported by a Formula One Grand Prix team, these were frugal days indeed. Eddie and Marie were as poor as anyone else, their joint income negligible, their prospects for improvement resting on the racing driver's ability to hustle and speed. Eddie was still full of self-belief and ambition, but life was now punctuated by bills and needs and he relied heavily on his native abilities to find a way of solving problems. Still, as Marie related, living in the Silverstone area, the newly wed Jordans found, naturally enough, that there were plenty of racing folk around them. But if this was stimulating for Jordan himself – which was to be expected, since he had set out to become a racing driver – for Marie, who had left a promising career in basketball and at Price Waterhouse behind her (not to mention her family in Dublin), it was, as she said, not easy to cope. 'That part of it was quite difficult for me. I remember a lot of the Irishmen, and Elio de Angelis. I remember him being around a lot and him being at the track a lot. We were impressed because he was in Formula One. There were others around too, like Bernard Devaney and Stefan Johansson, who were in the team but didn't live in the area. It was more the club guys who lived in the area. Then there was David Kennedy and Derek Daly, of course. We hung out with them. They were big boys then, they were around Formula One. We weren't. Not then.'

Discovering the dedication, hardships, requirements and sheer ability needed to make half a fist of a reasonable career as a driver in motor racing soon led Eddie to begin to give some serious consideration to his own future. He knew he had the ability to find money, the talent to run a team and the ambition to achieve things, but he was not sure his best path to success was as a driver. In 1978, he had juggled his way through a double life for most of the summer, racing and winning the Irish Formula Atlantic series and spending some time also away in England. He had found the backing to enter the British Formula Three Championship with Team Ireland, a team that used as its principal drivers Eddie Jordan and his friend Stefan Johansson, of Sweden. More of the same followed in 1979, when the men to beat included such talents as Andrea de Cesaris, of Italy, who later became Jordan's first Formula One racing driver, a very young New Zealand driver called Mike Thackwell and a very determined man from Upton-on-Severn by the name of Nigel Mansell.

But so long as there was no money coming in, he and Marie were forced to endure the life of squatters. 'For a couple of months, we lived with Alan Docking [who worked from Silverstone running an F3 team],' Marie recalled. 'That was when we came back for the second time [in 1980], and we still had no money and we were looking for a house. We were getting food parcels sent over from back home. That shows how bad it was! We lived in a room in his place for a while, but eventually we got our own place, a little two up, two down cottage in Silverstone. And it was like a train station there because all the young drivers used to come over to stay. John Walton, he came across then. We were unsure if Eddie could afford a house at first.'

As Eddie faced the realisation in 1979 and into 1980 that his talents as a driver were insufficient for him to realise his dreams, he had simultaneously to swallow the disappointment, keep Marie's spirits high enough for her to believe their future was bright and happy, and work out what was the best way forward. The way things worked out for him supplied him with the answer: management and team ownership. 'When we came over to England, there was a manager on the team,' Marie recalled, referring to 1979 when Eddie signed as a driver for Derek McMahon Racing, 'but the guy running it wasn't good enough so Eddie took over the running of the team. He ran it himself with Stefan and Bernard [Devaney] for a while. Then, the next year, he got the money for himself from Marlboro and he ran only himself with the money. So he had a team, but when things got tight and he was trying all sorts of things, he had a test in Formula One and he also went and did a bit of Formula Two. Then he retired from driving, because I had had our first baby and he still wasn't earning any money, started to put other people in his car and to charge them, and that is how we first started to earn a bit of money, and how the team started.'

5. BRACKLEY

'We never saw the business side of it. A young racing driver wouldn't. Interestingly, when I had some international success, winning the British Formula Ford Championship, I put an advertisement in the Irish motor sport magazine Michael O'Carroll used to produce, thanking all my sponsors. The next day, the sponsors rang up to tell me that one Eddie Jordan had rung them wondering if they would sponsor him, which I didn't take too kindly to, but that is the nature of motor sport. It is cut and thrust. If you are prepared to risk your life driving a racing car, it is no skin off your nose to pick up the phone to ring somebody and look for money. It doesn't enter the equation. You don't consider it immoral. You don't consider it uncivilised. It is a part of the world you are in.'

David Kennedy was working in a car sales company in the centre of Dublin in 1972 when he met Eddie Jordan for the first time. Kennedy was a young racing driver, competing in Formula Ford with some success and working during the week. Jordan was then employed behind the counter at the Bank of Ireland in Camden Street. He was interested in motor racing, having been to Jersey, and he was racing in karting events.

'I used to lodge the money in this bank beside the car company premises,' Kennedy recalled. 'I was racing Formula Ford at the time, and it was fairly unusual because there were hardly any single-seat drivers in southern Ireland. Prior to Mondello Park, which turned out to be Ireland's only motor racing academy, were hill climbs and sprints where you couldn't really learn your trade. So the advent of Mondello Park gave southern Irish racing drivers the opportunity to learn. Having got myself a Formula Ford car, I was probably one of the few drivers with any real single-seat experience in all of southern Ireland, and I was doing reasonably well. That meant I had a little bit of a profile, and I would lodge this money in this bank where, coincidentally, the manager was my uncle. He was also looking after Eddie Jordan! So, when I went to lodge this money, Eddie, having read about me, would interview me! "How do I go motor racing?" My first thought was "You've got a job, you can't be a racing driver"; my second was "You're far too old even to think about going motor racing". I think that I was about eighteen or nineteen at the time; he must have been all of 22 [24, actually], an ancient age to consider going motor racing. I don't think I imparted to him my conscious reasoning, or replied to him, "You're too old and too ugly, so don't bother." So he would engage me in conversation every time I lodged money in the bank. So much so that the queue would go all the way out of the bank and into the street and my Uncle Pat would come out and shout across, "Kennedy! Will you get away from that!" But Eddie showed an uncanny ability to withstand the pressure of this queue, some of whom would be barracking, saying, "Can we come on, please?" or "Can we lodge our money here, please?" There would be frantic housewives and little businesses trying to get their money in while Eddie was listening, talking and asking questions.

'That was where I got to know Eddie. It was once a week at least. I remember hoping, on occasion, that he wasn't there. I think I timed it sometimes so he wasn't there. Who was this lunatic, and why was he interviewing me? I mean, you had no idea he would go anywhere or do anything. But such was his passion for getting as much information as possible, you knew he was serious. But, at nineteen, you only have eyes for yourself. Anyone else doesn't really fit into the scheme of things.

'From those meetings, Eddie got to know the world of single-seat motor racing because he had previously raced some karts, but I don't think he really had any proper contacts to go motor racing. Eventually, through contacts of mine, he bought himself a Formula Ford car and then joined the fray – at the back of the queue! He was even further back than I was, but such was his knowledge of finance, something of which I had little knowledge, that he managed to leapfrog me and get a newer car. So, that is where I first met Eddie, and why I was so impressed by his neck!'

Kennedy was not the only hopeful young racing driver making his way in Ireland at the time. His contemporaries included Derek Daly and Bernard Devaney. Jordan, using his ability to find money, sell cars and then invest in his own racing career, was soon catching them up, age disadvantage or not. As mentioned previously, he was not one for giving up easily. 'The young crew at the time would probably have been myself, Derek and Bernard,' said Kennedy. 'We really wouldn't have considered Eddie then as one of us because of his gargantuan age, and where we were serious young professional racing drivers going places, Eddie was perceived as being someone who enjoyed it and did it for pleasure. Yet, you wouldn't have said that to him at the time! We raced against him and he raced very capably; he had newer cars than we had and therefore got better results. He was also generous, in a way. I remember, once, that he towed me to a hill climb all the way up in the north of Ireland, which was a little bit unusual because racing drivers are by nature selfish people. I was quite surprised at that and it gave me another side of his character. The fact that he rang me up the following week asking for some money had nothing to do with it; you could see that Eddie was cut from a different block of wood from the rest of us because he saw another aspect of all this business of motor sport.

'We never saw the business side of it. A young racing driver wouldn't. Interestingly, when I had some international success, winning the British Formula Ford Championship, I put an advertisement in the Irish motor sport magazine Michael O'Carroll used to produce, thanking all my sponsors. The next day, the sponsors rang up to tell me that one Eddie Jordan had rung them wondering if they would sponsor him, which I didn't take too kindly to, but that is the nature of motor sport. It is cut and thrust. If you are prepared to risk your life driving a racing car, it is no skin off your nose to pick up the phone to ring somebody and look for money. It doesn't enter the equation. You don't consider it immoral. You don't consider it uncivilised. It is a part of the world you are in.'

Kennedy might have bridled at this, but it did not stop Jordan continuing to manage his racing career with precious little sensitivity towards other people's welfare. Jordan had learnt how to make money, and how to make it work, and he was applying the lessons.

'I probably had more sponsors than he had,' Kennedy added, 'but I did not have the business acumen he had. I used to have a car called the "community car" because I had called so many people. I felt Eddie understood money. He owned a house before any of us had even thought about buying one and he always kept a foot on the ground, at all times. When the rest of us had nothing to lose, and when myself and the other drivers went to Australia to work in the mines, Eddie was, more wisely, trying to put deals together. Eventually, and ironically, it was a lead of mine at Marlboro, whom I had approached to put together a sponsorship programme for me to race abroad, who did so much for him. When I originally asked, they said, "No, we can't do anything abroad, but we can do something in Ireland." So I rang Vivian Candy, another young racing driver of Eddie's vintage, and said, "There's a deal out there, here is a lead, go and get them." Vivian went for that deal with Eddie and together they raced under the name Marlboro Team Ireland. Then Eddie used the connection to work with Marlboro in Europe and to start his Marlboro UK operation. That's where he took his Formula Atlantic. That was his real shot at the big time, because then he had the money to race abroad. That was the way he started his Marlboro operation.'

Eddie remembered it all clearly, and recalled that Philip Morris, owners of the Marlboro brand, had made a decision to build on their success with it in motor sport by taking it into the Irish market. 'They wanted to launch it in Ireland and it was a very different taste of cigarette. They knew what they wanted and they knew Formula One, and they had done it with the "cowboy" [advertising] package,' he said. 'Vivian Candy and I were involved in it, yes, but I don't remember David being involved in this at all. Vivian had won a couple of Formula Ford races. He'd never really done anything particularly great, but he came from an advertising background and he knew how to put a presentation together. He needed a two-car team because he'd realised he wouldn't get the Marlboro support by himself.

'Vivian and I went to Great Western House, near Heathrow, to meet George Macken, the then president of Marlboro UK, who were providing the money. We launched a car at the IRAC club in Dublin, with me doing Formula Atlantic and him doing Formula Ford. He was the original person who put the proposal together, with me as the senior driver, but he needed me to make his package look better. I needed him to make sure it was a really slick presentation because it was for an international programme. We were a reasonably formidable duo for a programme in Ireland, but after two years they decided not to go on with him – he just didn't have the success, and I'd won the Formula Atlantic

Championship. But we had raced. He raced one year in Formula Ford and one year in a saloon car, but, sadly, the results weren't there for him. My "prize" for winning was that I came up with the idea of having an Irish Marlboro team abroad. And they bought into that, which was terrific for me.'

In spite of all their on-track rivalry, the group of Irish drivers who emerged from the early days at Mondello Park remained friends. 'We would see each other at race weekends,' said Kennedy. 'It would only be a small nucleus of us. We would go to races at Silverstone together. The whole group of us would hop into a van and get over there. We would book into one room in a hotel under "Mr and Mrs Smith", and then what seemed like 48 of us would pile into the room and we would all sleep on the floor, in the bathroom and everywhere else to try to save money. Breakfasts would be quite amazing, because one person would go down and get 48 sandwiches and 48 cups of tea and bring it all back to the room. Money was pretty tight because there was no history of any sponsorship money at that time. All Irish people were interested in was indigenous sports like hurling and horse racing. We were ground-breaking, and it was very tough.

'At the circuit, one of us would go round the back and we would have one ticket going back 48 different times. Then we bought a couple of tickets, but they recognised us coming back 24 times. I remember, on one occasion, we climbed in under the fences. I think it was at Brands Hatch. And there was another famous incident when we all went to that British Grand Prix [in 1973] when Jody Scheckter spun coming through Woodcote and took out the entire field. We were down on the next corner, Copse, up on the hoardings. There were several hoardings placed in a line to that corner and each of the hoardings had maybe twenty or thirty people on it. Our particular hoarding was all Irish. We had all come over together. There was me and Derek Daly, who later raced with Williams, there was Bernard Devaney and Eddie Jordan, and we had all agreed that we would stay up if the police came over. One by one, the police came and cleared the hoardings. They looked at us, shouted, "Oi! Get down off that hoarding!" and in the bat of an eyelid Eddie was down and gone. Then they got a little bit more aggressive: "Come on, get down, or we'll arrest you." Then the rest of the guys got down. The only two who stayed up there were Derek Daly and myself. We subsequently made it further in our individual driving careers than Eddie, and we looked disparagingly down on him and the other drivers because they hadn't got the balls to stay up there! We would dismiss Eddie as being weak and cowardly because he obeyed the police. So these were the sort of things that stuck in my mind when I saw what Eddie achieved later on. Maybe, I thought, maybe it was wiser to get down and follow what the police were saying.

'But Eddie was no pushover. He had some very tough times when he was racing in Atlantic and he must have been on the bailiffs' operating table several times to escape with his life, his heart and his pockets to fight another day! And, of course, he used his experiences to go on to better things in later years in Formula One, and to withstand all the slings and arrows of outrageous misfortune and the terrible things that happened to him, like when he almost lost his team with the truck accident.'

This accident came later on in their relationship and in Jordan's career when he had become a team owner racing in Formula Three. In 1983, they were enjoying probably their best season in F3 with Martin Brundle; he had lost the first nine races of the year to Senna, but had then stormed back into serious contention. Eddie gained greatly from the increased prestige associated with his team's progress, but also suffered heavily and deeply when tragedy struck on the way back from the Austrian Grand Prix support race at the old, high-speed Osterreichring at Zeltweg. In that race, Brundle had beaten local prodigy Gerhard Berger. Afterwards, as the team began the long drive home, the transporter crashed over a cliff on a twisting and dangerous section of road. The team's chief mechanic, Rob Bowden, was killed.

Eddie, stunned and distraught, could barely believe it. He wanted to give up, but his friends persuaded him to carry on. 'I was racing sports cars in Japan at that time,' Kennedy recalled, 'so I would have been out of the loop a little bit, not in the UK on a day-to-day basis. Eddie was really getting his F3 programme off the ground and I was away pursuing my career, so we seldom overlapped. But I would have popped in if I had been around.

That was an awful blow for him.' Marie recalled how the trauma of the accident upset her husband. 'IRISH RACE TEAM IN DEATH PLUNGE, that was the headline. I read it and I just thought, "Oh my God, what's gone on?" Eddie came straight over to Ireland, just to get away from the press. And it was a bit like in Italy where whoever owns the team is likely to be held liable, so Eddie was very shaken by it all. Then Eddie's lawyer took over and he sorted it out and smoothed things over. But it was just horrible. It was very horrible for everyone and for Eddie. The second boy ended up in the Stoke Mandeville hospital. He came to after the accident, he struggled and he got himself out and let all the wind out of the bag. When he got out he said there were people all around looking at him, and not one of them helped him. They were injured. He had a lot of damage to a leg and lost all the muscle, and so on, and the driver, he got thrown and he had a lot of marks from the glass and some damaged ribs. The poor guy who died was in the back where all the engines and the equipment landed on top of him. It was just awful for Eddie. It was a very tough time, a very bad time.'

But, as Kennedy said, Eddie was a strong, determined man. Like many who knew him when he was growing up, Kennedy laid much of the credit for that at Eileen's door. 'She is fire and brimstone, a charismatic woman,' he said. 'My mother would have known her better than I would. As drivers, we wouldn't speak to other drivers' mothers. Our agenda was down in the muck and the mire of the mechanics of the whole thing, but I would get stories related back to me, from my mother, about Mrs Jordan. That her boy was a terrible boy, altogether, and she didn't know why he was going motor racing – typical mother stories! I can't give any terribly insightful information about her. I have met her, though, over the years, and she was always a great promoter of Eddie's career. Every now and then, when things don't shape up for Eddie, she's there for him. She's a stalwart person, all right.

'And Eddie himself, he hasn't really changed. In the financial sphere, he is in a different league to most. But, for me, what's really important is the person, and the personality, and Eddie hasn't lost any of that charisma. He's still a charming guy. Success hasn't turned his head, like it has done to a lot of people. To meet him now, and to compare him to the other managers in the paddock ... well, if you want some colour, you know what end of the paddock to go to! He lends a more lively aspect to motor racing, and an enjoyable one.'

For Kennedy, the old times and the contemporary times (in 2002 he was working as a commentator for Irish television) have no distinct edges where Eddie Jordan is concerned. The colourful, resourceful, determined bank clerk from Camden Street may have grown up into a colourful, resourceful, determined Formula One team owner, but not much else has changed. He remembered their shared days racing together in Formula Ford as vividly as if they were only yesterday. 'I certainly remember when he broke his leg at Mallory Park and he was going round in his plaster cast and getting everyone to sign it – getting as much publicity as he could, as usual. He always used all his energy to his advantage, and that's all a part of being a successful individual in this business. He was always doing things. Finding ways of making more money.

'When he was living in Silverstone, I went off to Argentina and Brazil. When I came back, I found half a dozen of his mechanics living in what was, effectively, my house, because I had rented it from Eddie. I think I came back a day too early to find that he had sub-let it! I didn't say a word, because he was very generous in giving it to me at a discount rate in the first place, but I should have known better. That was part of his way. Where other people would have kicked down the door saying, "What do you mean by this outrageous behaviour?" you'd say, "Oh, Christ. It's Eddie." In a way, we understood that we all have bigger agendas, and you accepted these shortcomings.'

Shortcomings, opportunities taken and missed, misunderstandings, laughter, accidents, incidents and music punctuated Eddie's life throughout these years. Marie Jordan remembers plenty of them. In his final racing days, at a time in his career when he realised his days in the cockpit were numbered, he had another accident. At the time – the late summer of 1980 – he had taken Marie back to Dublin so that their first child, Zoe, could be born in Ireland. 'I was mowing the lawn one day, taking things on and trying everything I could think of to have this baby – I was eleven days overdue, or something – and Eddie came home for the weekend. He was going to do a kind of a race, or show, at Mondello so he was practising on the Friday.

'I had nothing to do and I was utterly bored, so I went down to have a look. Well, we arrived, and they don't have any proper equipment or anything. So we parked and I bumped into Dave Benbow, one of the mechanics, and he said, "Hi, Marie, how's it going?" I asked him if they'd finished practice for the day, and he said, "Yes, we've finished. Eddie had a bit of a prang and the car is not useable any more." And so I said, "Well, is it going to be good enough to race tomorrow?" and he said, "Well, no, I don't know. Do you remember when Eddie hurt his ankle in that crash at Brands Hatch [a few months earlier]? Well, he gave it another bash, so we thought he ought to go and have it X-rayed." In other words, he'd had a big crash, hurt his ankle and they were determined not to tell me too much. I thought I'd go home then, but when I walked in through the door there is Eddie, sitting with his leg in plaster and the two grannies sitting beside him. They are all terrified I'm going to have the baby there and then. I just said, "So, you did break it, then, did you?" And the two grannies did not know what to say or what to do. He gave up racing very soon after that, I think.'

Marie's memory played a trick on her briefly in the midst of this recollection, but she soon corrected it. Eddie did indeed retire from racing soon after this, but first he indulged himself with a foray into sportscar racing that came to a conclusion with another tragedy. 'There was a terrible accident where a team-mate of his was in a big accident and burnt to death,' she added. 'I think Eddie was supposed to drive, but he didn't go. I think he couldn't afford it or he didn't have a sponsor, so he didn't go. And the guy who did, he died.' Herbert Müller was the team-mate who burnt to death when his Porsche 908 exploded at the Nürburgring. As Marie said, Jordan was absent that weekend, not having raised the sponsorship he needed for the drive.

Zoe was born in the Coombe Hospital in Dublin in September 1980. Jordan, the doting dad, had to make the journey to the labour ward on crutches, the two grandmothers having reassured him it was the right thing to do. Marie was not too delighted to see him. 'Get him out of here!' she called out. But with Zoe came a multitude of new responsibilities and understandings, not to mention new directions in life for her father.

Eddie Jordan's driving career was a short one, but one packed with memories involving people, incidents, statistics and victories. When asked in September 1989 to recall the 'race of my life' for *Autosport* magazine, Jordan selected a round of the Vandervell British Formula Three Championship run at Oulton Park on 15 September 1979, when he was in the Derek McMahon team driving a March Toyota 793. His recollections of it, as related to Tony Dodgins, are colourful and intriguing.

'I'd won the Atlantic Championship in Ireland the previous year, but that Formula Three season in 1979 stands out in my memory,' he explained. 'It was very intense with many excellent, mainly younger, drivers, on the way up. My own performances had been a bit grim at the start of the year, but I was getting nearer the front by then. Just look at the entry list: Chico Serra, who drove F1 of course; Mike Blanchet, who was no slouch; Mickey Roe – effing quick; Salazar; Brett Riley, one of my all-time heroes; Mansell, who is a world champion; Guerrero – good; Kenny Acheson – great driver; Bernard Devaney – the biggest waste of all time, a talent that should have gone into F1; Andrea de Cesaris; Thackwell – another real star. I was running in a team with Devaney and Stefan Johansson. It's always difficult to put a three-car team together, but Derek McMahon fired up so much enthusiasm it was incredible. Both on and off the track! He was a two-bottles-of-vodka-a-day man then, but I think he's got it down to a bottle and a half now. Anyway, it was hard because Bernard was Derek's main man and it's a great shame he was never given the opportunity to show how good he was. He was always hampered by lack of finance.

'All season, the racing was close. At Oulton Park, de Cesaris was trying to stop Chico from clinching the championship. They were good days, very friendly, very entertaining and very hard when you were driving. Suicidal, effectively! They always maintained I was worse than anyone else, but I don't buy that. Stefan and I had qualified within a tenth [of a second] of each other, me marginally quicker than him this time. We were struggling a bit because we'd done Mondello for Marlboro the previous week and we hadn't been testing. We were eighth and ninth on the grid, but the race was stopped when Guerrero and Rob Wilson crashed at the Old Hall. It was quite worrying to see the state of their cars, but the drivers were okay. In the first start, Andrea had come through from fifth and had dived past Chico to take the lead. But at the restart he couldn't do it again, and it was Thackwell who led, from Serra and Kenny [Acheson]. Then it was me, Mansell, Stefan and de Cesaris.

'Right from the start, I could see that de Cesaris was quick. He passed Stefan, and I could see that he was faster than Mansell and me. He was a bit of a desperado in those days. He'd had a sequence of heavy shunts and now he could see Serra up there ahead and the championship getting away from him. I got away a bit because Nigel and Andrea were battling. That allowed Stefan to keep up as well. I couldn't believe what I was seeing in my mirrors. One minute I'd see one car, the next minute there'd be cars everywhere. At the entry to Lodge and Old Hall, I don't think the spectators could believe what they were seeing either. Cars were banging wheels, climbing over one another, being launched . . . the mother and father of a shunt had to happen eventually. Often, it looked like there were two cars with a total of six wheels. I just knew de Cesaris was going to shunt with someone and I hoped like hell it was going to be Mansell because I was next in line, and there was no way he was coming by me either!

'But I couldn't have wished the shunt Nigel had on my worst enemy. I remember clearly what happened. I was about seven lengths ahead, keeping a close eye on them. They were being so wild, I could envisage a car landing on me at any stage. The shunt happened on lap four, but it seemed much later than that to me, probably because it had been coming for so long. De Cesaris must have got alongside going into Foster's and Mansell moved over. This time, Andrea decided not to let him and his front wheel went in under Nigel's rear wheel, and it's always the car in front that gets it. It was massive. It was like the end of the world. I was going into the corner and I heard this thing come skittering down the track. It was a shock to me; I remember thinking, "Jesus, he's going to be hurt." Later on, I remember I couldn't believe he only had crushed vertebrae. I remember thinking that they should have stopped the race. I lost my concentration; I know I had a problem for a while in trying to adopt the same tactics to keep Stefan behind me. Thackwell won the race and took a new lap record. Serra finished second and clinched the championship, Kenny was third and I was fourth.

'It was a memorable day, and there was quite unbelievable camaraderie. Maybe I'm getting old, but these days it doesn't seem quite the same. It's more professional and geared to hospitality and everything else. I was 31 at that time and a lot older than most of them. Many of them were on their way to F1. I was on my way there too, but not as a driver.'

Much later, in August 2001, Eddie sat down and reminisced with another former driver of the same era, Bobby Rahal, both men talking about their memories to *F1 Racing* magazine. It was instructive for anyone who had not followed Jordan's racing career closely. Rahal had raced for Chevron in Formula Two and Jordan for Chevron in Formula Three in the late 1970s.

'I remember being told that this guy Bobby Rahal would show us how to drive,' said Jordan, 'and you did! You were very talented, and F2 was going through a really good period. It was very hard. But that is what is often nice about these things. Friendships happen out of almost nothing – partly because we both picked the same uncompetitive car. I'm bound to say that because I didn't win any races in it.'

Rahal, who in 2001 had a brief spell back in Formula One in charge of the Jaguar Racing team, was generous. 'You were a good racing driver,' he told Jordan. 'We were all trying to make it and everyone was struggling. No one had two nickels to rub together, and maybe that's what was so much fun. Everybody was just hanging on. You could race hard, but you could also go out and have a dinner or a meal and have fun. But what I always admired was that you did it yourself. You put in a lot of hard work.'

These comments, made over two decades after the events they were discussing, were revealing and important. For Jordan, so keen to find a way of making his business acumen and love of motor racing profitable, they demonstrated the way in which he applied his mind to networking, in a genuine and sociable way, so that he could emerge as the first great drivers' manager, the Mr

Fixit of the paddocks. This was his knowledge, his vast and clearly remembered list of contacts and activities, and he was able to use it to his and his clients' advantage.

'To be fair,' he told Rahal, 'you were on a very different level from me as a driver. I started later. And I think you made a good point: we both considered ourselves lucky to be driving a car that someone else was paying for. If the money wasn't there, we weren't going to be driving – simple. Things have changed for the better, of course, but what I really admired back then was that very few drivers from the States even bothered to come and take on F2, where all the hotshots were fighting it out. Back then, F2 was probably more competitive than F1 because all the cars were so equal. The teams were running Hart or BMW engines and that was it. What I found in you was a guy who, for an American, didn't have a big ego. You were unpretentious, grafting and mucking about in the same pubs as we were. Nowadays you can travel by plane or helicopter to races, which is not conducive to making the kinds of relationships we had. We lived in Borstal-type places, but they were fun. We'd be on the road for maybe three or four weeks. We'd go to Taormina and have a bit of fun in Sicily, and then we'd be off somewhere else. Those kinds of things are so easily forgotten, but for me they're the cornerstones, where these friendships appeared from. You were there, and you saw different sides to the guys. I don't even see half of the drivers now.'

In the same feature interview, Jordan confessed that his decision to retire from racing was an easy one, because he simply wasn't good enough. 'I'd left it too late for a variety of reasons, and I didn't have a manager. It's much more difficult to tell people how great you are than for someone else to do it for you. That's where Eddie Jordan Management came in, and I was very fortunate . . . I remember Mark McCormack [the creator of the International Management Group (IMG)] coming to me and he couldn't understand how I had most of the drivers in F1 on my books. But when I came into F1 with my own team there was a conflict of interests, and that business had to be sold on. I'd like to have kept it going, I must say.'

Some people in the Formula One paddock of the 1990s might have believed he never truly did let it go, since even when he was running Jordan Grand Prix he still made it his business to enjoy a more than passing acquaintance with drivers' contracts and the general comings and goings of the racers up and down the grid. As Eddie Irvine has recollected many times, the man who made most money out of his move from Jordan to Ferrari was not Eddie the driver, but Eddie the team owner. In his autobiographical *Green Races Red*, Irvine explained that midway through the 1995 Formula One season he 'knew it was time to leave Jordan. I told Eddie Jordan that if his team stayed as it was, I would not be driving for him the following year.' The outcome was that, following a protracted series of contacts, discussions and events, Irvine joined Michael Schumacher at Ferrari as his number two and Jordan received substantial compensation for the loss of his contracted man – in Irvine's words, most of what was left in the Ferrari bank account to pay for driver acquisition went 'towards the buy-out clause and into the Jordan bank account'. This version of events proved that Eddie Jordan the team owner still knew how to handle drivers and turn a profit.

That should have been no more surprising in 1995 than in the 1980s when he was using his business brain and understanding of the motor racing business to such good effect. Once he had realised his days were numbered as a racing driver – albeit one who was only genuinely competitive on a few days each summer – Eddie threw himself headlong into other ways of earning revenue from motor sport. He became known as a man who knew someone who knew everything about everyone – either that or he just knew everyone anyway. His old friend and former sparring partner Stefan Johansson said, 'Eddie's got his finger on the pulse of everything. He loves it. If there's a Formula Libre driver in Zaire looking for a drive, you can be sure Eddie will know all about him.'

This depth and breadth of interest in racing stemmed from hours on the road, every weekend spent somewhere at a race meeting, and even more hours spent on the phone staying in touch. He grew to know and to be trusted by nearly every driver in the business. All his experiences were valuable to him. His love of karting and racing, developed after he had fallen for 'the power-to-weight ratio and the acceleration, both of which are better than that of a Formula One car', gave him something in common with every racer he worked with. His ability to see a deal ahead and make it happen, his experiences behind the counter at the Bank of Ireland, his sheer knack of surviving when things were tough – all of this prepared him well for the challenges ahead.

In the racing days, of course, before he slid gently into management, he had at first seen most drivers as rivals; only later did he see them as opportunities. 'Our friendship began as bitter rivalry,' Johansson recalled. 'Eddie's style of driving was something unique . . . he was very single-minded, shall we say. I think I lost more front wings battling with him than with anybody else in my career. But he never gave up. Never.' Jordan has admitted he recognised that what he lacked in talent he made up for in commitment and courage, not to mention resourcefulness. 'I have to say I was a little accident prone,' he reflected with a smile. 'If I had been a team manager and I had had me as a driver, I'd have sacked myself.'

His worst accident of all was the one at Mallory Park in 1975. It was, he has admitted, a 'big, big accident', and even allowing for Jordan's tendency to exaggerate at times, those who know him have concurred that this was a devastating collision. He broke his legs, had to spend three months in hospital to recover and had one of his heels rebuilt with plastic. After that, it was an act of courage to resume anything like a normal life, let alone return to a racing cockpit. It said much about Eddie Jordan that he did both with alacrity. His inner spirit had been warned, however, and things were never the same again for him. He was more cautious when he resumed his driving career, particularly when he began caring more for people other than himself. Further accidents followed, of course, a snowball effect that eventually persuaded him to reconsider his life following his marriage to Marie and the birth of his daughter.

As Marie recalled, he flirted briefly with sportscar racing before finally calling it a day and hanging up his gloves and helmet. 'I was 32 and our first baby was born,' Eddie said. 'I did not race again and I had no wish to race. I knew that it was more important to me to do something that I felt I could do well.' And in the middle of 1981, seizing a chance, he bought a Ralt RT3 racing car and hired it to a promising young driver by the name of David Sears. 'The very first race we ever did, he put the car on the front row of the grid,' said Jordan. 'I felt I had found the right thing for me to do. It was quite clear to me then that if I couldn't be a world champion as a driver, I was going to do it as a team owner.'

6. SILVERSTONE

By the end of the 1980s, Eddie Jordan Management was reported to be turning over around £3 million annually, and to have a portfolio of nearly thirty drivers, not all of them in Formula One. By the same time, Eddie Jordan Racing was drawing up final plans for an assault on Formula One. By anyone's measure, it was a remarkable achievement in a remarkable decade. But few who knew him were surprised. His progress was always remarkable and unpredictable. Always.

Almost as soon as Eddie Jordan made his decision to abandon life as a poor, sponsorship-chasing racing driver and become a team owner and agent, he began to taste success. He and Marie might have lived without substance, but they certainly had style. It came with the territory when anyone moved within the orbit of Jordan, the motor racing mogul of the future. To give his project a solid start, he rented at Silverstone a former Nissen hut, number 4A, a place with no water or toilet, cajoled old friends to help him out and invited anyone wise or witless to join the adventure at his own peril. He started his own team, Eddie Jordan Racing, in 1980, but the idea had been there in his mind, waiting for take-off, for some time.

His ability to wheel and deal was critical to the venture thriving. It was a case of finding someone else to pay for most things and scrambling through, with Marie's help, to keep the home running happily. 'We lived like nomads,' said Eddie, looking back on the days from 1981 onwards when he was competing in the British Formula Three Championship. 'We went from race to race in the truck, me driving, with two mechanics. By 1982, I probably had about £32,000 coming in and we probably spent about £36,000. But that was nothing unusual. We were good at making promises. From a banking point of view, most racing teams are illiquid. They shouldn't be trading. They're all mad. To stay in the game, you know, you spend everything you have and then you hope you don't have to spend too much money you don't have.'

His hut on Silverstone's industrial estate was the base for a team that was to develop splendidly from such impoverished beginnings into one of the best in the British Formula Three series. He contested the championship every year from 1981 to 1989, winning it in 1987 with Johnny Herbert, and finishing as runner-up with Martin Brundle in 1983, with Allen Berg in 1984 and with Maurizio Sala in 1986. In the other seasons, David Leslie was fifth in 1981, James Weaver fifth in 1982, Harald Huysman ninth in 1985, Paul Warwick eighth in 1988 and Rickard Rydell fourth in 1989. The Jordan team also entered the European Formula 3000 Championship from 1985 to 1991, winning it in 1989 with Jean Alesi, taking third place in 1988 and 1990 with Martin Donnelly and Eddie Irvine respectively, and seventh place in 1991 with Damon Hill.

But these statistical milestones all lay in the future for Jordan and his team at the beginning of the decade when, as a newly married man with a young family on the way, he had to organise and plan as he had never done before. Quickly, he made the most of his ability to juggle figures and books, to ease deals with sponsors, to find new markets and explore new ideas and to talk, productively, to everyone. He was involved in a deal that led to the Japanese tyre manufacturers Yokohama coming to Europe, and when he realised that one of the most badly managed assets in motor racing were the drivers' careers, he became more and more involved in that. He turned the fact into an opportunity, forming his own business in 1983 in partnership with the lawyer Fred Rodgers, Eddie Jordan Management, to look after drivers and their business affairs.

Together, using Jordan's wit, tongue and quick business brain and Rodgers' legal know-how, they built up an impressive portfolio of drivers. Eddie Jordan Management had the right to take a proportion of the driver's income (it was estimated at averaging 20 to 25 per cent) in return for managing his contracts and developing his commercial and business affairs. As the drivers' talents developed, so they commanded higher and higher fees, and so, of course, Jordan benefited. It was also in Jordan's interests to keep moving the drivers on to new teams, to bigger and better things, to keep expanding his business. Furthermore, any young driver who came to Silverstone looking for a chance in motor racing would, if they showed sufficient talent, be offered a drive with Eddie Jordan Racing, but would also be required to sign a contract with Eddie Jordan Management.

In this way, Jordan attracted young potential and made money. It explains, too, how during the 1980s he became connected to so many stars of the future including Martin Brundle, Johnny Herbert, Jean Alesi, Martin Donnelly, Emmanuele Pirro and Bertrand Gachot, not to mention Irvine and many others, and was involved in so many of their deals. In later years, it was commonplace to see Jordan shouting at a famous Formula One driver across a crowded paddock, 'Hey, you! I made you, and don't you forget it!' As always, such greetings were also accompanied by a generous ration of profanities, all issued with infectious humour and a twinkle in his eye. He was a talent-spotter, too, and revelled in the chance to find a future champion and help turn him from raw potential into a finished product worthy of Formula One. Alas, sometimes this talent of his was the one that left him short-changed when the driver moved on and Jordan was left out in the cold.

One of his smartest early moves was the signing of Martin Brundle in 1983. Brundle, from Kings Lynn, proved to be a clever, determined and strong driver with huge potential during the Formula Three summer in which he put unprecedented pressure on Ayrton Senna. The Brazilian, later to become one of the most celebrated multiple world champions in Formula One history before his death at Imola in 1994, won the championship that year, but it was a close thing. Brundle was immediately snapped up and elevated rapidly to Formula One, leaving Jordan to quip, 'I sold him to Mark McCormack's agency . . .' The comment, suggesting that a driver could be sold like horsemeat, was pregnant with meaning. The age of the agent in top-class motor racing was about to arrive.

When Herbert won the British Formula Three title in 1987, Jordan kept him as part of his own team to help head his assault on the European Formula 3000 series in 1988. He believed Herbert had all the natural talent, the feel and the speed to develop into another star of the calibre of Senna, but a dreadful accident at Brands Hatch in August of that year left him fighting for his feet, let alone his future. Showing huge depths of determination, he won the fight, and stormed back the following year in Formula One – with Benetton. Herbert's fourth place on his F1 debut at the Brazilian Grand Prix was perhaps the most courageous drive of the year by anyone and fully justified Jordan's faith in him, even though his dream of seeing Herbert fulfil his undoubted talent in a Jordan car was not to be realised.

'It's a mug's game and it's not really a good gamble,' said Jordan, reflecting on the drivers' management agency business with his usual mixture of mock gravitas and irony. 'You have to hunt around for the right driver. Then you have to pray that everything works out and he gets the right deal, gets into Formula One, gets properly paid and earns sensible money – and doesn't have any big accidents. After all of that, when you try to charge him your share, he doesn't want to pay.' Few who have heard that, or similar speeches, will have either believed it or found themselves overcome with sympathy for EJ. Those who know him well will also know that there was a clever use of argument at play in Jordan's mind as he spoke. His business with drivers flourished and served him well in the 1980s, to such a degree that it provided much of the funding for his growing racing empire and helped support his rapidly improving lifestyle.

By the end of the 1980s, Eddie Jordan Management was reported to be turning over around £3 million annually, and to have a portfolio of nearly thirty drivers, not all of them in Formula One. By the same time, Eddie Jordan Racing was drawing up final plans for an assault on Formula One. By anyone's measure, it was a remarkable achievement in a remarkable decade. But few who knew him were surprised. His progress was always remarkable and unpredictable. Always.

'He was determined to succeed, always so determined, at everything he did,' recalled his mother, Eileen. 'Even with his clothes, at home, in the house. All his shirts always had to be immaculate. He was so very particular about how he dressed. He had such energy and so much determination.' When asked if all this came from her, she smiled. 'Oh, yes, I would say. Oh, yes.' By the summer of 2002, she was 85 years old and still fizzing with authority and order. 'When I have to sign anything, or say things, I say, "Is it all right if I just say 'over seventy' on this?" "Oh, yes, you don't have to give the exact date," they say. "Over seventy will do lovely." So, that's it. I just had my new driving licence yesterday and up to this time I have always got it for three years, and when I went to my doctor, she said, "Oh, you know, Eileen, I can only give it to you for a year now!" I said, "That'll do me fine."'

Driving is a delight that runs in the family. Eddie has always made sure that, apart from involving his mother in as many supportive roles in his business activities as seem to be both legitimate and worthwhile, he looks after her as generously as he can. For one Christmas present, he gave his mother a new car. Unfortunately, an errant piece of driving by someone in the vehicle behind her one morning in May 2002 left it distinctly, as she put it, 'bashed up'. 'Now, Eddie gave me that as a Christmas present. He is very good like that. But I could do with a new one, now. Any time! But don't go worrying him with it. I won't worry him at all. I never do. It's tough enough for him to keep going with all he's got to worry about now. And he is so kind to the rest of his family. I was over on the yacht recently, with my daughter Helen, who also leads a very busy life. She was nice enough to come with me for four days because who else could you bring on the yacht? Only your relatives and that. We enjoyed it very much. The bedrooms on the yacht are so beautiful. Real luxury.'

Eileen's pride in her son's achievements is laced, of course, with anecdotes and incidents and memories. But she is utterly loyal. When asked about any of his bad deals in his younger days, or his wilder moments around Dublin, or even his difficulties when trying to sort out his career, she is stoic in his defence. 'Did he have bad deals? Oh, well, now, I would be the last one to hear about that. That wouldn't do for him to tell me any of the bad deals. I think the only bad deals he had were with the girlfriends, really. But, then, I think that's his business.'

Like most Eddie-observers, Eileen agreed that her son's best 'deal' was to marry Marie. 'I can't believe she was only eighteen when she met Eddie and at that time he was racing around the place,' she said. 'He said, "Go down there to my tent and have a cup of tea," and I went and Marie was there with her sister Ann, who is married to Des Large. So he said, "Did you see that blonde girl there then?" and I said "Yes, I did." And he said, "Well, she is one of two sisters and I like her a lot." I told him, "Well, she's very nice." And so, the next thing, she came with Eddie, and they went around everywhere together. He was in the bank in Camden Street then and every Friday night he would leave and go to race in Liverpool, or somewhere like that. And he was also down to Brands Hatch and places, and then he came back on the boat for Monday morning and went into the office. But of course I was not to know about any of that. He told the doctor and he told the bank, "If my mother rings, please say I am just out, but don't tell her that I've gone to England." So, well, that went on for ages like that, but the next big thing that happened was when this woman phoned me one night, from Liverpool, to tell me Eddie was in the hospital. He had gone into a wall, racing at I don't know how many miles an hour; he had broken his leg in two places and he had a heel almost gone. Well, of course, I had him home on crutches and he was like a devil to handle because he wasn't able to get around much at all.

'But we have a great love for each other and he is very kind to me now. I mean, he is more loving to me, I think, than he was to his dad. I'm not saying he didn't like his dad very much because his father would give him more pocket money than I would and that is what kept him very much in with his father. But, even to this day, he will tell me all his little secrets. So, he is very good like that with me. And, of course, we are alike. Very alike, really, in appearance and in everything. Very often, for all his functions when he had all sorts of presentations and everything to deal with, he would say to me, "Mum, will you come with me?" And of course I would. One morning, he rang me very early and he said, "Mother, I'm going for a photo shoot and I want you with me." I said, "Right. I'll have to have my hair done." So I sort of had the hair done, and we went to the oldest pub in Dublin for the photograph of the two of us drinking in it. It was very good.' The photographs, taken by Pip Calvert, were indeed very good. They accompanied James Allen's excellent feature article on the Jordans in the May 1998 edition of *F1 Racing*.

Eileen Jordan's pride in her son's business has been, of course, a major motivation for Eddie throughout his working life. He radiates her energy, shines with her humour and dry wit, and possesses all of her drive, but there is another side to him, a more serious and reflective side that comes, perhaps, from his father. He is a man of many dimensions who has, when asked, often talked of the many parts of his personality that he senses live alongside one another within him. 'They are like a lot of different characters, all struggling to get out and escape,' he said. 'It's a constant battle between the main two, and I think that's often the case with many people. Your upbringing is very important and gives you the road ahead. It shows how the track is laid out in front of you, if you like. In my case, which I suppose is true of many Irish people, I could see that the way my parents had brought me up was preparation for a well-structured, conventional life. My father was an accountant, and I was their only son. Still, my attraction to motor racing became as addictive to me as a drug.'

His time spent managing young drivers and helping them build their careers, albeit for a slice of the revenue, was time well used, but it put him in contact again with the feelings and ambitions he had harboured. He revealed, too, the feeling that, had he not been so well prepared for a conventional life and had he not spent so long working in the Bank of Ireland, he might have had a better chance of realising his unfulfilled personal dream to be a successful racing driver in his own right. That summer in Jersey, in 1970, when he had been earning money day and night during the Irish banking strike, he had also begun spending it – nearly all of it at the St Brelades kart track where he discovered the thrill of speed and racing. Yet he was aware that, even then, he was involved in a race against time – in his case, of course, lost time. 'As a driver, it was a definite liability for me because I was always older than all of my contemporaries,' he once told another former bank employee who turned to motor racing, the author and journalist Alan Henry. 'The likes of Stefan Johansson and Andrea de Cesaris were up to ten years younger than me; I was almost thirty when I needed to be almost twenty, so far as Formula Three racing was concerned. But then, in another way, that banking experience certainly helped me in a managerial role, within motor racing, later on, so it was probably not such a bad

EDDIE JORDAN

thing.' Like so many highly successful men, Jordan is a mixture of
startling humility – though realism is perhaps a better description
– and stunning resourcefulness and dedication. He can admit,
with ease, that he was late making a move in life to motor racing,
then with equal equanimity explain that he turned it to his
advantage.

'When I came to England, I think Derek McMahon was
probably a bit responsible for things that happened, but I believe
it was Marlboro who did the most and mattered the most because
they believed in me, then, as a driver,' he said. 'I was always a
hustler!' McMahon, who signed Eddie to race for his team in
Formula Three, was one of the most colourful men around on the
British motor racing scene of the 1980s. It was reported that he
had once enjoyed a visit to a basement disco in Austria so much
that he had returned with a partner to share the fun and
atmosphere. The partner, so the story goes, was a drunken
donkey. It was little surprise, as Marie Jordan pointed out, that
Eddie quickly became the effective manager of the McMahon
operation.

'As I said, I was always a hustler,' Eddie said. 'There was a guy
called Vivian Candy. We had already got together and we had got
some money from a company called Captain America. It was the
first of the Hard Rock Cafés, that type of thing. They sponsored
us, so it became Captain America and Marlboro. And off we went
from there, really. But I knew I wasn't going to make it [as a
driver]. My mind told me so at an early stage. But I wanted to stay
in the sport and I felt I could use all the experience I'd had as a
driver, and the experience I'd had when I was thrown in at the
deep end in 1979, to run Derek McMahon Racing in Formula
Three, which in itself was difficult. It was the experience I used
as the foundations.'

Keeping the McMahon operation running as smoothly as
possible in difficult circumstances required much of Jordan's
knack of putting together deals, his ability to build up team spirit
and his far-sightedness. His contacts on both sides of the Irish Sea
were critical, too, not least Vivian Candy and others, in developing
the operation that became Marlboro Team Ireland. These exploits,
these experiences in management and organisation, were central

to his ability to develop Eddie Jordan Racing in the early 1980s. The momentum he brought into the fledgling team was enough to carry it all the way up the scale to Formula One, particularly as he allied his team's progress to his other business activities and his willingness to travel far and wide for races in order not only to gain income, but also to learn more and more about the global business of motor racing. 'I have always been keen on broadening my own education and going anywhere to do so,' he confirmed. 'If, for example, there was a race on in Hong Kong, say a good Formula Atlantic race, I would want to be there. It was not simply because I liked travelling, but because I knew instinctively that I had to keep broadening my experience. It all helped.'

As the team developed, so the Jordan family drew closer. By the early 1980s, they were a close-knit group with responsibilities and pressures, but they enjoyed their life, particularly after having survived the difficult times. 'I remember those days very, very well,' Marie said. 'We were in a caravan. There was Eddie, myself, and the baby. I remember we had enough, once, to get us to Monaco for a race, and then, as far as we knew, we were finished. We had to go home, then somebody came up and they wanted us to go all the way up to Zandvoort [in Holland] to race the following Sunday. So, that night, John Boy left in the truck and we left with the car and we all ended up staying in a hotel. It just seemed to spiral from there. Somebody else wanted to race the car the next week, and, well, we were a going concern!' The 'John Boy' referred to by Marie was John Walton, from Dublin, the loyal and long-suffering mechanic who had travelled from Ireland to work for Eddie, along with 'Mal' from New Zealand, both men taking the rough and tumble of life on the road with this extraordinary motor racing family in their stride.

'I was not worried about anything after that,' Marie continued. 'That was the year when Zoe [the Jordans' first child] was around and it was the year of the famous old story, in Monaco, when we showered on the beach and I wore a dress from Oxfam – I can't remember what Eddie wore – and we went off to the Marlboro F1 Gala Dinner. She was only eight months old then, and we went straight up to Zandvoort after that. From then on, we were able to afford things a little more. We were able to buy a small house, for two or three thousand pounds, at Silverstone, and once we had a place to live in and a car and some money, we didn't need much more than that. Then things got better and better, slowly, and we went for a bigger mortgage on a house with five bedrooms, admittedly only a hundred yards up the road, but they didn't want to give Eddie a mortgage because he had no fixed income. So I said I would run it as a guest-house, as lodgings, and I took in four or five racing drivers for bed, breakfast, lunch, evening meal, washing and ironing for the grand total of £40 a week. It paid for all the food. It helped us with the mortgage, too. It also meant there was company for me as Eddie was away so much. If you did the European season and the British season, it meant you were racing from early March to late October just about every weekend. So the boys were great company, and they would baby-sit, too. They were all about eighteen, nineteen or twenty.

'He never talked about Formula One. Not then. Maybe he was dreaming about it, but he never said anything. But, you know, looking back, on our first date when I didn't really know him he did say he was going to go into Formula One; the second time, after about three or four years when he was probably beginning to think about going into Formula 3000, he told me he already had a team set up. I just thought, "Oh yeah, like hell!" He didn't really say more than that. I think when he is really working for something he thinks about it a lot, keeps it to himself and works it all out. Sometimes, you know, you can be talking to him and you can see he's not really listening, he's sliding off and thinking about something else. But he did mention Formula One and I did think then that it was way above anything we could ever be doing. I never paid much attention to him when he talked about Formula One. Then, suddenly, almost out of the blue, he said he was talking to Ford. He went out, came back and said, "I've got an engine." I think I was pregnant at the time, with the last one, and we were just moving in here, into Oxford. We were re-mortgaging the house and using up all the money we had – everything went into it. Eddie was about forty at the time, and I remember thinking he should take the chance and do what he wanted to do because at that age he could still start again. They were nervous times. We had another three or four years of it before it all settled down, really.'

Marie's reference to the Marlboro F1 Gala Dinner at the Monaco Grand Prix was made on the assumption that most people are familiar with the story. In motor racing circles, it is a famous tale, but here it deserves a bit more explanation. The caravan, for example, that she shared with Eddie, Zoe and the mechanics, was an old and ant-infested vehicle without any running water for showers or other such luxuries. That is why, when the invitation to the ball was made available, they went to the beach to take their showers. Eddie was obeying the old rule: miss the reception and you miss the deal. Legend has it that it was at that Monaco reception that he did the deal that led to Zandvoort and, afterwards, the sustained levels of half-decent cash flow that enabled him to establish his team. The borrowed car that had gone to Monte Carlo had paid for itself. The idea of having a car for hire became several cars for hire, single-race deals turned into full-season deals, and the business grew and grew, carrying him closer and closer to that long-cherished dream of Formula One.

In the early 1980s, during this period of growth and excitement, Eddie Jordan met and befriended hundreds, indeed probably thousands, of people. He made an impression on them all, and many of them made an impression on him. One who certainly did was the genial Gary Anderson, a tall, heavily built, easy-going motor racing enthusiast from Belfast. Anderson had learnt about Formula One and motor racing the hard way by building and racing his own Formula Three car, having previously worked at Brabham, under Bernie Ecclestone, as a mechanic. In the early 1980s, when Jordan was launching himself on the unsuspecting world of international motor sport via his fledgling operation from a Silverstone hut and an infant Formula Three team, Anderson was, in his own way, starting out on the same road. Inevitably, their paths crossed.

'When did we first meet? Well, that was in the early 1980s,' Jordan recalled over a pint of Guinness with Anderson in the summer of 2000 for a special feature published by the Jordan team's excellent *J* magazine. 'We were both running Formula Three teams and Gary told me not to be cheating!'

'And that's right,' said Anderson. 'The rest of us were running Formula Three and he was running Formula Three and a bit. As usual, he was doing things to his rules . . .'

'How can you say such a thing, Gary? You're only coming out with that because we were beating you!'

The interchange, as reported by Maurice Hamilton, the chronicler of two very different seasons in the Jordan team's later history in Formula One, *Race Without End* and *Against the Odds*, was typical of the men and indicative of the way they tackled the job and their friendship in those days. One weekend they might be out in Sweden, racing at Knutstorp; a fortnight later they might be in Italy, at Misano. This period was the one during which the Jordan family travelled together in a caravan towed behind a Transit. Anderson and his team slept in their truck and in local bed-and-breakfast accommodation. As everyone did, they lived from day to day, race to race, week to week like carefree gypsies, forever enjoying the moment.

'I probably knew more about Gary than he knew about me,' said Eddie. 'He had been a mechanic with the Brabham team in the 1970s, he was building his own Anson car and he was racing it. Gary was instrumental in me going to Europe, and, if I am perfectly honest, that would turn out to be the best time of my life.'

These two Irishmen, one from the north and one from the south, were friends as well as rivals and did much to help each other. They used converted furniture vans and various other vehicles in order to transport their cars and equipment around Europe.

'His mechanics used to come with me in my truck and we would all meet for dinner here and there,' said Anderson. 'At the races, we'd use Eddie's pick-up to get into town at night–'

'I remember travelling in your truck, at about thirty miles an hour!' Eddie interrupted. 'It was just *so* slow.'

'It had no brakes,' Anderson replied by way of explanation.

'It had nothing at all, if you ask me,' Eddie retorted.

On and on they went, this pair of motor racing aficionados who have shared so much, worked together and had fun together all over the world. According to Jordan, the sharing and the travelling was all part of the way of life. Anderson, he said, had a 'box van' that had once been used by a removals company, had no tail lift, and therefore required planks for loading and unloading cars.

'We'd loan each other mechanics to push the cars up,' said Jordan. 'I had an A series Transit with a hood on it and the car was almost vertical at the back. You would have the biggest guy you could find grinding the thing up on this winch and the others would be pushing the back. You would have the odds and ends, bits of spares, a nose cone, a set of wets, maybe a rear wing . . .'

'If you were lucky,' said Anderson. 'If something broke, you'd make bits. You had no choice. We didn't have two pennies to rub together.'

Once at Misano, Jordan revealed, after his driver Tommy Byrne had won the race, he found it extremely difficult to remove his car from scrutineering. He said this was due to the organisers wanting to strip the engine down in the paddock because, he said, they didn't have enough to pay the prize money. 'And we wouldn't leave without it, because the next race was in Sicily, or some place.'

Jordan was a customer team owner, an entrepreneur who traded for chassis, engines and drivers, while Anderson was a constructor, a maker of cars, a man who had to sell his products to keep his business afloat. 'You turned them out as quickly as you could,' Jordan told him. 'But you were always late.' He recalled one season-opening race at Vallelunga in Italy where he arrived with three new cars, none of which had turned a wheel. 'We weighed one for the first time at scrutineering and the thing was eighty pounds under weight. So we had to go to a builders' merchant in Vallelunga and find three times eighty pounds' worth of lead.' Such incidents were typical of the time as the two men used their talents to the full in different ways, Anderson selling cars, Jordan managing drivers.

Jordan was also to feel frustrated at times when his own ambitions were not fulfilled as he had hoped. In 1982, for example, he spotted a driver he believed could join him and become one of the best of all time. To back up this feeling and show confidence in his judgement, Jordan offered the driver a free test in one of his Formula Three cars at Silverstone, which was unheard of at this time and at this level of motor sport, let alone in the midst of the hand-to-mouth set-up that was Eddie Jordan Racing in 1982. The driver, however, was special. His name was Ayrton Senna.

'It was at Silverstone on the Club circuit in mid-summer that it started,' said Jordan. 'Senna was sweeping the board in two-litre, and one day I rang him up. I had begun racing my team in 1981, but 1982 was my first full season in competition. I was running James Weaver and we were having big difficulties getting money together. I wanted to get into driver management and I was looking for some young talent. I rang up several of the top promising young guys to offer them a test. Senna was one of the few I did this to for nothing, for free. In those days, I wasn't normally very likely to do things like that. He told me that his father had just come across from Brazil, he was driving for Rushen Green and he needed to get permission. He asked me if he could come on a Wednesday afternoon, because he'd be at Mallory Park doing a couple of laps that morning. I said okay, and he came down.

'Weaver had taken pole position the previous weekend with a lap which was, I think, 54.2 seconds, in the morning qualifying session. Ayrton arrived, did twenty laps and looked amazingly good. Remember, this was in the afternoon, and Formula Three cars always went a bit quicker in the mornings, in the crisp, cooler air. The warmer it gets, the more the barometric pressure increases and the engines suffer a bit. So, to equal in the afternoon a time set in the morning was significantly good. Well, he came in and made a couple of adjustments to the car, things he wanted to tune for himself. It had some slight understeer, and he moved it just slightly. He didn't change anything seriously. We had set the car up exactly the same as we had for Weaver. He didn't do anything with the tyres. Then he just went back out again, and after another ten laps he equalled the pole time. After another ten laps, he became one of the first drivers to drop into the 53-second bracket on the Silverstone Club circuit, and this was his first time in a Formula Three car. It was astonishing. Absolutely astonishing. Amazing.

'We kept Senna's adjustments on the car for Weaver, and he went on to win three races very soon after that, at Donington,

Jerez and Nogaro. Senna was something very special, but I knew, inside me, that he would not drive for me. To be honest, I just didn't have the pedigree he was looking for. I was thrilled with what he did in my car, but I felt he lacked something as a person then. I was full of admiration for him, but had other feelings too. He knew I had given him a free test, but in 1983, when we were fighting so hard against each other for the Formula Three title, he hardly spoke to me at all.'

So Senna slipped away from Jordan's grasp, just like another great Formula One driver of the future, in different circumstances, nine years later when, after a stunning debut at Spa Francorchamps in Jordan's colours, Michael Schumacher signed for Benetton. But all that lay in the future in those carefree, hazy summers of Formula Three.

7. OXFORD

In this period, 1988–91, Eddie did indeed become the motor racing world's most successful salesman. This is not a statement founded on gross turnover or sheer size, but on his extraordinary ability to make deals where none seemed to exist, and to lease those drivers signed on contracts to Eddie Jordan Management to teams and promoters all over the world. He had cash coming in from all kinds of sources, and the money came in very useful as his family life, his racing team and his various business activities grew rapidly together.

Towards the end of the 1980s, Eddie Jordan began to want more. He was making money, he was spending it, he was enjoying his life, but he knew how much more there was to be achieved if he could retain his focus, stay true to his goals and work hard to fulfil his dreams. He had, significantly, also formed a strong relationship with R.J. Reynolds (International), the tobacco company that made Camel cigarettes, among others, and which had developed a growing interest in motor sport. Jordan's reputation as a dealmaker and a man who delivered was good, his popularity rating was high, his ambitions seemingly limitless. He had also signed a clutch of highly promising drivers to Eddie Jordan Management, thus enjoying success on two fronts. By the end of September 1989 his hottest property, Jean Alesi, a fiery and fast French-born Sicilian, was being crowned as the F3000 champion and Eddie knew he was achieving his goals, leaving only the bigger and grander challenge ahead.

There had, of course, been hiccoughs along the way, when the rate of growth had outstripped his team's sapling strength. His first taste of intensifying the workload and the challenge for his men came in 1985 when he dipped into that Formula 3000 scene for the first time and found that the task of competing simultaneously on two fronts stretched his resources almost to breaking point. 'We went backwards for the first time and we had a very difficult year. It was pretty bad, and at one stage I felt it was bringing us to our knees,' he admitted. 'There were still plenty of big names around in Formula Three, some very well run and very competitive teams, people like Dick Bennetts and West Surrey

Racing and Dave Price, and it was difficult for us to compete. I suppose we did not have the right kind of funding. We did a lot of work. We tried hard and we earned some respectability in the end. But it was a steep learning curve.'

One of the key factors in the Jordan team's final resurgence and triumph in Formula 3000 was the competitive racing of the dashing Alesi. Shy, passionate, brooding, Latin, unpretentious and natural, he had the dark features, blue eyes and good looks of a golden-age matinée idol and the personality of the boy next door, in Avignon, where his family lived. In England, however, he was a little boy lost when he first arrived; Jordan and his family took him under their wing. Instinctively, Alesi responded to this. He was, and remained, a man who needed love, care and the comforts of home, wherever he was throughout his long and ultimately successful Formula One career.

In 1988, Alesi had endured a difficult year and a particularly stressful summer in F3000 with the Oreca team. He had been shifted aside by the French outfit and out of the protective support offered by Marlboro, the well-known American tobacco brand owned by Philip Morris Inc. that had funded much of the growth of motor racing in Europe and in Formula One. Alesi was facing an uncertain future when Jordan, one of his most constant admirers, approached him and offered him a drive for 1989. It was an inspired move. Alesi proved to be the catalyst Eddie Jordan Racing needed.

'For me, it was very tough then and I was worried that my chance had gone,' Alesi recalled. 'It was hard to believe it. I was disappointed, but Eddie came and he rescued me. This sport is one where you don't get too many chances, and of course I was scared that mine had all gone. I knew what I could do. I was just so desperate to have the chance to prove I could do it. And Eddie, he gave me that chance. I shall always be grateful to him for that.' In his first test at Vallelunga, Alesi drove a 1988 EJR Reynard car with such speed and passion that all concerns, on both sides, were allayed. He was faster than many of his rivals at the same test in 1989 models, including the highly regarded Pacific Racing team's new vehicles, not to mention his Jordan team-mate Martin Donnelly. 'That test was important and it meant a lot to me. I just drove as fast as I could. I pushed and pushed and pushed. It did a lot for my confidence.'

Alesi stayed with the Jordan family in Oxford, where he was given a warm welcome. But with a swarm of young children in the house and a business to run, not to mention drivers to manage, including Alesi, it was not ideal for Eddie. He did all he could, but contrary to much popular myth – which has suggested that the Jordans were his unofficial foster family in England – Alesi soon moved on to live in his own lodgings with another family in Oxford. His English was not good and he needed the assistance of his brother José, who acted as his personal manager. But, slowly and surely, it improved, and as it did so his confidence rose. After winning the popular race at Pau in south-western France, his personal levels of self-esteem were such that he began to commute from France to the races and left Donnelly to do most of the testing. This relaxed approach signalled that Alesi was happy and in form, and that Jordan should begin looking further ahead.

The summer of 1989 was a turning point. Alesi was storming through the championship and Eddie's drivers were growing up fast. 'It was a very happy time in a very happy team for me,' Alesi recalled. 'They were so fair for me. It is one of the reasons why I was always happy to work afterwards and have so much respect for British teams. I had equal equipment to Martin [Donnelly] and that is all that any driver can ask for. For me, winning the 1989 Formula 3000 Championship with Eddie was one of the best and happiest achievements of my whole career. I learnt a lot that year.'

Alesi's successful year coincided with Eddie learning more than ever before about Formula One. He had drivers on the books of Eddie Jordan Management who were rising stars, sought after by many Formula One teams, and carefully and cleverly he managed their next moves, signing deals to allow them to race in the top echelon while maintaining their F3000 careers. Alesi, for example, made his Formula One breakthrough on 9 July 1989 when, guided by Jordan, he took up an opportunity to replace the veteran Michele Alboreto at Tyrrell Ford for the French Grand Prix; a dispute over commercial commitments to tobacco sponsors between Alboreto and Ken Tyrrell had created the vacancy. Alesi, who lived literally up the road from the Circuit Paul Ricard at Le

Castellet, took his chance with aplomb. On his debut in a Formula One car, he finished fourth. It was a wonderful result and performance, for the driver, for the Tyrrell team and, of course, for Eddie Jordan Management. Even more remarkably, however, and memorably for Jordan, Martin Donnelly also made his Formula One debut that day by replacing Derek Warwick in the Arrows Ford team, the popular Englishman having collected minor injuries after an accident during an ill-judged outing at a kart track in Jersey.

All this helped to erase the memory of the struggles of the mid-1980s. Harald Huysman and Steve Harrington, of Norway and Australia respectively, had made the 1985 season in Formula Three more notable for accidents and problems than any cele-brated results. Still, morale at Eddie Jordan Racing was lifted in 1986 by the efforts of a highly competent Brazilian, Maurizio Sandro Salo, who fought valiantly in his EJR Ralt car against the superior and more modern Reynard cars of his competitors, led by Andy Wallace and Madgwick Motorsport. The momentum was regained that summer, and it was to continue into 1987 when Johnny Herbert, who had been appointed number one driver when Thomas Danielsson of Sweden turned down the leading drive, won the championship. By then, Jordan had moved from Ralt cars to the Reynards. Herbert, driving what was then known as an EJR Reynard-Spiess powered by an engine supplied exclusively to the Jordan team, revelled in the opportunity and established himself and the team as racers of the highest quality.

Herbert moved up to F3000 in 1988 and won his maiden outing in Jerez, in southern Spain. It was another milestone victory for the team and for the driver, wiping away the F3000 agonies of the past and, by dint of one of his most daring and risky business deals, securing for Eddie Jordan an unrivalled reputation as the top wheeler-dealer in that category of motor racing. It is a label he has maintained with much style ever since. But, before an explanation of this special deal, as a result of which he secured funding from the Camel cigarette brand, a brief foray into the team's previous history in F3000, and into the foundation of the formula itself.

Before Formula 3000 came into being in 1985, the recognised stepping-stone towards Formula One was the old Formula Two.

But by the start of the 1984 series, it was widely accepted that the costs of Formula Two were outweighing the virtues of the series, and that a replacement, a more modern and formally recognised pre-F1 series, was needed. Hence, the Formula 3000 Championship was created, the name of the series deriving from the planned use of the venerable three-litre Ford Cosworth DFV engine that had been the mainstay of Formula One throughout the 1970s. The formula introduced an electronic rev limiter to restrict maximum engine speed to 9,000 revs per minute, and this in turn reduced the power output to about 450bhp. In turn, the lifespan of the engines was increased and costs reduced.

Eddie Jordan Racing decided to enter Thierry Tassin, of Belgium, as their driver in 1985. The team competed in a handful of races and treated the adventures as a means of gathering experience as much as anything else. 'We tried to do it on next to nothing and did a reasonable job for Thierry, but he did a lot of hard work,' Jordan recalled. 'At the end of the year, we finished third with Claudio Langes [of Italy] in Curaço and we had an outside chance to win it, but to finish in the top three of the last race that year at least gave us some credibility. But the whole experience left me asking myself a lot of questions. Did I think I was good enough to carry on? Should I continue? It was a pretty close-run thing in my own mind, but I came out and said, "Yes, let's get on with it." I pushed myself harder than ever to do it.'

The outcome of Jordan's personal 'push' was that he motivated himself and his team to higher and higher achievements, culminating in the successes with Herbert and Alesi, all the time mixing his businesses, his talents and his goals in a constant demonstration of juggling that often had his family and staff scratching their heads in bemusement. Only he knew what was happening. Only he knew why it was happening. But it was working. That rare combination of motor racing enthusiast, sharp business brain, man-manager-and-motivator supreme and laugh-a-minute Dubliner was dancing through life, carrying all the joy of Ireland with him as he cut his own unique swathe through the English business of top-class motor sport.

The deal, mentioned earlier, that saw him secure the sponsorship of the Camel cigarette brand for his Formula 3000 team was a supreme and perfect demonstration of his brilliance at the time. Knowing that R.J. Reynolds, the owners of the Camel name, were looking at heavy promotion to boost the brand in Europe, and thinking that he had as good a chance as anyone of proving to W. Duncan Lee, the man in charge of Reynolds' marketing budget, that his team was the right place for a major Camel investment, Eddie decided to take a risk: at that opening race of the 1988 season at Jerez, as soon as he realised that with Herbert on pole position a major deal was in the offing, he had his cars branded with the Camel livery for the race. He had already begun talks with Lee in a bid to secure a contract for sponsorship and had told him he would show him the power and worth of Eddie Jordan Racing by securing him impressive coverage in the British motor sport weekly magazine *Autosport* the following week. Herbert's maiden Formula 3000 victory did just that; it was capped, of course, for Lee and Reynolds, by the unlikely and unexpected sight of Camel's colours and logos splashed across all the major highlight pages. Jordan, by an act of enormous faith in his own ability, judgement and good fortune, had delivered exactly what he had promised. W. Duncan Lee was unable to resist. At last, the Jordan operation had major backing, the support of a public relations budget that was massaged into existence, and an inflow of vital funds to ensure its ongoing growth.

'It was a pure, total, complete and utter gamble,' said Mark Gallagher, a long-time Jordan-watcher who graduated through association with the man and his team from admirer to rejected admirer, from fan to friend, from self-employed freelance writer and contributor to the Jordan cause (sometimes paid, sometimes unpaid) to one of the stalwarts of the commercial and marketing operation of the Jordan Grand Prix operation. 'He just risked it, stuck out his neck and the whole thing worked. It was a pure gamble, but you have to hand it to him – he did it and it worked out. I can't think of another man in motor racing who would have risked that.'

'There I was,' Jordan explained, 'my car was on pole, a great driver, but no money for the next race and no money even to get home! So that was when I phoned Duncan Lee, the man in charge of the Camel sponsorship, and told him that I had put a few Camel stickers on the car and that I'd win the race. We did, and we got a racing budget out of that one. It was a close shave though.'

That year, however, was not only about commercial success, goals achieved and ambitions clarified, it was also laced with deep sadness and a frustration that was not to be relieved until Alesi won the F3000 title in 1989. Herbert, after his win at Jerez, continued to demonstrate his blooming talent in Italy: at Vallelunga, where he qualified fourth but retired from the race; at Monza, where he qualified tenth and finished third; and at Enna, where he qualified fourth but retired. Then he returned to England and took pole at Brands Hatch for what turned out to be a fateful race on 21 August. Herbert was, by that hot summer's afternoon, challenging for the championship when his career – not to mention his life – was threatened as he became involved in a huge and ugly accident that left his car without any front wheels, front wings or nose section. Photographs taken at the time, following the second impact in what was one of the worst multiple collisions witnessed that year, revealed the sickening sight of Herbert's badly damaged legs hanging through the gaping hole at the front of his car where only seconds before there had been a chassis and bodywork. For Eddie, it was another dreadful experience, another terrible accident in a life that has been pock-marked by such events.

The collision involved several other drivers, notably Gregor Foitek of Switzerland and Olivier Grouillard of France. It was so appalling that it was a leading item on the national television news broadcasts that evening and in the following day's newspapers. Herbert's lower legs and his feet were so mutilated by the impact that the medical team at the hospital to which he had been taken considered at least one amputation. Herbert's appeal to the nurses and doctors encouraged them to do all they could to avoid that desperate conclusion. It seemed his walking and driving days were over, but, remarkably, his lower limbs were repaired and he was able to recover sufficiently to be carried to his racing car the following March and then to finish fourth in the Brazilian Grand Prix, in blistering heat at Rio de Janeiro, in a Benetton Ford.

Jordan had predicted that Herbert was a great star of the future, and his judgement was accurate, but the hugely popular Englishman was never to fulfil his destiny because of that terrible accident.

If Brands Hatch was a shattering blow to Herbert, it was an equally emotional shock for Jordan, but he and his team showed their toughness, their increasing levels of hard professionalism and their reliability by returning to the job for the re-started race and then successfully assisting Herbert's team-mate Donnelly in securing an outstanding and highly charged victory for the all-yellow Camel-liveried cars. Donnelly then went on to win again at Dijon, in France, and took third place in the championship.

As Donnelly's stock rose so, of course, did Jordan's. Donnelly had signed a six-year contract with Eddie Jordan Management, entering the Jordan team as a replacement for Thomas Danielsson, who had suffered a puzzling eye problem midway through the 1988 season. The Ulsterman was filled with his own ambitions, fuelled by much the same kind of dreams as those that had taken Eddie Jordan out of Dublin. When asked to explain why he had signed such a lengthy deal with Jordan, agreeing to hand over 15 per cent of his earnings, he said his attitude was that it was 15 per cent of nothing, so it had to be a good deal. He not only took full advantage of his opportunity with Jordan, he soon showed he was worthy of higher things when Lotus, then one of the greatest names in Formula One even if they were falling on harder times, began making enquiries about signing him. As a former winner of the prestigious Macau Grand Prix (for Formula Three drivers), Donnelly had established a good reputation. For Eddie Jordan, he was the perfect driver to manage.

On paper, at least, for Donnelly was clever enough to know how to play Jordan at his own game. According to comments made to David Tremayne, he was ready for the Jordan 'strokes' and had various tricks of his own to use. Having told Jordan that his drive with the F3000 team, valued at £30,000, would be paid by Mrs Rio Nolan, the widow of Dublin builder and Donnelly's former sponsor Frank Nolan, Donnelly then concentrated on the business of delivering results on the track. It was a shrewd move because the money from Mrs Nolan, not unexpectedly, did not arrive and Jordan was left to hawk the talents of Donnelly around the market place for the income he needed to fill the deficiency in his original planned budget. 'He sold me off to Vern Schuppan to drive his Porsche 962 sportscar at Spa Francorchamps, and then in Japan,' said Donnelly. 'Eddie was my pimp.'

Jordan, of course, had little choice in the matter, even if the description used by Donnelly was a shade inaccurate in the literal sense of the word. Close Jordan-watchers, however, will know that such a way of describing his activities would be no more colourful than most of his own language, particularly his often bizarre behaviour when it came to passing opinion on other people's activities. That said, Jordan was extremely successful at his work when it came to managing drivers and turning them into profitable investments. He found several driving deals for Donnelly. These included one in Japan, with Tokyo R&D, a testing contract for Lotus, and deals to do the Daytona 24-Hour race for Tom Walkinshaw Racing and the Le Mans 24-Hour classic for Nissan. It was all lucrative business for Eddie and good experience for Donnelly, but the best coup of all was the move that led to him taking Derek Warwick's place at Arrows, at the French Grand Prix, on the same weekend Alesi had his chance with Tyrrell. 'When Martin came to us, he had no money at all,' said Jordan. 'His racing programme was going to cost around £500,000 . . . In the end, we did some deals and he ended up being able to take a salary of about £60,000 to £70,000.' 'I didn't have a single free weekend,' Donnelly admitted, with a wry smile.

His willingness to gain the exposure and do the work, coupled with Jordan's ability to find the deals, not to mention Fred Rodgers' expertise with the paperwork, meant that his career moved from the slow lane to the fast lane in almost no time at all. By the end of 1989, he was installed as the partner for Derek Warwick at Lotus for the 1990 season, having learnt an enormous amount about negotiating, money, politics and sheer blarney in his time with Jordan. Citing one example from his time under Jordan's control, in 1988, Donnelly said he and Eddie went through a day of protracted and melodramatic negotiations, later known as 'the winter of discontent' according to Tremayne, but which ended with all parties happy. Doors would slam, Jordan would walk off saying things like, 'That's it, I've had enough!' only to return and say he had reconsidered and had a modified proposal to put forward. The banter and the theatricals continued for hours and was seen by those involved as part of the Jordan style of dealing.

'You just had to accept in life that if a deal was being done on your behalf by EJ, he would make money on it,' Donnelly told Tremayne. 'You had to accept that. You'd also make money for yourself, but EJ would always make money out of it. And if you couldn't accept that, he would mess up your head. He always was a wheeler-dealer. A very good and very shrewd wheeler-dealer. And EJ today is successful in life because he's a very good talker, he's a very good politician and he gets good people around him. I consider him a good friend.'

In this period, 1988–91, Eddie did indeed become the motor racing world's most successful salesman. This is not a statement founded on gross turnover or sheer size, but on his extraordinary ability to make deals where none seemed to exist, and to lease those drivers signed on contracts to Eddie Jordan Management to teams and promoters all over the world. He had cash coming in from all kinds of sources, and the money came in very useful as his family life, his racing team and his various business activities grew rapidly together.

Marie was using her high levels of energy and intelligence to keep an eye on her husband's overtaxed lifestyle. Eddie, having by now fully recovered, in physical terms at least, from his big racing accidents at Mallory Park in 1975 and at Mondello Park in 1979 and from the knowledge that he had peaked as a driver by testing a McLaren Formula One car, was living life like (some said) a man demented by his own livewire outlook on life. When the house in Silverstone, where they had taken in racing drivers as lodgers, became too crowded in the mid-1980s, the Jordans had moved again to a sprawling stone house in Westbury, Buckinghamshire, where, among the immaculate gardens, there was a tennis court and a swimming pool. For a family of five, following the arrival of Zak, a younger brother to Zoe and Michele (or Miki), it was an ideal home and a great base for the busier-than-ever Eddie Jordan to lie down, rest and think.

He was thinking, most of the time, about Formula One – how to do it, how to get there, how to find the funds, where to take the risks. Marie had listened to the dreamlike stories for months, if not years, and she was slightly amused by them. Then, early in 1990, 'I realised, quite suddenly, that he was serious. He had this plan to have a Grand Prix team, and he wanted to race it in 1991. And this was going to need total commitment. It was to be the toughest time of all for us because we knew we could end up losing everything.' By the time the team was launched, they were living in Oxford at the seven-bedroom house that was to become, with the addition of their fourth child Kyle, the Jordan family's final home. The risks they took to back Eddie in his £2.5 million plans for a stab at Formula One were the biggest they had known.

As always, however, Eddie depended not only on the loyalty and support of his wife Marie and his family, but also on the unstinting backing of the exceptional team he had built up around him at Eddie Jordan Racing. He was a shrewd judge of people and could inspire his staff in a way few others in the business knew how. It was this quality that as much as anything attracted people such as Trevor Foster, Ian Phillips and John Walton, not to mention the team's long-suffering secretary Lindsay Haylett and numerous engineers, mechanics and other staff, to stick with him through thick and thin as the Jordan story unfolded. It explains, too, how he could convince Anderson to rejoin him. The big Ulsterman had moved to the United States as an engineer in the American IndyCar racing series while Jordan entered Formula 3000 and laid the foundations for his unexpected (for many) assault on Formula One. Anderson had returned in 1988 to oversee Roberto Moreno's title-winning season in Formula 3000 with Bromley Motorsport, and a year later, in the same series, he saw Jordan celebrating a similar triumph with Jean Alesi (both had won driving Reynard cars). By then, the Formula One dream was moving into the first stages of reality. Not unsurprisingly, it was commanding the attention of both men.

'We were racing in Birmingham and Eddie came up to me and said he wanted to get something together for Formula One,' Anderson recalled. 'He said if it went ahead he would want me to join him. Typically, he was as good as his word. At first, I thought he was mad even to consider it; since then, I don't think I've really changed my opinion! I joined Eddie on 4 February 1990. We raced in Formula 3000 and at the same time started preparing a car for Formula One. By then, we had two units at Silverstone, but in reality they were nothing. There were no offices, it was just a fabrication shop. So after he had got me to join him, my first job was to find somewhere to work . . . I should have known better, shouldn't I?' Anderson was not the first and wouldn't be the last friend or associate of Eddie Jordan to articulate such a feeling. 'Ah, yes,' Jordan said, no doubt with a smile, in Maurice Hamilton's account. 'I recall that. We had this carpenter called "Plug" and we sent him to Brackley Sawmills to buy a set of stairs. Then we bought railings, and some breeze blocks, a couple of doors and built some offices. I dread to think what the fire people would have said!' For Anderson, however, it was good enough. And he admitted as much. He was a no-fuss racing man. He wanted every penny available to go into the speed of the car. The faster the car went, the better the results. His equation for success did not include luxuries for the management or staff working for the team. 'Even then, although I was convinced Eddie's F1 idea was worth a shot, I never thought he would actually put the money together,' Anderson recalled. 'Come November [1990], when the car ran for the first time, I thought, "This is really happening. We're going to go racing." A bit of sponsorship came in and Eddie was running around in his Porsche . . .'

And therein lies another story to make everyone chuckle. The Porsche's role in Jordan's birth as a Grand Prix team is now part of Formula One folklore and has been told over and again in many different ways. It is difficult to pin down the definitive version, but the gist of it, from Eddie's own mouth, is that 'we originally wanted to call our car, the first Formula One car, a Jordan 911. It was the year 1991 and it was our first car. Then, a writ comes through the door from Porsche, talking about the wonderful brand image they had built up over the years for their 911 car. They said they had the rights to this 911 title for a car. So we had a bit of a discussion and, would you believe it, our car becomes a Jordan 191. And then a Porsche gets delivered to Silverstone!' The 191, later to be dubbed the 'lean, mean and green machine', was one of the most attractive cars ever seen in Formula One. But in 1990 it was first seen as a drawing, then as a black machine without a spot of paint on it, long before the money arrived to decide what the colour scheme might be and whose logos would be spread across its bodywork. 'That car', said Jordan, 'was probably the most beautiful car of the decade and it cost next to nothing to build. Don't talk to me about quality control or expensive machinery. We barely had a ruler to our name. The point was that Gary and I both knew what two and two made – and it never made five. It only ever made four. Our past experiences told us that.'

Alongside Anderson was another of EJ's most loyal employees, John Walton, who had first caught sight of Jordan in the early 1970s on the bumpy track at Mondello Park in County Kildare. Walton, given the predictable soubriquet 'John Boy' after a character in the American television series *The Waltons*, was a Dubliner, from Coolock, a motor racing fan and a popular man with a certain way of looking at women that Marie Jordan succinctly described as his 'come to bed eyes'. 'He was waiting with a group of people, like David Kennedy, Derek Daly and Bernard Devaney,' Walton said as he recalled that first meeting. 'I knew Derek Daly previously because I used to do stock car racing at the same time as him. But I didn't get to meet Eddie Jordan on a one-to-one basis till 1979, when I came to Silverstone with a guy called Tommy Donnelly and went to live in Eddie's house. Eddie was driving with Derek McMahon at the time, alongside Stefan Johansson. I carried on doing Formula Ford for a few months until an opportunity came along and I went to work for Derek McMahon – and that's when I started doing work on Eddie's car and things like that.

'We became good friends and one thing led to another. We carried on like that for a few years and then I went off to do Formula One [as a mechanic with Ayrton Senna at Toleman, and at Benetton] and Eddie decided to hang up his helmet. We had a little joking agreement that if he ever set up a Formula One team I would come back and work for him. So in 1990, when he decided he wanted a go at being a Formula One team owner, well, we bumped into each other at the Monaco Grand Prix and we had a chat and that was it. I joined him, and it all happened from there.

'In those early days, when he was racing, he was obviously a great fun bloke to be with, but we had a lot of arguments. They were nothing too serious, obviously, only about racing or things connected to it. It was always like that. We never fell out. To me, EJ is still a great person. Apart from earning a lot of money and enjoying it and building up his team, he hasn't really changed at all. He is the same bloke I first knew around Dublin all those years ago.'

Talking at the San Marino Grand Prix at Imola in 2002, Walton recalled with enjoyment many early escapades with the enthusiastic young racing driver Eddie Jordan. On an afternoon of disappointment for himself and his team at the time, Minardi Asiatech, he rolled back the years in his mind and smiled. 'One funny incident, one I can remember a little anyway, was when we went to Phoenix Park for an Atlantic race, and we went with a navy blue car. Then, the night before the race, Eddie turned up at my mother's house, in Dublin, with the car and the trailer and dropped it off. He told me what he wanted, and it meant I had 24 hours to change it into a Marlboro car. That meant a complete change of colours from blue to red and white. And the funny bit was that obviously there was an agreement with the guy who owned this car that if there was any damage it would need to be paid for . . .' In that particular race, said Walton, Jordan managed to reach second place before he was forced into retirement. 'It was quite an old car, but of course, when it broke, it was all my fault. I ended up catching his helmet – and that was quite funny, really, after all the work we'd done that weekend. But, again, it was typical Eddie. He was so competitive. And he gave it everything.'

Asked if Jordan had true talent as a driver, Walton said, 'Yes, I think he did. In the Formula Atlantic series, in Ireland, he showed what he could do. But when he came to England, to do Formula Three, the races were a bit too short for him. I think it used to take him a few laps to get up to speed. But even in Formula Three, you know, he was racing with the likes of Nigel Mansell and the car he was driving at the time wasn't exactly the most competitive one around. But then, I remember, the manufacturer brought out a new car, which everyone had to have, so he ended up on the front row of the grid at Silverstone for the European race. I think you would have to say he did have some talent, but not the talent of a world champion, and he obviously realised that very early on and that was why he decided to quit racing, which I think was probably a more ballsy attitude to it than anything else he could have done. One thing I will definitely say in his favour, having lived with him for quite a long time, is that he and Marie risked the lot. I know the kind of sacrifices they had to make and he did put everything he ever had, or could put his hands on, on the line to achieve what he set out to do. So, I think you need to give credit where it is due. He deserves everything he has got now that he has become successful.'

Jordan was always a popular figure, well known for the stunts he could pull, said Walton. 'Oh, yes, he was pretty sort of popular and famous as an Irish national racing driver, and probably he was as well known as a wheeler-dealer, too, but some of the things he used to wheel and deal in I am not sure whether it is fit to print. I've got to say, I do admire the guy a lot. He has a lot going for him and I genuinely like him, as a friend and as a boss. I like working with him. I just think he is quite amazing, really.'

As in any conversation with or about Eddie Jordan, it is difficult to stay on a fixed agenda and proceed in a predictable course. His low threshold for listening to other people, his short attention span and his jack-in-the-box energy are legendary qualities associated with him, but they seem to spread and affect all those who have been close to or continue to work with him. Hence, any dialogue about Jordan tends to jump backwards and forwards, side to side and up and down as the conversationalists attempt to pin down their subject. It is difficult also to establish clear and certain facts, backed up for accuracy. Indeed, as time passes, the legendary incidents and activities of Eddie's life become more and more vague and colourful, less and less precise. Walton was happy to add to the vault of legendary tales.

'There was another funny incident – not when it happened, but towards the end of the relevant weekend. We went to Mondello. It had been arranged that we would have a Formula Three race there so most of the English teams decided to go. We got there, I think, on a Wednesday or something, and they arranged some free practice for us. Out on circuit at the time there was EJ and Bernard Devaney. EJ went out, only for a few laps, but then he didn't come back for a while. Bernard Devaney came back into the pits and said that EJ had had an accident, so we drove round and the car was actually over the embankment and they were really struggling to get him out because of the way the car went into this ditch. Unfortunately, he had broken his leg again, so he got taken away to hospital and we packed the car up and everything else. The car was in the back of the truck for the weekend, parked at Mondello.

'When he got sorted out and he was let out of hospital, he was going to do the commentary on the race, on the Sunday. Before the start of the race, he came down, and I remember I was just sat at the side door of the truck, talking to some people, having a cigarette. He wanted to show some people the car, on his crutches. And he started ranting and raving: "I told you not to be smoking in this area", and this and that. Anyway, I got a bit upset about it and sort of jumped off down the truck. I think he thought I was going to jump down and cop him one, so he moved backwards and sort of slipped over on his crutches. It was funny to see him, so mad and angry, down like that on his crutches when really he should have been calm and preparing for his commentary job. After that, when we had got the car back to England and we had rebuilt it, we went to Mallory Park. He was still on his crutches. We had to lift him into the car at the start and out of the car afterwards!

'I suppose the best run I have ever seen him do was at the British Grand Prix at Brands Hatch that same year. He had an accident in practice, I think, as well, and totally wrote the car off. We borrowed a car from Derek McMahon, who was in Formula Three at the time, and again this happened to be another navy blue car that we had to change overnight into a normal red car. Of course, then he couldn't fit into it because Derek was quite a bit bigger, so we just got some jackets and things off various people, stuffed them in behind him and strapped him in. Then he actually went out round Brands Hatch quicker than he had ever been in his life.'

As a Dubliner, Walton has grown up as an observer of the Jordan story. He has seen his friend change from the accident-prone but fast racing driver into the ambitious driver manager and team owner. I asked him, 'Has he ever done anything generous or kind?'

'Not to me, he hasn't,' came the quick, quipped reply. 'Yes, I think he has donated to a couple of charities and I think he does a lot of work for a charity Marie is involved in. I know he is very kind and very good to his mother. She is a fantastic lady, very much a character in her own right. You know his mum, and you can see where EJ gets a lot of it. She is certainly a very fit lady for her age and very active. I didn't know his father that well. I only met him on one or two occasions. I know that he was a very intelligent man, and when he [Eddie] first went to Spain to build a house, his father did a lot of the architectural work on it, and the design work. But, sadly, as I said, I never got to know him that well, but I think that he was a bit of a character as well.'

I asked another question. 'What is he like if you fall out with him?'

'Sensitive,' said Walton. 'We've had a few fallings-out over the years, as you can imagine, but they never lasted very long. He always had a nice way of turning things around, shall we say, and maybe even bringing you round to seeing things his way. He is very persuasive and charming, really, but he doesn't hold grudges or anything like that.'

Walton worked with Jordan as a mechanic and general life-support system assistant from the early racing days at Silverstone until he gave up driving, then he returned to join the Formula One team from 1991 to 1996 before leaving again. Why did he leave the second time?

'To be honest, I felt that it was time for me to move on. I had got an offer I felt I couldn't refuse. At the time I felt like we were getting a bit stagnated at Jordan, and that basically was the real reason.'

If he came back and asked you to join him again, would you go?

'If the price is right, he can have me. I suppose it is like unfinished business. I was very pleased for them when they won their first race [in F1], and I was one of the first people to congratulate him, but things change and circumstances change. I left because I felt I needed more. I needed to get more experience.'

As one of the men who worked closely with Jordan in all areas of his operation over many years, Walton knew better than anyone how stringent Eddie could be about cost controls. He hated to see money wasted. 'You had to make sure that everything had the right number of miles on it,' he explained. 'He wouldn't be allowing anyone to take risks; put it this way, he wanted to get his pound of flesh! In 1992, the year that was probably tighter financially than any of the others, the people who helped to make the car found out what he wanted. The manufacturers and suppliers in 1991 had to work with inflation and all the prices went up, so when things started to get really tight he called each individual supplier, banged the table, haggled and bartered with them, and ended up paying less for most of the parts than we had been paying in 1991. That's the kind of guy he is. But one thing I have to say about him, he always said that the day he couldn't afford to pay the people, that was the day the doors closed. And he was always as good as his word. That was something we never ever had a problem with, wages. And I take my hat off to him for that.

'There were some very bad times, too. The worst time of all came, probably, at the end of 1992 when he broke with Yamaha, found some more money from somewhere and had the balls to take a flier, a real gamble, with Brian Hart's new engine, which nobody else had ever seen or heard of. That was probably one of the best packages and teams he ever put together. We used that for two years and had some very good results with it, then the Peugeot deal came along. He always seemed to be able to pull it out of the bag when he had to.'

Walton's admiration for Jordan is genuine. Midway through the 1991 season, when Walton was a stalwart in the Jordan garage, he was in Magny-Cours preparing for the French Grand Prix when the following interchange took place, a dialogue typical of the banter in the team at that time (at any time, actually).

'John Boy, why did you leave Benetton to come back to work with me?' said Jordan.

'Cos you're my hero.'

'Stop messin' about. Why?'

'I'm tellin' you. Cos you're my hero. I always said I'd be back when you came into Formula One.'

Clearly played to an audience, this interchange was recorded for posterity by Paul Kimmage of the *Sunday Tribune*, who was then privileged to enjoy a pit lane stroll with Jordan.

In that morning's French daily sports newspaper *L'Equipe*, Frank Williams had offered kind words and encouragement to the new Jordan team after their impressive start to the year. Jordan wanted to know why such a ruthless and wily old competitor as Williams had done so. 'Eddie, a man with your drive and energy can't be stopped,' came the reply.

As they strolled on, Walton having returned to work, Jordan halted to admire the McLaren garage. 'This is it. This is the cream,' he said. 'If you asked me if I had a hero, I would probably say Ron Dennis because he has won more Grand Prix races than I probably will ever win. But he is the target. He has always been the target. When he was in Formula Three, I wanted to break all his records, and I did. In Formula 3000, I wanted to beat what he did, and I did. So I'm after him, and he knows that. He's quite nice to me and it's no problem because he respects what we are doing because we are a very professional team. The way I look at it is this. It will take me time to beat Ron Dennis because he's amazingly professional. You can see it all around his garage.'

'But, does what Frank Williams said in *L'Equipe* today make you feel good?' asked Kimmage.

'No,' said Jordan. 'Not really. Why would it make me feel good? Do you think he meant it?'

'Well, he obviously meant it if he said it.'

'He probably meant it, but he probably finds it easier to give us praise than his closest rivals. I don't mean that badly against Frank because that's maybe his opinion, but I have to live up to that. You see, it doesn't matter whether they love me or hate me. It doesn't make any difference. I have a job to do, and that is to make my team the best team in the world, and that means getting the best engine, the best engineers, the best drivers, the best people, and if I'm not good enough to do the job I do I'll have to get the best person who can do my job. But that would be sad, because I think I can do the job myself.'

'I read once in an interview you said you'd never pay millions for a driver like Senna.'

'Yeah, never.'

'But if you want to be world champion, and Senna is the best . . .'

'Then I'll pay it. Nothing can stand in the way of the end result.'

If Walton had heard this, it would have been amusing to see the look on his face. Jordan and drivers is a specialist subject, a place for the brave or the foolhardy. When asked, Walton was less than enthusiastic about the Jordan system of selection. 'He can certainly impress you at times, and at other times he can totally mesmerise you because some of the stuff he does is unbelievable,' he said. 'But at the end of the day, it seems to work in the favour of the team. He just has a knack of finding the deals.'

What, then, has been his craziest, least expected deal of all?

'I thought that when he pulled off the Peugeot deal, that was quite impressive. I thought at that stage that we could go somewhere and do something special as a team. But there were things happening in the team that didn't work, so it took us a few years to pick it up again and make it happen. But Eddie never lets the pressures reach you. Sometimes, when you know him very well and you socialise with him, he might open up to you and you can see the concerns and worries, but most of the time he does a good job of keeping it to himself.'

Walton's favourite memories are of the on-the-road fun that consumed them during the chaotic early years, in particular the way in which the Jordan family would always muck in, whatever the circumstances. He recalled one particular run down to Monaco when, in his own words, he 'lost half a caravan'. 'I can't remember, but I think we had a guy called Brett Rally driving the car, and that year we would basically just go from race to race and then someone would come along and they would have a few quid and they would want to go and race somewhere else. We were borrowing this caravan from a guy in the local pub near Silverstone, and we put it behind the van. On the way down, somehow I lost half of it, but I didn't notice until we got there. It was the bit that holds the gas bottle to the front. We had gone from Silverstone, on the Bank Holiday Monday, from the race, and driven all through the night straight to Monaco. We got there and had to put the awning up and everything. They had Zoe, their eldest daughter, who was only a baby at the time, with them, and there we were, living in the remainder of the caravan.'

At times like these, Eddie was prepared to fall back on some of his old salmon-, car- and carpet-selling practices. Since their 'Grand Prix' tickets lasted only until the Saturday night (when their racing was over), they were of little value, but this did not deter them from selling the remains of their tickets to 'unsuspecting punters' in town in order to raise the funds for their own supper and a few drinks. Then it was back in the van and the car, load up, and drive away again, on to the next race in the next country the following weekend.

But then, being careful with money was ever Jordan's lookout. He might have earned a small fortune by the end of the 1980s through his F3 and F3000 teams and his driver management business (as a result of which he had become an expert on the drivers' transfer market, contracts and the machinations around the F1 paddock), but he knew too, as he made his preparations for Formula One in 1990, that he did not have enough funds to throw money around freely. He spent much of that year doing his sums, and things added up to a tight squeeze: he would need to register his team for the championship at a cost of around half a million pounds; to hire an expert designer and engineer (Anderson) and a team of mechanics (such as Walton) and others to help him design and build the car; to acquire an engine, a supply of tyres and a motley collection of incidentals to make sure the whole thing came together and worked. His discussions with Ford about an engine were fruitful, but engines were to cost Eddie around £6 million in 1991 alone. Thankfully, he consoled himself before the season began, he had a good friend in W. Duncan Lee, a backer to pay the major bills. It was tight, but it would work out, he told himself.

Then, almost like a bolt from the blue, came the shocking news that Camel's plans for 1991, as announced to the media at the Belgian Grand Prix at Spa Francorchamps in August 1990, did not include a budget for Jordan. Instead of maintaining their previous strategy, the American-owned company was switching its colours and its sponsorship in Formula One (where it had backed Lotus) to the Benetton and Williams teams. In short, it was determined to be associated with winners and front-runners. When asked about Jordan's role in the future Camel programme, Lee said merely that there were no plans for Jordan to be involved. 'Not at this time' was the phrase he used, and it reverberated back to Oxford with the devastating pain of a drill to the brain. According to Lee, there was no agreement to supply Jordan with F1 sponsorship, private or formal.

Eddie was aghast. 'We were guaranteed money with an existing sponsor – Camel – and that is what made it so much easier, relatively, to press the button to green and build the car,' he was quoted as saying. In fact, Jordan had been keen to take over the ailing Lotus operation entirely and had commissioned several reports on the Lotus business. It did not happen. And the Camel cash went elsewhere, too. From Jordan's point of view, having committed himself to Formula One for 1991, having signed a deal for the Ford Cosworth HB V8 engine, the final act of 1990 could not have been worse. He was so upset that he went and stood outside the errant sponsors' American headquarters before being moved on by the police.

'I always knew it would be an interesting ride with Eddie,' said Marie, with the kind of dry understatement that could only come from someone who had experienced it all. 'Good fun, yes, with lots happening all the time. Never a dull moment. He always said he would go into Formula One. Even when he went off to America and said he was looking for an engine, I just thought "Yeah, yeah", and then a few months later, we were knee-deep in preparations. It was tough. We were on a tightrope for two years. At one point, we were down personally by £3 million; all it needed was for one of the banks to close in and we could have gone under. But I never gave up. I never told Eddie not to go into it, but I remember my stomach being permanently full of butterflies. I used to wonder what we would do if things really folded. We had four kids, all in private schools, and a big house. I knew it would all have to go. We'd already sold off all the extras. I knew that it could sometimes be just a matter of days, maybe even hours, whether a company survived or not. It was tough for us because we were supporting ourselves. It only settled down after two years. It was that long before we could relax at all, financially. It was maybe three or four years altogether before we could feel easy about it all. I never really asked too much about it, though. I never found out just how much in debt we were. I was better off just cruising around doing my own thing. I could see that he had big problems. It was easy to see. But my worries were more about the family and just keeping things going. I didn't need any more than that. And Eddie managed to stay pretty cheerful, really, all the way through it.'

Staying cheerful was, of course, a Jordan trait he has maintained throughout his life. It is the quality in him that makes him most endearing to people the world over. And he manages it with plenty of his unique trickery and humour. He has also maintained a lifelong belief that if you can have some fun for little or no charge, it is not necessary to throw money around. He has applied this philosophy in many an amusing situation. He was, for example, an expert at boarding British Airways and other aeroplanes with an economy ticket and through his own knack of mixing humour and resourcefulness ending up in business or first class. He also carried a press card – thanks to his artistic contributions to the Irish media over the years, one presumes – and used this to gain entry to some of the most overbooked concerts and entertainments around. On one occasion, however, as Marie was prepared to divulge, he almost came unstuck. They had gone to Edinburgh to see Scotland play Ireland in the Five Nations Championship. 'Eddie and I stayed on to see the Boomtown Rats,' she recalled. 'They were playing a concert. We arrived at the door and Eddie took out his card, saying he was there to cover the rugby and the Bob Geldof concert. The guy said, "I'm sorry, you'll have to speak to the manager." So Eddie said, "Who's the manager?" And he said it was Kayo. Kayo came out, looked at Eddie – and at this time Eddie was quite a well-known driver – and said, "Where are you from?", knowing from how he spoke that he was from somewhere in Ireland. And Eddie said, "Synge Street." And the guy said, "Oh, I went to Synge Street as well." And then you start thinking, knowing that Eddie is going to get caught at this sooner or later. But it didn't happen that time.'

Jordan's readiness to take a risk won him rewards, deals, dividends and friends, but it also upset a few people whose egos were too sensitive. Alesi, however, another maverick in the sense that he was always ready with a smile and liked warm company and a good time, understood him, even if they could barely communicate in a common language for a long time. Their relationship summed up both men in many ways, but Alesi's warmth and gratitude towards Jordan as the man who rescued his career has remained genuine. 'For me,' he told journalist Gerald Donaldson, 'Eddie Jordan did a fantastic job because he tried to give me the English mentality. It is very different from the Latin, like me. If you remember a long time ago when Jesus Christ came to Nazareth. When he first came, everyone said he was fantastic. Four days later, he was crucified. That is the Latin mentality. Up and down. Too much. Inside, I am still a little bit like that. But, for one year, I also lived with an English family, in Oxford, to try to understand the language and the mentality. For me, this was a very good experience. I try to be a calm person. Sometimes, when I am very angry, I want to explode. But I try to remember the English way. I try to stay quiet and I try to understand what happens around me.' It might have been Jordan talking, not Alesi.

In the summer of 1990, in the *Sunday Times*, the motor racing correspondent Norman Howell profiled Eddie as someone 'ready to make his mark in Formula One'. In Alesi's view, Jordan had already done it, but by means other than having his own team. He had been preparing the ground, sowing the seeds that were about to grow and flower. Howell recognised this, remarking, for instance, on Jordan's 'uncanny ability to spot young drivers and to maximise their potential', though in the same article he also reported that Jordan had sold his option on Johnny Herbert's services to Benetton during the winter of 1988–89 in order to finance a race, omitting to mention that the little Englishman's future was at that time seen as questionable due to his injuries. He praised the Irishman for having 'confounded all by convincing Ford to supply his still nascent team with fifteen of the company's latest-specification V8 engines, the same ones which until the end of this season are the unique preserve of Benetton. A number of F1 teams were after the same engines, but Eddie got them.' Jordan said he was 'in the pink', and the reporter noted that this was perhaps because his eyes were hidden, at the time, by pink sunglasses. Above all, the important fact was that Eddie was being written about in a major feature interview in one of Britain's biggest and best-known quality Sunday newspapers, long before the time when he first hit the asphalt as an active contender in Formula One. It was the first of many times Eddie Jordan would enjoy high-profile publicity.

Howell noted, too, that Jordan had 'the look of a record producer rather than a prospective F1 team manager', and informed his readers that Eddie believed he was of 'the next generation'. 'Music is my hobby, but motor racing is my business,' EJ declared. 'Frank Williams and Ken Tyrrell are my heroes. But I admire Ron Dennis. He is brilliant. I may not respect him in the way I do the older guys, but you have to look up to him and try to emulate what he has done.' His first opportunity to do just that came in March 1991 in Phoenix, Arizona.

8. FROM PHOENIX TO MEXICO

'After Phoenix, we sat down and discussed where we were. We talked of what we thought we were good at and what we were not good at. After thinking about Phoenix realistically, I know what the potential is. We realise where we are good and where we are bad. We've tried to improve in these areas, but by no means have we cracked it yet. Everyone in F1 is striving to move forward, and we have so much to learn. Hopefully our learning curve will be steeper than other people who already have a bank of knowledge. There are so many pieces of intricate information that are required to be the best in any formula it is difficult to have all that knowledge in a hurry.'

'I shouldn't say this, I know, but if we don't get twelve points out of a season's racing, if we don't finish sixth or so, what the hell are we doing in Formula One? I certainly don't want to make up the numbers.' So said Eddie Jordan in February 1991, a month before the season-opening United States Grand Prix was held on a hastily assembled street circuit at Phoenix in Arizona. The grandstands were temporary, the 'track' was created using normal everyday American roads, all at right angles to one another, the surrounding scenery was atypical of the hot, deep south and south-west, and the climate was a shock to the system for travellers from Europe who were leaving a cold, damp and gloomy winter behind. The distance from London to Phoenix was great, too, and carried its passengers through several time zones; it was tea-time in Northamptonshire when it was breakfast-time in Arizona. But for golf lovers, or for people seeking an early-season sun-tan in the scorching desert rays, it was a good place to start the year. It was to be the maiden outing for the new Jordan Grand Prix team; the date 10 March had been underlined in red in Eddie Jordan's diary months before.

In fact, Eddie had been thinking of almost nothing else for longer than that. His serious moments, his silences, had filled his life for a year. Those close to him knew he was at work when he went quiet or lost interest in anything else that was happening. 'Most of his work, his ideas, his thinking, his deals, he does all of that on his own,' said Marie. 'He does it all in his own way. It's often difficult to get an answer from him, and that's because he hasn't worked it through in his own brain, his way, how he is going to approach it, or in what way, or how he's going to handle it. Or maybe which angle he is going to use. He has to think it all out for himself his way first.' Marie believes that Eddie, with the way his mind works, could and should have become a brilliant golfer. It is a sport she loves and understands. 'He is such a very competitive sportsman. He still is, with his golf. I can see it. Sometimes he sends the ball everywhere, but then, when it comes to his putting, he is something else. It's just amazing how good he can be. It's all about focusing your mind and concentrating on nothing else, and he's got it. He could have been a brilliant, brilliant golfer. But he didn't have the patience for it. Sometimes, you can see it with him. You can talk to him but he's not there. He's gone.'

During the dark nights and long dismal days of the winter of 1990–91, as the Phoenix race drew closer with alarming speed and the Jordan team worked feverishly to find the budget required to paint the black carbon-fibre body of Gary Anderson's beautiful Jordan 191 in the colours of generous and supportive sponsors, there were plenty of times when Eddie was silent. He was not talking. He was out for the count. The confirmation from R.J. Reynolds that there was not going to be any Camel sponsorship for Jordan Grand Prix had given him a big problem to solve. He was feeling a lot of stress. When the news release confirming the team's plans was sent out in December 1990, it was accompanied by a photograph of a plain black car. It carried no advertisements. Jordan had little option at that time but to hand the deeds of his Oxfordshire house over to the bank. He collected together all his personal savings and accumulated items of wealth and deposited them all in a gambler's belief in himself, in his own ability to solve the problem and find a sponsor, to spin the wheel and get lucky.

For the Irish, who were aware of the enormous risk he was taking and the great challenge he was meeting, Jordan was a hero. In the *Irish Times* of Saturday, 9 March 1991 he was profiled as 'the man behind Ireland's first entry in a Formula One Grand Prix' and photographed wearing fashionably large spectacles, a dark polo shirt and a chequered sports jacket. Even when times were hard and stressful, Eddie knew that appearances mattered, and he followed the dictum he had obeyed since his teenage years to turn himself out smart. By this time, of course, he had met the challenges of the winter, overcome the problems laid at his door by the non-appearance of the Camel support he believed he had reason to expect, and he had found replacement sponsors. The most important of these was 7UP, the refreshing drink owned by Pepsi-Cola, but there were plenty more, including Fuji Film, BP, Marlboro, Philips Car Stereo and others. Somehow, in the final months of an eighteen-month rush to the grid, he and his team had hustled together a budget of nearly £12 million for the season. It was enough to start, but nobody really knew if it would be enough to complete the job.

Remember, however – as so many people obviously did at the time, reminding him of his wilder days in Dublin – that this man Jordan had scratched around for a few extra pounds many times before. Just fourteen years earlier, it was reported, he had been sighted at the height of the international rugby season at the top of Grafton Street, fully dressed in a colourful chef's uniform, hawking his smoked salmon below a large placard that read SAUMON FUMEE ICI. TRES BON MARCHE. The French tourists were happy, but not the local gardai, who were constantly employed in moving him on. He had suffered, too, in lots of other ways (though the idea of seeing Eddie suffering is one that tests the imagination since he is one of those men who always finds amusement and pleasure in life whatever the circumstances). His late love affair with motor racing had led to many errant adventures on the race circuits, a long series of accidents and many injuries. In the space of eleven years, he said, he had broken his legs so often they were barely recognisable as the limbs he was born with. He had broken his left leg a total of thirteen times, and it had been so badly damaged that his left ankle and heel had been rebuilt. Most of it is made of plastic, he will heartily inform anyone who asks, but it seems to do little to slow him down.

Indeed, the story of Eddie Jordan's vicissitudes and his rise from ad hoc street trader and bank clerk to Ireland's first Formula One team owner was so romantic and exciting that it made him everyone's favourite Grand Prix chief long before he reached the grid in Phoenix. His fresh approach, his effrontery, his language and humour all helped develop a unique appeal that was as attractive to seasoned sponsors of rival middle-of-the-road teams as it was to the fans and the media. He was a good talker, as everyone knew, and he used this gift as frequently as possible. Though he had been living in England for over a decade, he remained wholly Irish, undeniably a Dubliner. His entire spirit reverberated with his Irishness. He ribbed reporters from the start about their accuracy and their work, making friends immediately. At the initial launch of his car, when his friend John Watson – the great Northern Ireland driver who was one of Eddie's heroes and who drove in 152 Grands Prix in his long career with Brabham, Surtees, Lotus, Penske and McLaren, won five of them, notably the famous 1977 British Grand Prix at Silvertone in hot sunshine, and later became a highly respected F1 commentator – gave the vehicle its shakedown test, he offered warm, low-key hospitality in his Silverstone hut and a brand of smiling enthusiasm that won him many supporters. It did not matter a jot to the reporters who were served tea and biscuits rather than the normal heavy luncheon served by a London hotel that they had missed out on a gastronomic experience. Instead, Eddie served up some life in the raw. He smiled too, as Watson recalled. 'It was a very important moment really, for Eddie, and and for me. It was the first time that a Jordan car had turned a wheel out on the track and, of course, all of Eddie's aspirations and ambitions hung on how that first drive went. I came in with a smile on my face and I think that said an awful lot. The car was good.'

His drivers for the 1991 season were his old friend and former track rival Andrea de Cesaris, then a veteran of 150 Grands Prix out of which had come just one pole position, two second places and a host of spectacular accidents (he was nicknamed Andrea de Crasharis), and a little-known Frenchman by the name of Bertrand Gachot, the Luxembourg-born son of a French European Commission official. Gachot, 28, had a reputation as a temperamental and difficult individual, and he had raced in just five Grands Prix, but he was valuable to Eddie in that he brought money with him to the team. So, too, did the older Italian (he was 31), who, though unpredictable on the track and full of humour and tantrums, was easier to understand than the highly strung Gachot. Indeed, as the season unfolded, so did Gachot's temperament.

For Jordan, however, there was no time for predicting the future, analysing psychology or having the luxury of many second thoughts. He needed to move from one decision to the next in a seamless flow, hoping none of his decisions was wrong. 'Quick decision-making is particularly important in motor racing,' he said in a press conference during the run-up to the opening race. 'Fortunately, that has never posed a problem for me. Ireland has a wonderful motor racing tradition, which made us famous internationally after the First World War. That tradition found new life in the opening of Mondello Park, which did wonders for the confidence of our drivers, who went to England to try to make their names.' Every interviewer from the assembled media was likely to have heard most of the Jordan stories several times over before the season began, but his was the tale of the year, so far as previews to the 1991 championship were concerned. Several so-called experts decided that he had no chance, one in particular having to eat some humble pie because he had predicted, following the shakedown and initial launch of the car in the winter, that Eddie Jordan had no chance and would fail. That journalist was the celebrated French writer Gerard 'Jabby' Crombac, a man who showed that he knew less about Jordan than he knew about motor racing when he said that the Dubliner's forlorn approach to the task was doomed to failure.

'Apart from my ventures into smoked salmon, I would sell rugs and carpets out at Ashbourne market and so on,' Jordan continued to his audience. 'Now, you would probably say "God, you're mad", and maybe I was. But I couldn't help it. I was totally besotted with the world of motor racing and it was like being caught up in something that was much bigger than any love affair . . . Finding myself impoverished and married with a baby daughter living in a one-room flat in Buckinghamshire, I thought of returning to Dublin and going back to my old job in the bank. Then I decided to give it one last shot. This time, I decided, I would enter management. I borrowed £7,000 from a friend who is now my business partner, Fred Rodgers, a solicitor . . . That set me up in management, and my first driver was an English lad, James Weaver. I also had David Hunt, James Hunt's brother. And all the while I knew I had developed a good eye for a driver . . .'

The words poured forth, and the Formula One world learnt that, for Eddie, the telling of the story is more important than the actual facts. He erred only marginally from the original truth, of course, embroidering as he went, so it was always forgivable. The problem for those trying to see through the mists of time and nail down a reliable and accurate version of affairs has been that the embellishments have become part of the folklore, and his versions of incidents often do not tally with other people's recollections. It is without argument that he played a part in the management of many drivers' careers, but his claim that 'the young Brazilian did all my testing for the remainder of 1982' conveyed the idea that Ayrton Senna had worked diligently for months to improve the Jordan cars' performances, when in fact he had completed just the one test-drive, and a free one at that, having already signed a contract to drive for Dick Bennetts' team West Surrey Racing.

There is little doubt, though, that Jordan did make money from his drivers. All of them have answered questions about his activities on their behalf with the look of men who have just found out their numbers came up in the lottery, only to be told the ticket was bought by Eddie. According to various reports, he negotiated a three-year deal, for example, on behalf of Martin Brundle with the Tyrrell team for 1984–86 after his sensational F3 season with Eddie Jordan Racing in 1983 when he pushed Senna all the way in the championship. This was worth a reported £800,000 to Eddie Jordan Management and provided many of the funds on which his early successes were built. Indeed, Brundle probably has every right to claim, as Jordan so often does when he meets drivers who were once under his control, that 'I effing made you!'

When his management company was at its peak, Jordan could boast – as he did on the eve of the 1991 season when he spoke repeatedly about his own business acumen – that he had brought in the Japanese tyre company Yokohama and a Middle Eastern petroleum company known as Q8 (both, it transpired, after some assistance from other parties). He had handled drivers such as Jean Alesi, Martin Donnelly, Stefan Johansson, Gachot and Johnny Herbert, and his motor racing portfolio of clients made him a bigger agency in the field, it was said, than Mark McCormack's IMG, arguably the biggest of its type in the world, so the *Irish*

Times was told. Of all the drivers, it was Alesi who had the most potential in terms of future revenue to Jordan. Again, it was reported, Alesi could have been worth £2 million to Jordan during a ten-year career in Formula One after he moved on from his Formula 3000 team. The Jordan system of the time certainly worked, too. In the 1980s, three outstanding drivers scored points in their maiden Grand Prix outings: Brundle (fifth for Tyrrell in Brazil in 1984, a result that was scrubbed from the records for technical reasons); Alesi (fourth for Tyrrell in France in 1989); and Herbert (fourth for Benetton in Brazil in 1989). All of them were Jordan drivers.

But all these past achievements, these landmarks in his team's development and in his own progress from street hawker to team owner, were worth nothing unless he could pay his bills and steer the 7UP Jordan Ford team to stability and success. His home in Oxford was on the line, along with the house he had built by the sea in the Spanish resort of Sotogrande, where he and Marie enjoyed their passions for golf and sailing, not to mention a flat in London. As Marie has explained in earlier chapters, there was also the more important matter of the children's education and future. Eddie had attempted to buy into Lotus without success; now he had to start his own operation from the bottom up, and to find the cash to pay all the bills. That he did this was, in the end, a greater achievement than all he managed to inspire his loyal, exhausted and extraordinary team to do on the track.

But the journey to Phoenix, in both the physical and metaphorical sense, was strewn with obstacles, not least the need to raise funds and fend off predators from other teams who, having been made aware that a new kid on the block was finding fresh meat in the highly competitive financial waters that are Formula One's life-stream, had begun to make their own approaches to steal sponsors away. Still, this was a signal to the Jordan team that they were being taken seriously.

The critical recruitment by Eddie of his friend and right-hand man in commercial, marketing and public relations affairs Ian Phillips was the sign to those in the business that this Dubliner was not to be dismissed or treated lightly. Phillips was a veteran of the British motor racing scene, a former journalist who had been the youngest ever editor of *Autosport* magazine (at the age of 22), who had worked at Donington Park as managing director from 1976 to 1978, who had become a well-paid and successful freelance motor racing media consultant and reporter, and who had also been general manager of the Leyton House March F1 operation. He was seasoned in every aspect of the business at this level, he understood the need for money, he knew the sponsors and he was skilled in communications. His was a vital signature. He became a critical partner in helping develop the strategy of the business.

Working with Jordan was never likely to be a straightforward job, but long before he signed up, Phillips had a very good idea of what to expect. When interviewed at the Jordan Grand Prix headquarters at Silverstone in May 2002, Phillips' answers were punctuated frequently by gales of laughter as he recalled the hustling style of Eddie in his early days. Asked, for example, when and where he first set eyes on Jordan, Phillips replied, in a deadpan style and without delay, 'Windsor Castle, Camden Hill Road, London W11.'

Why do you remember it so vividly?

'He gave me a headache.'

When was it?

'It was in 1975, which was when I was editor of *Autosport*. We used to run the magazine from said hostelry and everyone in the business, basically, knew that if they wanted any chance of a mention in the magazine they had to turn up there on a Tuesday, Wednesday or a Thursday night, at the Windsor Castle. In those days, there was a fairly big Irish contingent of rally drivers and racing drivers, and one night, of course, Edmund Patrick arrived. I remember him coming back to my house that night. The man just would not go away. He had to tell us that he was going to be Ireland's first world champion driver. He took all night at it, too. And that's how it all started for me, really.'

As editor of *Autosport* in those days, Phillips was as influential in the media, publicity and communications side of the business of British motor racing as anyone could be, and he knew many people in all areas of the industry all over the world. This made him a man of influence and an attractive contact for all the drivers, managers, team owners and ambitious new entrants to the sport. It also meant he was approached frequently to be involved in various projects as a consultant, or to help certain people or companies find the appropriate deals and opportunities. When asked about his first such dealings with Eddie, he scratched his head before recalling, from the depths of a plethora of agreements during three decades in the business, one he believed was the first he did in which Eddie was involved.

'I guess I did my first deal early in the 1980s when I was a sort of consultant to Philip Morris, to help them with their work in the junior categories. One of my "patches" was Macau.' Here, he smiled broadly and chuckled. 'Well, of course, EJ managed to turn up, as part of Marlboro Theodore Racing, with Teddy Yip. Dickie Bennetts genuinely had the Marlboro money, but Sid [Taylor] managed to get Teddy and Dickie to share a garage and I've no doubt Eddie got paid ten times more than Dickie ever did at that race! And that was the start of it. Various other things that he said he got, I had passed his way. He earned a fortune, for example, out of a guy called Maurizio Sandro Salo, who he was managing; I got him a job, through March, driving in Japan. I think he got a ten-year living out there and I don't know how much of that went back to Eddie. And then I helped swing his Bridgestone tyre contract for Formula 3000 in 1985, and Thierry Tassin to take his Debic budget there, and that was quietly swept under the carpet, though I do remind him from time to time. Really, I'd say that Eddie was around and busy all this time and I was doing things working for various people. So it wasn't until I actually joined him that I realised I could have earned money out of all the things I had done for him.'

Did you do any business with him, or for him, when he was a driver?

'No. I don't think I did any. No. He was always blagging his way into these various drives. I remember he drove one of the works Marches for one or two races and it was sponsored by Marlboro. So I think I must have been involved somewhere along the line. He had done his deal and then it became my responsibility to put a cover-up patch on him, or something like that! But no, not deals as such. We just knew each other, and went to some parties together.'

What was he like as a driver?

'He had accidents! Lots. I remember going over to Mondello for a non-championship Formula Three race, or was it an Atlantic race? I can't remember exactly. I can't even remember if he took part, or if he had already broken his leg during testing in the week. But, as usual, there was a drama about his involvement. That's the long and the short of it. As you would expect, there was always a lot of drama around Eddie when he was racing. And, always, an awful lot of noise. There was always so much noise and fuss going on around anything Eddie did that half the time it was difficult to know what he was doing or trying to do. I think I probably first appreciated his energy in Macau when he raced there in Formula Atlantic, and there was another Irishman who was there who was even noisier than him, and his name was Gary Gibson, who, God bless him, is dead now. It became a bit of an Irish expedition because you'd got Sid Taylor involved with Teddy Yip. It was a wild weekend. Well, more than a weekend, because we were there for more than a week sometimes.

'I think as a driver on a national level he was okay, but he was a bit out of his depth when it came to international racing. But to be fair, as Eddie is with anything in life, he soon realised that it was a blind alley to his ambitions and he switched his aims to the management side. First came the racing team, I think, and then he set in train all that has continued until today. He always used to say to all the drivers, you don't sign for my team unless you sign a management contract. Well, I think he ended up signing more management contracts than he did running cars. But all that has stopped now. It has been gone for a long time. Still, there are other people doing the same, like Flavio [Briatore, the Benetton boss]. I think EJM [Eddie Jordan Management] got folded at the end of 1991. Fred [Rodgers] is still around, I think, helping young drivers.'

And how did you get from there to here, working for Eddie at Silverstone?

'Well, during my last years as a journalist, he was running his F3000 team and I'd got various contacts so I had to listen to most of his drivers whingeing about him [loud laughter]. It was then, also, that we had a lot of stuff we inadvertently put his way. I helped steer Q8 his way because I did a deal for them to supply the fuel to Leyton House March and they were looking for a manufacturer association. My best mate at the time was a guy called Chris Witty and he sold them a Formula 3000 involvement, using the name Ford, on what was very much a customer Cosworth engine [more loud laughter]. And that deal went to EJ, of course. There were lots of contacts through people in the paddocks, and he was lurking around Formula One races, you know, for a long time.

'I remember once going to Le Mans, before that time, probably around 1983 to 1984, and I was going out there with Marlboro. I went with Graham Bogle from Marlboro and, I think, John Wickham and Gordon Coppuck, who were [the F1 racing team] Spirit at the time. And, of course, we had to give a lift to Mr Edmund Patrick Jordan, who had a grand total of eleven drivers he had rented out to all sorts of people at Le Mans. Well, we went out there, I think, on the Thursday, and he was going there to collect! I should think he collected about a quarter of a million in envelopes and then he rushed home again. I don't think he was there for more than twenty minutes! Of course he got over there free of charge, and that was the way he operated all the time.

'When Eddie went to a race meeting and he was not competing in any way, shape or form with any of his drivers, he never had a hotel room. He was always looking to blag rooms or to sleep on people's floors. Sometimes, because he used to collapse before anyone else, he'd sleep in their beds until they got back to their rooms! Then he had to sleep on the floor, or the other guy who'd lost the bed did.'

Phillips' arrival sent a clear message to all the established Formula One teams that Jordan was going to be a thorn in their commercial side as well as their racing one. In turn, Jordan knew, especially once he learnt of the approaches by other teams to his new sponsor 7UP, that he had made a strong early mark on the scene. What he did not know, not then, was just how vicious and Darwinian the commercial jungle of the sport really was. He had told the *Irish Times* that his target for the season was 'sixth in the constructors' championship – we will then aim for the world title in 1993–94'. Those who laughed might have found themselves choking as time wore on, because Jordan not only began to deliver decent results, he also made mincemeat in his first few months of the particular difficulty of having to pre-qualify merely to take part in each Grand Prix. This was the chief reason why the bigger teams were irritated by his success, his coup, in delivering the 7UP sponsorship package, which blended perfectly with his intention of having a perfectly emerald green car, a vehicle that showed off the colours of Ireland and his sponsor brilliantly. The sponsorship deal was worth barely £1 million, but it was with a recognised name that would have nicely decorated any other team's portfolio of backers. The establishment, therefore, did their best to scupper his plans. The last thing they wanted was a new kid on the block causing them any embarrassment. That's why they hoped pre-qualifying, that early-morning test of nerves and potential, would trip Jordan up.

The pre-qualifying session was scheduled to take place between 8 a.m. and 9 a.m. every Friday morning before the start of each Grand Prix, from Phoenix in March to Adelaide in early November. This was necessary because eighteen teams, each with two cars, were entered for 1991; restrictions kept the numbers admitted to the practice and qualifying sessions down to 32, of which only 26 would actually start the race on the Sunday afternoon. This meant that in March it was possible for Eddie and his team to travel from Silverstone to Phoenix, take part in one hour of pre-qualifying and end up among the luckless group of four cars destined not to play any further part in the weekend's action. Even for the silver-tongued Eddie Jordan it would be a demanding job to explain away such an exit to an American sponsor like Pepsi. But Eddie was ready. 'I pulled no punches,' he explained before the flight to Dallas and on to Phoenix. 'I had to make a presentation before 47 of the company's executives and I told them there was a risk with this business of pre-qualifying. I explained how, despite your cars and drivers being potentially among the quickest, an unforeseen mishap could wreck your chances. I also explained that we genuinely believe we can get through pre-qualifying more often than not. Our potential is unbelievable. But, most important of all, I said that 7UP could grow with us and be part of the success of Team 7UP Jordan. If they went with one of the better known teams, with massive sponsors, their identity would be lost.'

However, the greatest coup of many coups for Jordan in his preparations for the 1991 season was his success in persuading Ford to supply him with their best engines. Benetton, backed of course by Camel's sponsorship, had believed they had an exclusive deal with Ford for the new Cosworth V8s. It was no wonder, then, as we shall see, that later in the year the Benetton management took the opportunity, when it arose, to ensure that Jordan did not continue to receive such a supply of engines the following year – and, in the bargain, managed to poach Eddie's greatest driver, Michael Schumacher, after only one race in green.

But before that, Jordan's much admired 'lean, mean and green' machine made a near-perfect F1 debut in the hands of Gachot, the Frenchman finishing tenth in Phoenix to lay down a marker for the team. Poor old de Cesaris failed to qualify for the race, but his performance was auspicious enough. Respectable efforts by both drivers followed in the next three races at São Paulo, Imola and Monte Carlo, then the breakthrough came in the Canadian Grand Prix in Montreal on 2 June, only the fifth round of the year, de Cesaris coming home fourth and Gachot fifth. It did not matter a jot that Nelson Piquet, in a Benetton powered by the same Ford engine, won the race, nor that Nigel Mansell, a championship favourite and race leader, had suffered a gearbox difficulty while preparing to celebrate victory on the final lap and so ended up sixth. The Jordan team had scored points and was among the elite.

More than anything, it was a massive psychological fillip to the whole team. The partying in the little caravan parked in the paddock, close to the Olympic rowing lake on the Ile Notre Dame where the Circuit Gilles Villeneuve is laid out, was understandably unrestrained. This was the critical result for Jordan and the team, the answer to all the questions and the reason they had all joined forces. At the next race, the Mexican Grand Prix in Mexico City, de Cesaris finished fourth; at the French Grand Prix at Magny-Cours in central France, the Italian took sixth place; and at Silverstone, for the British Grand Prix, Gachot came sixth before they repeated their form from Canada by taking fifth and sixth at Hockenheim on 28 July. It was thrilling for everyone, especially as the form of the team in the first half of the season (up to Silverstone) earned relief from the need to pre-qualify in the second half.

Eddie, aware of the stakes involved in all aspects of running his successful team, experienced elation mixed with trepidation as the prospect of paying performance bonuses was entwined with the value of his team's successes. As ever, he had prepared himself for all eventualities and had taken out a special performance-related insurance policy that would, he hoped, deliver some of the cash he needed to meet the bonus claims. Indeed, this was how the aftermath of the Canadian Grand Prix was reported in the *Daily Telegraph* of 4 June: 'Eddie Jordan and his fledgling Formula One team stand to earn a substantial bonus from a unique perform-ance-related insurance policy if they continue to show the sort of form which brought them their first World Championship points in Sunday's Canadian Grand Prix. As he celebrated the efforts of his drivers, Andrea de Cesaris and Bertrand Gachot, who finished fourth and fifth respectively in Sunday's race, Mr Jordan con-firmed he was paying in to a policy which insured his Team 7UP Jordan against finishing in the top six of the Constructors' World Championship in their debut year. He said, "It is a special insurance policy. It is performance related and will pay, but if we are particularly successful. When I looked at my budget for a development programme for 1992, I thought we did not have enough to do it properly. So, I decided to use the money in a different way, and when I heard of this policy I went for it. Of course, I cannot give you any figures."

'Mr Jordan, Ireland's first Grand Prix team owner and a man with an innovative style even by Formula One's standards (he obtained his engine deal with Ford before he had built his first F1 car), is believed to be the first man in the sport to have taken out such a policy. If his team remains successful – Sunday's five points take them to equal sixth in the championship – then Mr Jordan, it is believed, could become the recipient of as much as £1 million, which would make a healthy contribution to his team's budget next year. This kind of indemnity has been utilised before in soccer and speedway, and was used by Belgian Eric van de Poele, who finished second last year in the International F3000 Cham-pionship, recording three wins along the way . . .

'Mr Jordan offered praise to everyone. "We have a close-knit team and that result said it all about them and the companies we work with. Everyone has worked so hard. I had a lot of stick when I signed Andrea and he has proved me right. He has made only one mistake all season and he has done a great job.'"

Unfortunately for Eddie, and for the reporter (the author of this book), the policy described above was never to pay out. The agreement entered into by Jordan with such wholehearted enthusiasm was with a Belgian company that not only wanted to keep its identity secret, but also to ensure that the whole deal was subject to a confidentiality clause. Once Eddie had talked about his arrangements, the clause came into effect and the deal was made null and void.

His euphoria remained, however, and was identified with by every man, woman and child in Ireland, a fact which elevated him almost overnight in their sporting spectrum from a hopeful also-ran to a cult figure to rank alongside the imported hero who managed their national football team, the Englishman Jack Charlton. By the time his team had made collecting points a matter of fortnightly habit, it seemed half the emerald isle wanted to join the party and travel over the Irish Sea to Silverstone. 'They think the cars are all in Irish green, and as I and several team members are Irish, they see this as a World Cup campaign all over again,' Jordan explained on the eve of the annual Silverstone invasion in which he had participated with glee and joy only a dozen years earlier. 'Instead of Jackie's green and white army, it's Eddie's army.' Estimates of the Irish contingent at Silverstone in 1991 circled around the 20,000 figure, and still the race turned into a Mansell-mania celebration, typical of the times.

Yet it was Jordan who seemed to command just as many column inches and television minutes as anyone else. 'They can't make up their minds whether I'm a flannel merchant, whether I'm clever, whether I'm a hustler, or what,' he said in interviews with the British media in the run-up to the British race. 'To be honest, I don't really know myself. I would do anything to help my racing. The more money you have, the better chance you have, no matter what level you're at. The Irish people are good hustlers, you know. But I don't think I could handle drivers if I'd not been one myself. I don't stand for any garbage, I treat them as normal people. I don't put them on a pedestal. Once they know you know how they feel, that you understand the pressures, the highs and the lows, you can work together. I very much doubt I'll change the way I am, or the way I operate, if we get to the position where we have the top drivers here. They're not angels. Neither am I. It would be nice to think we might one day have Senna here. We pushed him so hard in the Formula Three Championship with Brundle. There's no doubt in my mind that Senna's the best in the business and our target is to be the best and perhaps go for the championship in three years' time. I'm the biggest optimist there is, and I suppose some might say my optimism is unrealistic. But you've got to have targets and we've done pretty well for starters. That's all it is, though. Starters. I don't think there's any secret to this game. You work hard, you get good people, get on with it, but try to keep a smile on your face.'

This was a more measured response than that given to his happy inquisitors after the Canadian Grand Prix when, in a manic hour awash with champagne, he had talked himself virtually to a standstill. Yet, as ever, even in his most emotionally unrestrained moments, he talked with great fluency and passion. When asked if Montreal was the pinnacle of his career, he said, 'Well, I've had some other good days. Obviously, winning the championship with Johnny Herbert and winning a championship with Jean Alesi. They were very special days because, you know, to win a championship is quite difficult because it's a year-long fight. This obviously is very important for everybody in the team because we are the only team here to finish with both cars in the points and that is quite special because it is for the best when both drivers get points. And I can feel it is a complete team effort and that everyone is part of it. We set ourselves a task to have so many points by this stage and I think we are now on target, or maybe one point ahead! Up to this time, it has been frustrating. We were not quite as relaxed as perhaps we should be and this has given us the belief and the kind of complete confidence we need to have in ourselves. We can move forward now from this position. We want to progress, and we want to progress quite well.'

On the subject of reliability, he said, 'Well, it's very early days yet and it's easy to get blasé about something. The performances of these cars are such a very delicate edge, in terms of reliability, that it is always something to get the maximum performance. So, for us to say we have licked the reliability problem would not be right; it is a bit too early for that. Having said that, we have sorted out the problems we had in the first couple of races and we addressed that very quickly. The design team and the engineers back at base have been superb. We attacked that side very quickly because we knew that if we could finish races we could finish in the points. I think the performance of the engine and the car right from day one has been there, so it was a matter of making sure that all the pieces went together properly.

'Pre-qualifying is like something you cannot imagine. It is like two races in one because you have to peak at eight o'clock on Friday morning and then, if you don't perform, you are out for the rest of the weekend. It's as easy as that. We know what it is like to miss out in pre-qualifying because at the very first race we had a problem. Andrea's engine was over-revved and he didn't make it through. That's how difficult pre-qualifying is. It is hard to equate, but I think the team will become great in stature as a result of doing pre-qualifying because of the detailed attention that is required to perform well there, so I don't think it is that negative. But I'll surely be glad to be out of it.

'For me, now, my mind is on the future. I am always thinking about the team, the strategy we need as a company, the structure we need. From my side, which is the commercial side and the operation of the company, this year is almost finalised. That's put to bed. I have to think about the future, and the future for me is not next week, the future for me is 1992. How can I try to win races? And 1993. How can I possibly win the championship or something? That is where my mind is at the moment. It won't change. I was quite emotional at the end of this race, I have to say. It is such a great day for everybody. For me, personally, I feel very excited about it. But mainly because, you know, the mechanics and the drivers and the team have really achieved something. They all committed to us before the car even turned a wheel, and that's quite a brave thing to do. The mechanics we have, and the engineers, they have all been with me for a long time and we brought them through the formulae and we didn't hire in a lot of people just for Formula One. We wanted to do it our way, and I feel very happy and very proud for them because they have stuck with it, and this is justification for what they have done over the winter. I think, though, on the day, we had a lot of luck. I thought we looked strong in the test at Magny-Cours and I thought we looked strong here [Montreal] in the race situation. Our strategy has been that we want to be reliable. We can sacrifice some performance at the beginning just in an attempt to make sure we finish, and that's what we have done. Finishing is important.'

Eddie, of course, knew he had been working as hard as possible to achieve his goals. Even after the Brazilian race, only the second of the season, he wore the relaxed look of a man who knew things could only get better. 'I think I was confident from the beginning,' he said at the time. 'I think the team had a reasonable amount of reality attached to it from day one. When I made the decision to put together a lot of borrowed money and a lot of my own money, it was not a decision that was taken lightly. At Phoenix, I hadn't given enough thought to the possibility of not pre-qualifying. I think I misunderstood how traumatic pre-qualifying can be, but that's not to say we underestimated it. Eight good cars arrive and try desperately to be on the pace. Before you start, half of them are excluded! I entered knowing this to be the case, therefore it is impossible to say it is fair or unfair. They are the rules, and you have to abide by them. I don't feel sorry for the teams that haven't pre-qualified, but it is a very hard pill to swallow. In Phoenix, it made us go on the defensive rather than on the attack. In Brazil, the thing that impressed me the most was that we had an engine gearbox problem after pre-qualifying and we had to change the whole back end of the car. What was so pleasing for me was that we were strong enough to endure these setbacks. We had both cars in the race and we pushed strongly. We're aggressive and we are arrogant. We are saying, "Where are the bastards? Let's go get 'em." But not in a nasty way, in a competitive way.

'After Phoenix, we sat down and discussed where we were. We talked of what we thought we were good at and what we were not good at. After thinking about Phoenix realistically, I know what the potential is. We realise where we are good and where we are bad. We've tried to improve in these areas, but by no means have

Above There is never a dull moment in Formula One, particularly in a Grand Prix paddock, and especially for Eddie Jordan. As someone who is as at home with musicians as with politicians, he is comfortable talking shop with Max Mosley, the president of the sport's ruling body, the Federation Internationale de l'Automobile (FIA). They may be discussing music or racing, but are most likely to be thinking about money, the lubricant that keeps the business on the road.

Right Relaxed, serene and stylish, Marie Jordan has never been anything other than totally positive and supportive to her husband's career and ambitions in one of motor racing's most successful and happy marriages. Her calm demeanour has won her many friends and admirers, some of them baffled by her ability to survive alongside such a bundle of energy as Eddie.

Above Few people were happier than the Formula One 'ringmaster' himself, Bernie Ecclestone, when Eddie Jordan finally delivered his first Grand Prix win in Belgium, in 1998. The man in charge of the sport's commercial business affairs knew better than most that Jordan's team were good at the box office, but admitted that his maiden triumph would make him unbearable! The sport's most colourful pairing are pictured at Silverstone during the 1996 British Grand Prix.

Above Never mind the quality, listen to the noise! Johnny Herbert and Martin Brundle join Eddie Jordan on stage to provide a memorable evening of entertainment at the post-race party at Silverstone, in 1996. Both drivers spent time racing for Eddie in their early careers and enjoyed great success. Predictably, Eddie reminded them regularly of this in his own inimitable fashion.

Right Music is the first real love of Eddie's life, ahead of sport, and there is nothing he loves better after a stressful day than to beat the hell out of a drum kit. He is pictured doing just that in public during one of his famous, successful and inimitable post-Silverstone parties in the paddock at the British Grand Prix.

Below Two of the old school, Ken Tyrrell and Eddie Jordan, meet to ponder the present and the future for the privateer independent teams at the German Grand Prix in 1996. Eddie had great admiration for the self-made team owners of the past like Tyrrell and Frank Williams. Tyrrell won world championships with Jackie Stewart, but his long career at the top of motor racing ended when he sold his team to the emerging British American Racing outfit.

Left What Eddie Jordan does not know about music is not worth knowing. Here is Eddie pictured giving the hugely-successful singer Phil Collins a few words of wisdom on the music business and Formula One just before the start of the 1997 German Grand Prix at the Hockenheimring.

Below Making his point and putting his message across, Eddie delivers his views with a clear sense of direction as Ron Dennis listens in May 1998. Eddie has never been afraid to speak his mind and has high respect for Dennis, the McLaren International chief who coined the phrase 'Welcome to the Piranha Club' after Jordan had lost Michael Schumacher to Benetton in September 1991.

Right If his family had had their way, Eddie may have become a professional golfer instead of a Formula One team owner. According to his wife Marie, he is a very competent and competitive player who had a great talent for the game. Here he is pictured during a round at The Oxfordshire course during a pro-am event before the Benson and Hedges International Open in May 1998.

Below The first, the greatest and the wettest ... Eddie takes a champagne shower courtesy of the efforts of his outstanding race winning driver Damon Hill and runner-up Ralf Schumacher after they had finished first and second, so delivering his team's maiden Formula One triumph, at the 1998 Belgian Grand Prix. Eddie was so stunned he barely knew what to say or do after the race, but this experience gave him the lift he needed for the night that lay ahead.

Above They come in all shapes and sizes, Eddie seems to be thinking, as he listens to an explanation of something special from the Hollywood film star Sylvester Stallone during practice for the Italian Grand Prix at Monza in September 1998. Stallone was asked what he was doing spending so much time at Formula One races and replied: 'I'm an Eddie Jordan groupie'.

Left Sitting pretty and waiting for action, Eddie's boat 'The Snapper' is pictured soaking up the sunshine in the harbour at Monte Carlo where it serves as both the hospitality headquarters for the Jordan family and as sleeping quarters during the weekend of the Monaco Grand Prix.

Right Eddie mixes easily with people from all walks of life and even made the deputy British Prime Minsiter John Prescott feel relaxed when they shared a joke on the grid prior to the British Grand Prix at Silverstone in 1999.

Below Eddie is not only a Formula One fan, but also a lover of football and other sports. He is a regular at Coventry City, the club he supports, and an ardent follower of the Ireland national team. Here he is pictured at Lansdowne Road, Dublin, where Ireland played Yugoslavia in September 1999 in a Euro 2000 qualifier.

Left Enjoying a rare moment of relaxation together during the rush of a Formula One weekend, Eddie and Marie posed in the harbour at Monte Carlo during the 2001 Monaco Grand Prix. As this picture shows, they were quite at home in the magnificent and unique surroundings and had come a long way from the days when they showered on the beach and changed into 'Oxfam fashion-wear' for the traditional balls and parties in the Mediterranean principality.

Below Eddie's great energy and strength is drawn from his family roots and, as this photograph taken at the 2001 Belgian Grand Prix shows, he is never happier than when surrounded by wife Marie and their children Kyle, Zak, Miki and Zoe. Together they are a formidable and loyal team and provide Eddie with the love and inspiration that has been the bedrock of his momentum since leaving Dublin for Silverstone and a life in motor racing.

we cracked it yet. Everyone in F1 is striving to move forward, and we have so much to learn. Hopefully our learning curve will be steeper than other people who already have a bank of knowledge. There are so many pieces of intricate information that are required to be the best in any formula it is difficult to have all that knowledge in a hurry.

'But we've made progress, and that is the kind of thing I need to see. I also need to see the background. I need to see if the team is working well. We are nowhere near the potential I think is there. We have good equipment, but not mountains of it. We have a good technical programme. I don't want to look ahead and say it's all going to be easy, because there are going to be setbacks. We know we are being talked about now, but we've had to work hard for it. We've done it our way. I'm not saying it's the best way, but I feel satisfied. I hope we can grow into a bigger and happier team. There is no doubt that the bigger we get the less personal it becomes. That, in itself, is a worry, because I have always felt that I have been very close to my team, in a hands-on situation. Of course, whether I like it or not, I cannot do it like it was before because it is a bigger operation, but I would be very reluctant to give up the things that have made us successful in F3 and F3000 because I believe in those principles.'

When told that Benetton were due to receive a new HB V8 'series five' engine from Ford Cosworth for the San Marino Grand Prix a month after the Interlagos race, Jordan was unflustered. It was plainly not his style to shout and throw his toys out of the pram. 'No, I am not disappointed at that at all. In fact, I am massively supportive of the Benetton programme. I honestly believe, and hope, they will win races. I hope the new engine is like they believe it is, because that will work back into our system. It would be very naive and foolhardy to try to outdo a team like Benetton. We are not in that position. We are the new kids on the block and we are not even starting to be in that position. Of course, if we get the chance we will try to beat them. That's normal racing sense. They have the official works Ford deal and we have the Cosworth deal. The engines are made by the same people, but I have no problems in accepting the terms of the agreement. All the new development and technology when it is available will go to Benetton first. I have no problems in accepting that. We can lend support and feedback to the ultimate benefit of both ourselves and Benetton.'

When pressed by some reporters, when he looked relaxed and people thought his guard was down, to reveal how he had managed to scoop so many so-called sponsorship experts in Formula One and sign 7UP, he was just as cagey as ever. 'Well, I'm not going to tell you how I did it because then everyone else would know! And I think you'll be surprised by other commercial activities we are planning. We are very commercially orientated. We have always had major corporate sponsorship and we've been able to hold on to it. I feel comfortable this way. I like to work with professionals. Our philosophy is that generally the sponsor is always right. I think they also have to be made aware in a professional way of what their role is, in the most diplomatic and beneficial way for both parties. Each then knows where they stand and what is expected. I think it is very important to have a set of ground rules which is accepted by both parties. They are easy to adhere to. There are times when there are differences of opinion, of course, but it is how those differences are sorted out that gives the strength to a relationship.

'I think we've achieved a lot in everything we have done so far, but we want to be the champions. We want to be champions like McLaren and do it continuously. We have to be careful that we don't arrive at a plateau and accept it. We have to be careful not to accept just being comfortable. That is going to take time. In motor racing, clever decisions have to be made continually, from a technical point of view, a financial point of view, in logistics and in operations. Getting it right gives you a great sense of satisfaction. It's very easy to be blasé and big-headed in F1, but it can turn and smack you in the face so quickly. To be anything other than humble in this business, I think, is a gross mistake. Fortune can dictate so many of the borderline issues. You can have the best of everything, and you should win if that is the case, but we're all human and we all need Lady Luck on our side.'

His response did nothing to lift the intrigue over the signing of the 7UP deal. Just how had he managed to achieve something that had eluded so many others? The answer, as usual, belongs in the folklore of Eddie Jordan's life and comprises a cross-section of his strongest interests stitched together by his outgoing personality and willingness to do virtually anything to earn money.

For more than a year before the start of the 1991 season, indeed as far back as 1989, he had been planning his entry into F1. He had approached Gary Anderson and told him he had £800,000 to begin with. That *was* enough to begin with, but, as Anderson pointed out in his direct style, sponsors and engines were needed. For the next year, although Eddie pulled off one of his master deals by landing the Ford HB V8 engine, Anderson was left to work through the difficulties with which we have already become acquainted (lack of preparation, offices, organisation and low funding), and with only 27 staff. These loyal members of Eddie Jordan Racing were travelling all over Europe to race at weekends in Formula 3000 and helping build a Formula One team in between. After the Camel débâcle, there was no strong prospect of a major replacement sponsor, and the bills were arriving. 'This was a tough time for us,' explained Jordan. 'I'd managed to raise £3 million of my own money for the project, but it wasn't a lump in the bank that we could just go and draw on. It came in dribs and drabs. I had to do television commercials at the same time to make £20,000 or so. It was not a lot, but it was enough to pay the wages for three weeks.'

It was these television advertisements that helped bring Jordan and 7UP together. In 1989, the American soft drinks company had sponsored Benetton; at that time, the Anglo-Italian team had asked Jordan if he could help them in the shooting of a commercial. After that, Jordan kept in touch with them, particularly avidly after reading that Pepsi-Cola had taken over 7UP. And then came a slice of luck thanks to his strong interest in music.

'I always loved music and I used to be a bit of a rock journalist,' he told Norman Howell in late 1991, the last part of his opening sentence stretching credulity a little. 'I was at the Tina Turner concerts and I ended up backstage, chatting to some people from Pepsi. We got on well and we talked money. They wanted more control than I was prepared to give them. So, the trail went cold . . . for a while. But then I had a call from Marlboro, who helped pay for my drivers, and they said that 7UP were getting interested again.' He knew, without any doubt, that he had to go for this. By late 1990, he had sold everything of any saleable value. The Formula 3000 cars, for example, went, along with his personal toys, including at one time a Ferrari. For Eddie, now, there was no going back.

He went and made a successful presentation to 47 delegates representing 7UP and was requested to return, to a London hotel, with his driver, Bertrand Gachot, one of his former clients. Eddie agreed to the arrangements, made the plans and duly arrived at the hotel on the pre-determined day. Unfortunately, Gachot was nowhere to be seen. The deadline arrived and Jordan, not to be put off by anything, went out in front of his audience and again gave a dazzlingly persuasive speech on just why 7UP should invest in backing his team in the Formula One World Championship. The worst over, the presentation made, Jordan was just starting to relax and consider his prospects of clinching the deal when he received an urgent phone call. It was Gachot. He was ringing to say he could not come to the presentation because he had been arrested for assault and was now in the police cells. Please, asked Gachot, could Eddie come and organise his release?

It was a year since he had started talking to Anderson, it was nearly Christmas, and the bank had only recently asked Jordan for the deeds to his home in Oxford as additional security. His position, financially, was perilous, and now he had to cope with a driver who was in jail instead of with him, helping him to secure the vital sponsorship that would solve his problems. Pepsi, 7UP's parent company, understandably took their time to reach a decision. Ford's state-of-the-art engine was working beautifully, and in early January 1991 the car posted impressive lap times, but money was needed, not the aggravation of a driver without a clue about normal civilised behaviour in a city full of busy people rushing to do their Christmas shopping.

Jordan made sure his driver was released from the cells and did his best to draw a quiet veil over the affair, but it came back, with a vengeance, later in the year, when things were harder than ever for the fledgling team that was often left fighting for survival off the track while shining on it. Looking back on how he felt as he gambled everything and just hoped for some divine help at this time, Jordan said, 'I've learnt to live with risk, but I have four children and it wouldn't have been fair on them or my wife to put them at risk. So, I formed a limited company. It felt safer that way. But until 7UP signed the sponsorship deal at the end of January, I did feel very vulnerable. Remember, I was the one who told the others not to worry. Let them concentrate on the car, I said. I'd do the money. Well, they'd got the car on the track and I still hadn't delivered my end of the deal. If it wasn't for the fact I owned the team, I would have had to sack myself!'

Surely only Eddie Jordan, of all team owners, could have produced a scenario such as that in which he found himself in the winter of 1990–91? He knew another team was working hard to steal the 7UP deal from under his nose. That was normal behaviour in Formula One, as Ron Dennis confirmed when later in the year, at the height of EJ's most publicised difficulties, he strolled towards the Irishman in the paddock at Monza and said, 'Welcome to the Piranha Club.' That, however, is another story. At this time, in January 1991, as Eddie said, he was busy with another fight on his hands. 'I had to tussle hard to get that money. I used to go in all guns blazing; I hadn't learnt to be restrained, or more calculating. Now, I don't let people know I'm upset. It's a hard lesson to learn.'

In that respect, at least, he might have had some sympathy for Gachot. Few in the Formula One paddock offered him much once the true story of the events in December 1990 in London emerged almost nine months later.

9. SPA FRANCORCHAMPS I

Little did Gachot know of the chaos his moment of madness at Hyde Park Corner had caused during the weeks he was in prison and dreaming of regaining his liberty. Indeed, only those who were there know exactly what happened at the Villa d'Este on the night of Thursday, 5 September 1991; moreover, few who were there, as a complex 'transfer deal' was struck that saw Schumacher leave Jordan for Benetton and Roberto Moreno move in the opposite direction, albeit reluctantly and despite winning a court action against the Anglo-Italian team, have revealed the full truth. But it was there, in the imperial foyer of one of the most spectacular and famous hotels in northern Italy on the edge of Lake Como, that F1's clandestine wheelers and dealers became the Piranha Club.

According to one of the rumours circulating about Eddie Jordan's entry into Formula One, he had so much confidence in his team that he had placed a bet of £50,000 on them finishing in the top six in their maiden championship season. That bet, if my reasoning is correct, was, in effect, the amount of cash he paid as a premium for the unique performance-related insurance arrangements he had made with that Belgian company. It was an arrangement Eddie, in his enthusiasm, often referred to as a wager he had made on himself and his team. Unfortunately, as we know, he came unstuck. The deal did not work out. Nor, as it unfolded, did the contract with Bertrand Gachot, whose unpredictable temperament had always been regarded as suspect, and a possible weakness.

Born in Luxembourg on 23 December 1962, Gachot was the son of a French official working at the European Commission. He had raced karts from the age of fifteen, attended the well-known Winfield School for racing drivers in France and dropped out of university to race in Formula Ford. He found some success with the Pacific Racing team in Norfolk, England, and won the British Formula Ford 2000 title in 1986, but his career, though promising, never took off fully. He was as well known for his associations with strange sponsors such as the extraordinary Belgian anarchist Jean-Pierre Van Rossem, who claimed never to brush his teeth or wash his own hair, who ran the Onyx Formula One team in 1989. This relationship foundered when even Van Rossem, a fat, eccentric figure with long hair and an unkempt face, found some of Gachot's forthright views on life and motor racing were not in line with what he could tolerate or indulge within his team.

By the time Gachot signed for Jordan, in 1990, he was reputed to be a volatile character with an inconsistent record, but Eddie, who had had previous dealings with him through Eddie Jordan Management and who knew about his many interesting connections in European financial and political circles, believed he could handle the difficulties while at the same time profiting from a decent driving performance and a steady cash flow. Gachot, it must be said, could also be charming, urbane, entertaining, kind and very good company. And indeed, all had seemed rosy enough until that fateful day in London when Gachot failed to arrive at his appointment to support Eddie's presentation to 7UP in London.

Gachot, running late and hurrying, had become entangled with a taxi-driver after a minor road traffic altercation in central London, reportedly close to Hyde Park Corner. The two men had exchanged heated insults and some vigorous comments on their relative driving styles, which had led to a physical confrontation during which Gachot had sprayed the taxi-driver with the contents of a CS gas canister he kept in his car for emergencies. Gachot maintained he had acted in self-defence, and that he had had no idea the use of such things was illegal in Britain. All this was going on while Jordan was doing his best to convince the people at 7UP that his team was the one for them.

Gachot's arrest and subsequent trial, after he had been charged with causing actual bodily harm, led to a chain of events that caused a furore in the Formula One paddock and beyond. In the circumstances, it is noteworthy, then, that Gachot, despite all that must have weighed on his mind during the first eight months of the 2001 season before he went to trial in August, drove with unfailing commitment and great enthusiasm for the cause. It is entirely typical, also, of the roller-coaster nature of Jordan's first year in Formula One that he had one of his drivers arrested before the season began, sent to trial and, most stunningly of all, sent to prison. Gachot had finished sixth at Silverstone, sixth again at Hockenheim and ninth at the Hungaroring near Budapest, where he set a new lap record, before his case was heard. It was one of the most extraordinary chapters in the history of Formula One, as well as in the life of Eddie Jordan.

In short, when Gachot was imprisoned – and we shall see shortly what he thought of it all – his absence created the vacancy into which Michael Schumacher made his jaunty Formula One entrance. This happened at Spa Francorchamps on 25 August, and he became an overnight sensation. He qualified seventh, broke his clutch at the start and went back to his family home at nearby Kerpen in Germany with a reputation as the best German driver, potentially at least, the sport had ever seen. Eddie and his team were overjoyed at their luck. Besieged by debts, with Cosworth chasing anxiously for payments on the Ford HB V8 units that had been powering the team to decent results all season and with doubts surrounding the team's survival into 1992, Jordan suddenly felt like a man who had accidentally fallen into a gold mine. Unfortunately, the feeling did not last. Fewer than eleven days later, Schumacher was 'transferred' overnight to Benetton on the eve of the following Grand Prix at Monza. It was a dark deed, hidden in wreaths of controversy and intrigue, and it was the source of the soubriquet 'Piranha Club' that became attached to the business side of Formula One thereafter.

A taste of how this happened, and what it was like for Jordan and his team as they lived through that hellish fortnight in late August and early September 1991 before, during and after the Belgian Grand Prix, will follow shortly, but first to Gachot, the man whose moment of madness with a CS gas canister triggered the entire episode. The Frenchman had been sentenced to six months for possession of the canister and eighteen months for assault. In an interview with journalist Joe Saward later that year, he said, 'I just couldn't believe what was happening. For me, it was a clear case of self-defence, and I think that people who know me know I would not aggress anybody. The judge considered that I used too much force on someone who came only with his hands. I cannot understand his judgment and I will never accept it. It was an incredible sentence.'

He explained that he was held in Brixton prison in south London initially, and was later moved to an open prison. 'It was a prison, like you would imagine,' he said. 'But it was worse because you were locked in 23 hours a day. You didn't have a table on which to eat. You didn't have anything. You didn't have a toilet in the cell. You could not even switch the cell light on and off. You were trying to look out of the windows to see normal life, or people. You wouldn't treat an animal as badly as that. I had to be philosophical about it and laugh about it and not get miserable. At the end, I was surprised how man can adapt and how other prisoners were actually not such bad people at all. I discovered things which I never believed were possible. Afterwards, they moved me to another prison which was not at all what I imagined a prison to be. We were quite open, quite free. We had to do some gardening, but at least I had fresh air and was able to see outside. I was able to keep training, physically preparing myself for the day when I would finally get out.

'Initially, I was not interested in racing at all, I didn't want to know. I didn't want to see F1. Then the virus took over and I started to watch the GPs. I was riveted to the TV. It is something you have inside you. It's difficult to take it out.

'About 99 per cent of the people were really kind and thought it was wrong that I was in jail. They helped me, made life easier. Obviously you have the one per cent who are really bad people and they say, "Why does he have it easy? Why should he be treated differently?" But most of them made my stay in prison relatively bearable. One thing that was fantastic was the support I got from people all over the world. I had the most letters from Belgium, France and England, but many from America, Japan, Australia. I really enjoyed reading them all and I will reply to them. It was good just to know that I was not alone. It kept me calm. When you are in jail, you cannot think too much. You cannot get angry. You have to control yourself at all times. All the support did help me. The other thing which kept me going was that I was convinced I would get out on appeal because somewhere along the line I still believe in justice. We live in free countries after all, and I don't think anyone is interested in putting innocent people in jail.'

Gachot's appeal was finally heard after he had spent two months in prison and missed four Grands Prix. The Court of Appeal did not quash the conviction, but considered the sentence too harsh, and he was released. He flew immediately to Japan to watch the Japanese Grand Prix.

On arrival at Suzuka, the first thing he wanted to do was find Eddie Jordan. He wanted to know if he could have his seat back, but so much had happened, so many commitments had been broken and new ones made, that it was impossible. 'That disappointed me a lot,' he said. 'It was a drive I thought was mine, but he didn't want to do it because he had commitments with other people. He decided to interrupt the contract. I don't know what the grounds were, but I have had enough of lawyers and things like that. I'm not going to look into that. It's going to be my advisers who will do that. I don't want to get involved. I am left with a lot of destruction around me; everything that I have tried to do in the last years has been wasted.'

Little did Gachot know of the chaos his moment of madness at Hyde Park Corner had caused during the weeks he was in prison and dreaming of regaining his liberty. Indeed, only those who were there know exactly what happened at the Villa d'Este on the night of Thursday, 5 September 1991; moreover, few who were there, as a complex 'transfer deal' was struck that saw Schumacher leave Jordan for Benetton and Roberto Moreno move in the opposite direction, albeit reluctantly and despite winning a court action against the Anglo-Italian team, have revealed the full truth. But it was there, in the imperial foyer of one of the most spectacular and famous hotels in northern Italy on the edge of Lake Como, that F1's clandestine wheelers and dealers became the Piranha Club.

All this could not have happened at a worse time for Jordan Grand Prix. If ever Eddie needed to wheel and deal, to duck and dive, to borrow and beg and find some cash, this was the time. During those late summer days in 1991, the bills continued to pile up, and the budget was exhausted. Financially, Jordan knew his team was on its knees. Debts were all around him, including a worrying and growing figure owed to Cosworth for their engines. Cosworth were pressing for their money and threatening legal action. Without Cosworth, Jordan could not continue; even if they managed to struggle through to the end of the season, he needed engines for 1992. It was a grim scenario, now made worse by

Gachot's idiotic arrest and the attendant bad publicity. The likelihood of this Irishman, with his hard-working, fun-loving team of men in green, developing an outfit to challenge the likes of McLaren Honda, for whom Ayrton Senna was on his way to the drivers' title, or Williams Renault, for whom Nigel Mansell and Riccardo Patrese were heading towards second and third places, seemed remote.

'When we arrived at Spa, the cars were sealed away,' he explained, referring to the Belgian Grand Prix at Francorchamps in 1991, in which race Schumacher made his debut. 'The local bailiff had taken action. Well, we had just had a torrid two weeks. We had Gachot go to jail. We needed to find another driver, and when Michael Schumacher and Ian [Phillips] were trying to get the contract finished, on the Thursday night, we went to the track to find that local Belgian bailiffs had locked up the trucks and the cars. So we couldn't get them out. They claimed we owed somebody some money.' Jordan's memory of the sequence of events, he admitted, was hazy. According to Phillips, money was owed to a Belgian driver, Philippe Adams, and his claim resulted in the local courts approving an order to prevent the team from using their cars or trucks for fear they would leave the country without clearing the debt. Action was taken by the bailiffs, said Phillips, on the Saturday afternoon after qualifying. 'We found a way of clearing it up so we could race,' he added.

By this time, both Jordan and Phillips were deeply entangled in a desperate bid to keep the team going, to hang on to the dazzling talent of Schumacher, and to try to find an engine supplier for 1992. It was a juggling act, in terms of energy and resources available, every day for both of them. It had started when Schumacher tested for the first time, immediately before the Belgian race, and it continued through the following two weeks to the Italian weekend at Monza. Phillips was busy trying to tie down Schumacher while Jordan was seeking engines, and Cosworth, fed up with waiting for their bills to be paid, issued a winding-up order on Jordan Grand Prix. To make matters worse, Schumacher's management team were suspicious of Jordan's plans for the future. They were being fed information that suggested the team was in a perilous financial state, which was designed, deliberately, to persuade them to avoid signing any long-term contract. Schumacher, happy enough at the time to stay in a breezy holiday chalet he shared with his new team chiefs in Belgium, was also reminded that other teams had higher standards of hotel accommodation on offer. Few leading outfits, after all, would have considered asking one of their Grand Prix drivers to share quarters, including the bathroom, with commercial or marketing staff. To his credit, Schumacher was never troubled by this and always said, later, how much he had enjoyed his brief time with Jordan.

But Schumacher, like Moreno, was a mere pawn in the moves made by the major players at the time. His value was not only in his talent, but also in the fact he was German. Formula One needed a good German driver, but in a successful team with real prospects for the following season, not a team facing a winding-up order from its engine suppliers with little prospect for sustained success. Furthermore, Benetton, owned by the Italian fashion chain, were looking for ways of using Formula One for marketing their products, their image and the services of the other companies in their group. It was obvious, in hindsight, that Benetton had wanted Schumacher immediately they saw how fast he was on the opening day of practice in the valleys of the Ardennes, if not long before.

Walkinshaw, who was then director of engineering at Benetton where he worked in alliance with Flavio Briatore, knew all about Schumacher. Having run Jaguar in the Group C World Sportscar Championship, he had enjoyed close quarters experience of him. He had seen him racing for Mercedes-Benz in the same series and knew he was an exceptional talent. He was also in close contact with Jochen Neerpasch, an agent working on behalf of Mercedes-Benz as their competitions chief, as well as with IMG and their drivers, particularly Schumacher, who remained under contract to Mercedes-Benz, where he had been developed as a junior driver. 'Neerpasch had been canvassing several teams to see if they were interested in Michael, and of course I had been impressed with his performances in the Mercedes sportscar and I was keeping an eye on him,' Walkinshaw admitted. 'I said I was interested in running him [at Benetton], but understood he had a prior commitment to

Jordan. I was only interested if the Mercedes lawyers could give me clear legal advice that he was not committed elsewhere. I would want my head examined if I didn't go after a driver of his obvious calibre.'

It was the beginning of the end for Jordan's interest in retaining Schumacher long term. Walkinshaw, a resolute Scot with a reputation for winning at all costs, was not a man who wasted words. He was well connected within the paddock and through-out the global automotive industry, entirely aware of who was approaching whom for drivers and engines for the following year, and together with Briatore he was building a team to win at Benetton. He had recognised in Schumacher a driver he needed to help achieve his ambitions. Like Jordan, he was a proven entrepreneur, but a man also of widespread success throughout many parts of the motor industry. He had enjoyed success in many automotive programmes ranging from touring cars to sportscars and road cars. But success in Formula One had proved elusive until he caught sight of the potential of Michael Schumacher. With him, in a car packaged to provide the power and the performance he needed, Walkinshaw knew he could direct Benetton to the world championship.

He saw all he needed to see in just two days at the Belgian Grand Prix. Walkinshaw was unhappy with Moreno and he wanted to replace him. 'I wanted someone in the second car who would liven things up a bit,' he explained. With that in mind, he contacted Neerpasch, regarded by most of the players in this particular game as the man in control of Schumacher's future, alongside his manager Willi Weber, of course. When he telephoned Neerpasch, he interrupted the German while he was soaking in his bath. Still, they talked. 'Jochen agreed to come over to London to discuss the possibility of Michael coming to Benetton for the next race at Monza,' he said. 'They came over with their lawyers and a contract and we examined it and satisfied ourselves that, indeed, there was no agreement with Jordan. The only thing was that there was a block in the contract that if Mercedes-Benz came back into F1 racing in the following three years, then they would have the right to take him back. I thought it was worth taking that risk, and we signed him for Monza.'

Briatore, like Walkinshaw, saw Schumacher as a key figure in Benetton's future. 'The first time I saw Michael was at Spa,' he said. 'The first time I spoke to him was in London a few days afterwards, in my house. He was with me and Neerpasch. We discussed Michael's position with Jordan and it was confirmed to me that there was no contract. It was only a one-race deal. I told Michael I was ready to put him in the car and that we didn't need any money from personal sponsorship and that was how we did the deal. It was very important for him to get into the car immediately. For me, that was no problem. I felt it was important to find someone for the future of the team. We all felt very strongly that he was our driver for the future. My only worry was that he would not have enough laps, but we did not expect instant miracles. We knew, too, that we did not have the best car, but we were working on it. We wanted a driver for the future. I knew my situation at the time was not a winning one, but we were looking ahead and Michael was the first really important step. Nelson [Piquet] and [Roberto] Moreno were our other drivers at the time. I had already decided what to do, and two weeks before I met with Michael I had told Moreno what I wanted to do in the future – that he would not be driving with us any more and that it was not our intention to renew his contract.'

Briatore's and Walkinshaw's matter-of-fact approach to the signing of Schumacher made it seem obvious that Jordan had no right to believe he had any hold on him. In this age of harsh legal realities, any notion that Jordan, having been the man to run him first in a Formula One car, would have a moral first call on his services was treated as an irrelevance. A naive irrelevance. 'I had no problem with Eddie applying to the court [in London, for an injunction to stop Schumacher signing for Benetton],' said Walkinshaw. 'He tried on several counts and the judge dismissed every one of them. I think there's been a lot of nonsense on this. The fact is that Schumacher, for whatever reason, had no contract with Jordan. He was a free agent. How anyone can allow a talent like that to be walking around the paddock, I don't know. That's their business. When we were informed of that we went about the proper way of securing him.'

To a tough, experienced operator like Walkinshaw, this manoeuvring was all in a day's work. To the struggling new boys at Jordan, fighting on all fronts, every hour was a scrap for survival. Having 'found' Schumacher, thanks to some help here and there, having received £150,000 from Mercedes-Benz to give him a drive in Belgium and knowing that they were prepared to pay £3 million the next year to keep him there, and having survived the legal and financial difficulties of racing at Spa Francorchamps, Jordan had allowed himself briefly to build up high hopes for the future. In theory, they had secured a driver of huge potential and the backing of a dependable supporter. But then they became engulfed in other problems that distracted them from the more urgent need to sign Schumacher promptly, beyond agreeing a deal in principle, and prevent him being charmed away in the night. And these distractions, together with the information exchanges that are all part and parcel of the dealers' market that is the paddock in Formula One, undermined them.

'I had a call from Weber on the Friday afternoon,' explained Ian Phillips. 'Michael was due to come for a seat fitting on the Monday [eight days after the Belgian race and three days before the opening of the Italian Grand Prix meeting]. Then, instead of Michael, Neerpasch and Julian Jakobi turned up. We wouldn't let Jakobi near the place. He was working for IMG then.' As Phillips explained the story, carefully running through his memories to recall clearly these days now a distant decade away, Jordan interrupted to add his own recollections. 'I refused to let him in. I'd just come back from Japan with a deal for Yamaha engines, and at that stage we were skint. Absolutely skint.'

'Neerpasch presented a contract to us,' Phillips continued, 'and said, "These are the conditions for Michael." He had, basically, taken the space on the whole car! So we worked all night on a version of the contract we *could* sign. And then, in the morning, we were sitting around waiting for them to turn up when a fax came through from the lawyers with two lines, from Michael: "Dear Eddie, I am sorry I am unable to take up your offer of a drive. Yours sincerely, Michael." At that very time, Michael was at Benetton having a seat fitting. We knew because someone phoned somebody at Benetton.'

By the end of Tuesday, on the basis that they could prove he was having a seat fitting at Benetton and after having settled heads of agreement with Jordan, Jordan requested his lawyers to apply for an injunction against Schumacher driving for Benetton. The case was heard in London the following day, Wednesday, 24 hours before they were due to arrive in Monza. 'We had heads of agreement, which under normal law would have been good enough,' said Jordan. 'But what happened was that the judge said he could not restrict someone's right to work unless we had signed that other contract, which was unsignable. "On the basis that that contract is flawed, I cannot give you the injunction to stop him driving for another team until this contract is settled and signed," the judge said. But they had no intention of signing that contract. So it was a mistake I will always remember. But, in the heat of the moment, no one was at fault.'

Neerpasch recalled it all, at the time, with some detachment. 'Michael Schumacher signed an agreement with Eddie Jordan on the Thursday before Spa,' he said. 'It was an agreement to talk about an agreement. What he signed was a letter of intent. Eddie Jordan offered him the drive, but he needed money. Mercedes-Benz agreed that money and asked for sponsor's space. We talked with Eddie about the rest of the season and also the future, but only on the condition that our money would guarantee a certain space on the car. I went to see Eddie Jordan on the Monday and we could not agree. A number of teams were interested in Michael and we went to Benetton. They wanted him, and it was a straightforward deal. He is paid as a driver. I think the Jordan was a very good car for this year. There was no need to change. Michael wanted to stay with Jordan, but Eddie would not agree with our requirements for sponsor space and he wasn't prepared to discuss our contract. He wanted Michael to sign before Monza. Michael was still a Mercedes-Benz driver, but we released him for F1. At the end of it all, I think it is very important for Germany to have a competitive driver in F1.' Neerpasch also said that Mercedes-Benz wanted to have Schumacher back for their planned re-entry into Formula One in 1993 with Sauber. 'It would have been against our strategy to release him,' he said. 'We built up the drivers and we wanted them for our own team. It was sensational, of course, for the F1 people to see Michael at Spa. Everyone was interested in him. We discussed a lot of things. In the end, though, Eddie said he was using Yamaha engines and we discussed this and we decided that Yamaha were not going to be reliable or victorious. We wanted Michael to have a season in F1 and we wanted to finance the season for him. We wanted him ready for the following year, for the new Mercedes team for 1993. At that time, we saw 1992 as a preparation year. We wanted both Michael and Karl [Wendlinger] to get F1 experience. We discussed this with Michael and he decided to stay at Jordan. They were a very nice team and made him feel welcome. He did not want to change. But we discussed it for a long time and, finally, he decided to change.'

The whole episode, known at the time as the 'Schumacher Affair', threw a shaft of stark light into one of the dark corners of Formula One and contributed towards the creation of the Contract Recognitions Board, an organisation to formalise the legitimacy of drivers' contracts with teams. But that came later.

Prior to Neerpasch's visit, Jordan recalled, 'Flavio was restricting us a little, too, because we were a bit embarrassing to Flavio's Benettons with our Jordan, with a customer engine, so he made sure that we got stung. He made sure we wouldn't get the [Ford Cosworth] engines the following year. But it was worse than that [because of the winding-up order]. I had to run like hell to find an engine! I had heard from Herbie [Blash, a senior figure in F1 management and adviser to Yamaha] and Bernie [Ecclestone] that Walkinshaw and a few others were desperate to get this Yamaha engine and that if I didn't move quickly I would never get it. So, I'm gone to Japan, and Ian is looking after things – and all this is flying around the place when I come back on the Monday to find out that Weber had actually had the good manners to ring us and say, "Look, please, be careful." By that stage, Bernie and Flavio and Tom had, I believe, concocted how they were going to get a German into Formula One their way. There had not been one for such a long time. It was a very big market that was sportscar orientated, and this was their big opportunity. And it was no secret. Bernie will tell you. He helped to cement the deal between Flavio and Benetton to get Michael Schumacher to join them. At that stage I could, possibly, understand, because the chances of Jordan surviving were in our view quite good, but in anyone else's view quite limited. He was probably aware that there was a winding-up order about. Flavio would have told him about that. But we had a Yamaha engine at that stage, untried and untested.'

The significance of the engines was one of the critical issues in the story. Phillips explained, 'There was something else. Neerpasch, on Sunday morning in Spa, came to us and he said we had to run Ford the following year. We were all sworn to secrecy on Yamaha and so we said, "Oh, yeah, we will be." But what we didn't know was that Tom Walkinshaw, who was the engineering director at Benetton, was so involved by then. He had run the Jaguar sportscars against the Mercedes. He was the only other person in the world who knew how good Michael was. At this time we didn't know of Bernie's involvement in all of this. After Spa, Bernie disappeared to Sardinia, I think, where he was buying some land. He knew we had got the Yamaha deal because he had been instrumental.' Ecclestone had helped Jordan by using old contacts and advising each to help the other to make the deal work. 'We had been lying about Yamaha, because we had to! So they [Neerpasch and Weber] were using the big Ford angle, and when they went to see Bernie and said "What shall we do?" he told them Jordan had got a deal with Yamaha. He squared that away. No problem.'

Jordan joined in again, adding his own personal recollection. 'So then the fun starts! We said, "F*** this!" I knew it was happening. I had spies at Benetton, and they must have had spies at Jordan. Everyone seemed to know exactly what was going on, so it went straight down to court injunctions. They fought it like crazy, so we collared Moreno. We paid Moreno to use the same injunction to save his arse, but in the Italian courts. He won. We lost.' The court action in Italy was concluded on Thursday, 5 September, a day of simmering drama and comings-and-goings in the Monza paddock. 'At that stage, they were reconciled to losing him [Schumacher],' said Jordan. 'The financial penalty for losing Piquet was so huge that they would have had to retain him. And they had to give a seat to Moreno. Then we were all invited up to the Villa d'Este.'

'No, we were summoned. Summoned,' Phillips corrected.

'I'd never seen so many lawyers coming in and out like that,' said Jordan.

'And we didn't find our own hotel until Friday night.'

'Ian and I shared a single bed, and Flavio paid for it! He sent sandwiches to the room and they were mouldy old things! And Ian is not easy to sleep with!' At this point Jordan added descriptive reasons relating to odours and habits to back up this assertion. They are too colourful for publication. 'To do this in a small, single bed in one of the staff out-houses at somewhere like the Villa d'Este is not very pleasant. On top of losing your driver.'

Phillips continued his version of the story. 'We got summoned to the Villa d'Este. When I got to the circuit, I saw Bernie and I told him about the courts and what had been happening. He had got the plans for his house in Sardinia out and he said, "This looks great", pretending he knew nothing about it. Then he said, "Leave it to me. I'll sort it out." Then, at seven o'clock that night, he said, "Get up to the Villa d'Este," so we drove up to Lake Como in our little Fiat 126 rent-a-car. Bernie was there, and we saw Michael.' Phillips was immediately struck by the change in circumstances since the last race. 'In Spa,' he said, 'we stayed in a holiday camp. Five pounds a night. I shared a bathroom with Michael and Willi. It was a bit like a dormitory! And the next time I see Michael he is in the Villa d'Este! And they were all sitting there, having dinner, and we were outside. Eventually, Bernie came out. I'll never forget it. Eddie, Bernie and I went round the side of the staircase and there was this lovely glass cabinet there. We had told Moreno not to settle, and Bernie told us he had to settle, that there was no money. I pointed out to him that if nobody was sitting in that car by the time official qualifying came on Saturday, at one o'clock, then Benetton would be excluded from the championship. They could not take *force majeure*. Moreno was going to sit it out. Half an hour later, he came back and said they had offered Moreno half a million dollars.'

'No,' Jordan interrupted, 'they offered it to us first. But we are not a team that is going to be bought. We were not going to prostitute ourselves on an issue we felt so strongly about. And we said we wouldn't take it.'

'And we told Moreno not to take it,' Phillips added.

'And, to be fair, the lawyer believed he wouldn't take it,' Jordan continued. 'Moreno needed to keep his seat, and we needed money, but we weren't prepared to take the money. And we were so strong about not taking the money that they then offered it to Moreno, who did take it.'

Phillips said, 'Yeah, at two-thirty in the morning Moreno took the money . . .'

'That is correct,' Jordan confirmed.

Having been forced to leave the job he loved at Benetton to make way for Schumacher, Moreno then offered Eddie $125,000 to fill the vacancy at Monza for Jordan Grand Prix. 'And we did the deal that night,' Phillips said.

'You just couldn't believe how many lawyers there were present there that night,' Jordan said. 'There were waves of them coming into that place. There were Benetton lawyers, Flav's people and Bernie's people. They were all so shocked that the family was upset that, in Milan, we had won a case against Benetton!'

'Everyone had been looking for Moreno the whole of Thursday,' Phillips added. 'But he was there all the time, holed up in our motor home. Nobody but us knew where he was. And, of course, the other thing was that we had Marlboro begging us to take [Alessandro] Zanardi, but Walkinshaw had told us, "You can't have Zanardi because I've got him under an option."'

'Yes, but at three in the morning we couldn't afford to take another risk,' said Jordan.

'When we left at six-thirty, having had just three hours' sleep in that single bed, we had to go and tell Trevor [Foster, team manager of Jordan] what was happening and to get Moreno fixed up for the car and all the rest of it,' said Phillips. 'Then we pull up at this set of traffic lights on the way to Monza and there's Maurizio Arrivabene, the Marlboro Italy man. He pulled up and said, "Why don't you take Zanardi?" We told him he had an option with Walkinshaw. And he said, "No he doesn't." The first time we meet Zanardi, he turns up at our motor home at half past eight in tears. "I really want to drive this car," he said, but it was too late then. Walkinshaw had told us what he did to stop us having Zanardi.'

Zanardi, the runaway leader of the International F3000 Championship, was waiting for his chance to step into a Formula One car, and he had pinned his hopes on Jordan. But on that Thursday afternoon, Benetton had given Zanardi a seat fitting. Clearly, Zanardi was being lined up as first reserve had the team failed to land Schumacher cleanly. Another driver's career was affected by the deal, too. Stefan Johansson, Eddie's old friend, was also in Monza during the Italian Grand Prix build-up waiting for a call from Jordan. As a Marlboro-backed driver, he hoped the fact that Jordan were a Marlboro-sponsored team would help him slip into the vacant seat created by Schumacher's departure. He never received the call.

'And then Ron came out with this thing about the Piranha Club, just as we were walking across the paddock at Monza,' Jordan added. 'He said, "Welcome to the Piranha Club." I can remember the moment.'

Phillips went on. 'Everybody was agog. Bernie pretended he knew nothing about it when he had orchestrated the whole thing. He was able to say we had Yamaha.'

Ecclestone, it appeared, had also had the vision to see how valuable Schumacher would be to the show as a whole. His talent, in a successful team, would open up a vast new German market. According to one German source, Schumacher, at the time, was under contract to RTL, the big German broadcaster, whose arrangement with Formula One dictated that if a German driver entered the sport it would double the fee paid; if a second entered, it would increase again. In short, Ecclestone knew his television business would profit from the arrival of Schumacher in the Formula One paddock – and Benetton were considered a more powerful and successful operation than Jordan, with a stronger brand image, too.

Senna, the great and glorious champion of the time, was disgusted at what had transpired. At the hotel, when he learnt of what had happened, he told Briatore what he felt about the way his compatriot and friend Moreno had been treated – like a pawn in a grandmasters' game of high-octane chess with stakes to match. On the Saturday afternoon, he claimed pole position. At the subsequent news conference, looking serious and thoughtful, he took the opportunity to give vent to his feelings. He spoke with controlled passion. 'It's difficult to comment in a clean and fair manner, without knowing all the clauses in the contracts, but, as you know, even the best contract in the world, drawn up by the best lawyers, is only worth anything if both sides are really working for it . . . What has happened was not correct. It's always the people in the top teams who are written about the most. So, I feel that unless one of us speaks about it, something like this just goes by and people get away with it. Moreno is a good driver. He's dedicated. He's a professional. And he had a contract for the whole season. But people just push others who are maybe not in a strong position and they threaten, use their apparently strong position to get a driver to change his mind and to accept things. As a principle, I don't think this was a good move. There were commercial interests involved and future prospects which made certain people do these things . . .'

Moreno, the fall guy, the man pushed out of Benetton to make way for the *wunderkind*'s arrival, deserved a word. Upset, threatened and cajoled to take money and give up the seat he had proved was his through legal action, he turned to God for support. 'I think everyone in the paddock was surprised by what happened,' he said. 'Unluckily for me, I was alone at the time I was told, as my wife and my daughter were in Brazil. I didn't even tell my wife afterwards because I thought it would hurt her too much. It is very difficult for a person to go through all that alone. Fortunately, I am a religious person. I believe in God. I opened the Bible and I asked God to put me in the right direction, and it opened at a good page. That gave me self-confidence and I kept myself together. It was very stressful. My only problem [in the 1991 season] was that I caught a virus before the race in France, in July. I went to the doctor and took some penicillin. It upset my stomach and I was not recovered for the race. I think it is the only problem I had this year. I took legal action because I just wanted to defend myself. I had to defend my rights on the contract I had for this year. On the Thursday night, I slept for only two hours and had my seat fitting at seven in the morning. I got in the car, I concentrated, and I tried to do my best.'

That Thursday night, said many long-standing observers of the sport, Formula One changed for ever. The once Corinthian world of Grand Prix racing, a world of pleasure and danger fuelled by adventure and funded by private means, crossed an invisible and barely perceptible line, shifting irretrievably from sport to business, from competitive rivalry to something more Machiavellian. It was the end of the last vestiges of the golden age, of gladiators in cockpits, of mortality, parties and fun, and the start of a new era of money, politics and intrigue. Schumacher had driven in just one Grand Prix meeting for the Jordan team after being hired as an emergency replacement for Gachot. Moreno was a journeyman, but he had a contract – a source of scant protection once the lawyers and power brokers set to work on that hot night late in the Italian summer. It was a night that left many unwritten codes trampled in the dust and dew of a magnificent September morning, a night that confirmed Formula One's future was in the hands of ruthless businessmen and ambitious competitors. It was, for Eddie Jordan and Ian Phillips, a final confirmation of the ruthless business in which they were competing to survive.

The story of Schumacher's switch from green to blue, from the blarney boys to the knitwear family, stunned the paddock the following day at Monza where Milan's beautiful people, including many models, several racing enthusiasts and soccer stars, had gathered with the regular circus of drivers, owners, engineers, mechanics, reporters, friends, cooks and motor-home staff to prepare for the annual Italian Grand Prix at the Autodromo Nazionale. Throughout the night before, amid a flow of smoked salmon sandwiches and fine wine, such men as Flavio Briatore, Tom Walkinshaw, Eddie Jordan and Bernie Ecclestone, not to mention the Schumacher entourage (including lawyers from IMG) and other legal representatives (on behalf of Moreno) and agents, filled the hours with persuasive talking and financial offers. The upshot was that Schumacher – then just a tyro from Germany barely ready to accept his mantle as the *wunderkind*, still growing accustomed to the place settings and purpose of his cutlery at formal dinners – was moved from one team to another after just one weekend as a Grand Prix driver. It was a late-night agreement manipulated by many deft hands, and one that ensured the outcome was that which the sport's controlling interests had sought.

Despite every effort they could muster in the fight to retain Schumacher, Eddie and his men were unable to hang on to the best young driver of his generation. Their application in London for an injunction preventing Schumacher from driving for Benetton had failed. Moreno's, with Jordan's support, had succeeded. He had, it seemed, thanks to the Italian legal system, kept his seat. Benetton were duly informed that they had to keep him in their car, alongside his friend, mentor and team-mate Nelson Piquet, for the Italian Grand Prix; furthermore, they were warned that they faced possible expulsion from the championship if they failed to do so. Indeed, on the Thursday afternoon, Italian bailiffs visited their garage in order to ensure that the cars were impounded and the law, and with it Moreno's right to a chassis, was upheld. But, by power of attrition, the weight of pressure and the lure of money, Moreno was weakened and overcome and Jordan's scrap for Schumacher was defeated. Benetton, with Briatore, Ecclestone and Walkinshaw working for a mutual interest, made sure that their multifarious international marketing interests would be able to exploit the young German's burgeoning popularity in his fatherland, and television broadcast rights for coverage of Formula One in central Europe leapt in value overnight. The Schumacher era had begun, and Eddie, outmanoeuvred, had been taught a very harsh lesson.

It was a decisive move in the creation of the so-called Piranha Club's reputation, one act in a drama that was part of a far grander play many felt was a scheme to develop Formula One into a global television spectacular. Significantly, for Jordan, a man of natural intelligence, warmth and sharp instincts, it was also a bitter learning process as he discovered that, in his first season as a team owner, it was wise to move with alacrity and, to borrow a phrase from professional football, get your retaliation in first for the sake of self-protection. This truly was the night when the lawyers and moneymen took total control of the sport. The rich men with helicopters to convey them above the morning mist and dew early that Friday morning to Monza were the winners; those like Jordan and his right-hand man Phillips, who, after standing to watch those helicopters whirr into life and rise into the sky, drove themselves down the valley in a hired Fiat 126 road car, were the losers. It was a lesson they heeded. Like the rest, they knew the Piranha Club would be running the sport from that morning onwards. And they knew that, as in the old phrase, if you can't beat 'em, you have to join 'em.

The whole episode left Eddie Jordan with every right to feel confused and dazed, but he had a season to see out and a team with a future to provide and plan for, even if that future was difficult to predict after the madness surrounding Monza. In the race itself, on 8 September, de Cesaris finished seventh and Moreno spun off after only two laps; in Estoril two weeks later, de Cesaris was eighth and Moreno tenth; in Spain on 29 September, de Cesaris retired after 22 laps with electrical problems and Alex Zanardi, at last making his debut as a replacement for Moreno (who'd been signed only on a short-term basis), finished ninth at the new Circuit de Catalunya. Then came Japan and Australia, the flyaway finale in Suzuka and Adelaide, where neither man scored a point, de Cesaris suffering an early accident in Japan and Zanardi being forced to retire with gearbox trouble, and the pair running eighth and ninth respectively when torrential rain ended the Australian Grand Prix after just fourteen laps.

So, in an utterly drenched afternoon of not a little chaos and confusion, the 1991 season came to its end. The maiden Jordan championship season, with Eddie leading from the front all the way, ended with his team fifth in the constructors' championship and de Cesaris ninth in the drivers' series. It was a creditable result after an unforgettable campaign, but none of that was much consolation to Jordan. He had seen his team grow up, he had seen one of his drivers go to prison, he had watched as another of outstanding talent was lured away by a top team after just the one sensational outing, and he had reached the end of the season with debts he knew he would struggle to pay off. Most of this debt, estimated at £4.5 million at the end of the season, was owed to Cosworth for the engines supplied for the year.

Eddie needed help, and in his hour of need he turned to Ecclestone, who was able to help make arrangements for income due in 1992 from television rights and prize money associated with his successful showing in 1991 to be brought forward. It was an act of 'gap plugging'. Eddie had bought some time in which to go out yet again in search of backers for the next challenge. Given all that had taken place, it was no surprise really that Eddie opted to take the Yamaha factory deal. In truth, he had no choice.

10. SUZUKA

There was something apprehensive about Anderson's mood, and something equally woolly about Jordan's prognosis for the season ahead. 'Our objective is to consolidate on the fifth place last year,' he said. 'Any improvement on that will be a bonus.' The distinct lack of confidence was not due to modesty, it came from the knowledge that the car was not a perfect creation, rather a compromise created out of financial and technical necessity. Cash flow remained a problem. Sponsors of the right quality were difficult to find. The new Yamaha engine was bigger, heavier and less proven in terms of performance and reliability than its predecessor, the Ford Cosworth, and the introduction of a semi-automatic gearbox with seven gears, a design that had its source in motorcycle gear-changes, only added to the concerns about reliability. Eddie knew all of this and decided to work, work, work. The high hopes engendered by the excellent debut performance in 1991 were a heavy weight to bear.

After 1991, things had to change. Eddie had spent a lot of money, the family were feeling the strain and he knew he would welcome a metaphorical charge over the hilltop from the financial cavalry, so long as they were on his side. He knew, also, that he had to steer the business through the stormy passages in the hope that success would reap its rewards. It is one of the unwritten rules of Formula One that the rich and powerful are looked after much better than the aspiring and the poor. It is a Darwinian business. He learnt that at Monza, more than anywhere else. He learnt it whenever he came under pressure. Now he had to make the lessons pay. The other problem was that the economy was taking a nosedive. A recession was sweeping in, Formula One was feeling the pinch and the sport was approaching was one of its periodic moments of uncertainty, of political sea-change, when the establishment rewrote its rule-book for the foreseeable future. Eddie, however, knew just what he wanted – survival. 'The situation was very clear as far as I was concerned. But I'm not saying that one thing was right or one thing was wrong. In 1991, I felt that Jordan had done a reasonable job and deserved a place in Formula One. The team was different. We had a different attitude, the whole thing had a bit of a buzz to it and the potential was always there. At that time, F1 teams were falling out of the sky, or beginning to – they were going out of business. Teams like Fondmetal, Brabham and Lotus were just a few examples, just a handful, of those who did not survive much longer. It wasn't clear then that we were going to survive either.'

To make sure he was part of the championship in 1992, Jordan had to balance his books at the end of 1991, which is why he accepted Ecclestone's loan. 'Yes, Bernie baled me out,' he said. 'But I don't think there is a team in F1 he hasn't helped or baled out. That doesn't buy loyalty, but it helps when it comes to making some decisions. I have worked in the risk business for a long time, most of my life really, and I could have been bankrupted sometimes by the risks I have taken. By the end of 1991, I had spent £10 million. I had just over £3 million coming in from buying and selling drivers, bits and pieces that could be put together, and £3 million from our group of sponsors. If I had not had a fair degree of experience in banking, in terms of structuring a repayment campaign, it would have been very easy for me to close the book and to have said, "I've done F1, sorry guys, I owe you a lot of money. Adios. It's too hot in the kitchen for me now." But I didn't. We fought on to do the job and do it well.'

Jordan Grand Prix was, by the end of 1991, at the very centre of Eddie's daily life. He was living for it and squeezing the rest of his life in around the edges, but still managing to have a good time and keep his family life in place. He worked prodigiously, but the way in which his team was demanding cash forced him to gamble and run his empire almost on the run. He knew changes were needed in management, structure, operational style, but with a growing team and incessant demands on his time he found it difficult to allot the right amount of time to the right kind of decision-making. Professional consultants were called in for advice, but it is not known whether or not they had any great influence on the running of the business.

Doubtless, the advice was expensive and, as always, Eddie would have found discussion of the cost a touchy subject. He has never been one to enjoy talking about his earnings or his spending. If he telephones home to Dublin and speaks to his mother after a race, not only will she call him Edmund, when she chooses, she will also introduce the tasteless subject of money. So, you had a good result, she might say; and how much did you make? Eddie finds this amusing and irritating at the same time. 'Irish people are the only people who ever ask in detail about money. It's just buried into them. I don't know what it is, and it just kills me. I hate it. I don't want to know how much you have. I couldn't care less. A lot of the newspaper articles probably don't mean to, but they come across as "he jets here and he flies there and he has millions and he has this and that and the other and he is such a rich man he doesn't even know his own wealth". Well, I find that whole thing very distasteful because it portrays me as being way above the ordinary person. Listen, I *am* the ordinary person. I went to school in Synge Street. And, from my side, there is nothing that any kid in Ireland couldn't do. Nothing, I promise you.'

When he is angry, or frustrated, Jordan becomes impassioned. His temperament is pure Irish, fiery and fast. But he is balanced and fair, too. When he feels cross about money, he can recall easily the desperation he battled to control during the winters of 1990–91 and 1991–92. In the first, of course, he had been chasing money after feeling he had been let down by Camel, knowing he was committed to Ford for $5 million. And costs were forever spiralling. In his final season in Formula One in 1961, when he won the Monaco Grand Prix, Stirling Moss earned a reported £6,000. Thirty years later, Jordan was spending £11 million and ending his first season in the business with a debt of more than £4 million; at the same time, McLaren were spending a budget of around £50 million and pushing for more, while their engine suppliers Honda were said to spend twice as much. But as costs rose, as competition became more intense, as recession cut in around the world, so the ferocious interest in the sport as a television spectacle and advertising medium ballooned rapidly. Up to 250 million viewers were believed to be tuning in to watch Formula One regularly in 1991. Sponsors wanted to be with the big teams and make the most of the television shows. It was this golden egg, growing bigger by the year, that the established teams in Formula One were keen to wrest, partially if not entirely, from the control of the sport-business-circus's ringmaster Bernie Ecclestone. This was why, when they found that Jordan was a nippy pest to beat on the track, they went for him instead behind the air-conditioned motor homes in the legal, financial and contractual conflicts that had turned Monza into a celebration of dark conspiracies.

Between that unforgettable Italian Grand Prix and the end of the season, Eddie's team had been left limping, metaphorically at least, and after using two drivers in a settled line-up for most of the year he found himself switching names around so that by the end of the season five drivers had raced his cars. He was also out of spare parts, exhausted, and searching, with some desperation, for the sponsors he needed for a budget of around £20 million in 1992. Stretched on all fronts, you could say, for he was also completing the building of his new factory just outside the front gates at Silverstone.

Eddie was never short of ideas, though. One of his schemes was to involve front-line Irish businesses in his team as high-profile Irish sponsors of the only Irish cars in Formula One. He spoke to a selection of different people, many state bodies and several companies – IDA, Bord Fáilte and CTT, for instance – but without any serious success. 'He needs more than £20 million and our total promotions budget, between the three of us, is less than £3 million,' said a spokesman for the IDA. Phillips, speaking on his boss's behalf during the 1991 season, said the team had not given up on the idea and would continue to pester for Irish money. 'We never take no for an answer,' he explained, an Englishman using perfectly acceptable Irish logic.

Inside the team itself, the 1991 season had been a rollercoaster all the way. The travel, the drama, the celebrations, the incidents and the ultimate joy in going the whole distance and finishing in the top six at the first attempt brought an elation that had been unexpected. It also brought problems, because with the end of the first racing season came the realisation that the preparations for the second season had started already. The Yamaha V12 engine was coming free, but it was bigger and it was different from the highly reliable, fast and much loved Ford Cosworth. This meant, also, that the 'small is beautiful' approach taken by the team had to change, albeit subtly, and that was a worry to many within the team. Hitherto, racing for Eddie had been a pleasure because of the tight-knit nature of the whole operation.

'There are people in other teams who are perhaps worn down by the politics and the systems,' one of the team's three designers, Mark Smith, an Englishman imported from Reynard, told journalist David Nally. 'Because of that environment, there are always going to be cases of personality clashes and egos. In a big team there is always a danger of little empires developing with internal rivalries and jealousies. Three people designed this year's car. That's unheard of, in design terms. If you had half a dozen, though, you'd need two managerial positions to control that and the whole thing would become unwieldy.' Smith said that Eddie had given his designers, and most of the rest of the staff, a free hand to do their work. 'But he does chase us quite regularly. He likes feedback. He's good to have a chat with – apart from when he's under pressure. He's fun to be with and he's fun to work for.' This was a general theme in all quarters of the original Jordan team. They liked the smallness, the nimbleness of their operation, and most believed it was reflected in the car. It was a fast, nimble car. It produced good results. 'We don't have any superstars who think they're better than the rest,' said Steve May, one of Jordan's ten race mechanics in 1991. He had joined after working at Benetton and Leyton House because he wanted a job with more direct involvement with the racing team and the cars, rather than on the test team or in the background. This was typical. Everyone at Jordan in that first season felt they played an important role in the team. The team did not carry any excess baggage.

Eddie himself loved it this way, but he recognised, afterwards, that he had been lucky. Had he waited longer than he did to enter Formula One, he might not have been able to experience it at all. 'I think you could say that we marked the end of an era,' Jordan remarked in 1999. 'An era when the independent team owner could make that huge leap to Formula One. Even then, as I can painfully testify, he would spend the first few years clinging by his fingertips to the edge of the dream. I'm not saying this to prove how wonderful we are – actually, I am! But, please, keep it to yourself! The point is that the best Formula 3000 team could not begin to contemplate the move today without having either an engine manufacturer on board or a very big sponsor. You are looking at minimum costs of £50 million to run for a year. In 1990, as reigning F3000 champions, we thought about making the F1 move and we reckoned on a budget of no more than £5 million. It was simpler then, but only on paper. We actually arrived in the middle of a recession, on top of which a major sponsor let me down late in the day. That's why our first car, when we rolled it out, had nothing on it but the maker's name. At our launch, we had fewer than thirty media people arranged on plastic chairs in the workshop. It's hard to believe that now. We were literally living from day to day in 1990, and it didn't end when we got to the first race. In fact, the heartache had barely started, even though we had found a few sponsors by then. The worst of it was the pre-qualifying. It was bad enough on its own, but we were also caught up in the middle of a tyre war as Pirelli attempted to take on Goodyear. At certain circuits, early in the morning, when it was cooler, the Pirelli proved to be a slightly quicker tyre. It meant, sometimes, with us on Goodyear, there were particular and excruciating sets of circumstances that made us feel, just once or twice over the whole weekend, that our whole future was in the balance. It seems a long time ago now, but the memories come back quickly enough. To this day, I can honestly say it was the most difficult time I have ever had in my entire life. It aged me fifty years in six months.'

Even in the worst of times, Eddie always had his music and his friends. Like any true Dubliner, he could always find a smile. It might be a wry joke, a funny lyric, or a filthy rhyme. He could have some fun, a bit of craic when the time was right. The whole team knew it. Some of them were victims of his humour, almost voluntarily. It was, after all, infectious. He had a look he often used to help him escape punishment, in a social sense, for outrageous words or deeds. But, most of all, he had his music and his mates. So, when times were not so good, he could cheer them up and they could, and would, do the same for him.

One of Eddie's best friends was Dave Pennefather, one of the group of Irishmen who grew up together with him in the city, crossing paths at music clubs and nights out and in the pubs and on the street and standing at the bar at the best gigs of the weekend. Ask Pennefather about it, then take a deep breath. 'Being such a small place, everybody knows everybody. You know, Ireland is a village, and you can't help but meet people, particularly in music circles, at the places everybody would play and bands and musicians or whatever would hang out. At the time we were all growing up, and there was a super kind of musical fraternity, if you like. It was, you know, at places like Stellar, and all the tennis, rugby and football clubs where they used to have lots of gigs. Any club, really, even parish halls who raised funds for parishes. So it was inevitable that over this period of time everybody would bump into one another. When Des Large set up with Ann McCarthy, Marie's sister, it became even more so; we were all crossing paths, though at this stage Eddie sort of moved out of town and was operating from the UK. But any time he was back in town, we would always try to get together.'

You probably know the story about Eddie's involvement with Des getting married to Ann?

'Do I? Oh, yes. Ha, ha, ha. The £300? Is that what you mean?'

Eddie says it's a good story, and you're the man to tell it.

'Well, there are so many variations on this one, now. So many various denials and so on. But Des is convinced that, for the introduction to her, Eddie charged him £300. Eddie, however, will tell you that's not right. He'll say that was for services rendered, for something he got for Des. He means some wheeler-dealing he did to purchase something for Des. My own belief is that the first one is right. He charged Des the money to introduce him to Ann.'

I think Eddie has decided it sounds better if that story doesn't go to print.

'Well, it's spread too much. It has spread like butter over here. It's a great story.'

But Eddie's version of the story is three times worse than the one he is trying to deny!

'Exactly!'

Pennefather is no ordinary friend of the family, and no ordinary music fan. As the managing director of Universal Music, Ireland, he handles a lot of the big names on the Irish music scene. He is also a hugely supportive friend of the whole Jordan family and the team.

'Eddie is a fantastic music fan, as you know, and over the past few years he has been very kind to me in relation to Grands Prix. He gets me tickets and he always looks after his chums, as they say. However, it is nice to be able to reciprocate and get him tickets for concerts. Eddie enjoys nothing more than to go to a concert and meet the band afterwards, creating a bit of havoc. However, there are one or two funny incidents around that are worth telling – like the night we were in the Olympia Theatre, which is a reasonably small theatre, and one of our artists, Ocean Colour Scene, were on stage. We organised for Eddie to sit in a box, which was kind of overlooking things. It was one of the old theatres, and the box was sitting just in front in three tiers. The place was absolutely jointed. It was hopping. The band were playing their hearts out and it was just one of these absolutely great gigs.

'However, midway through the gig, in typical Jordan fashion, he's standing up there and he's playing air guitar and whatever, and the crowd downstairs noticed him. And let's just say Eddie was absolutely flying. He is one of our top sportsmen, as you know, but at this particular time things were really hopping for him, it was tremendous. And Jesus, the entire audience start cheering and chanting at Eddie, and Eddie is air-guitar playing and he's giving it the lash. The band on stage are looking at this, never having met him. They knew that this guy Eddie Jordan was going to the gig all right, but they were from England and they weren't that aware. He begins to take over the entire gig, and he is doing shag all up there except standing there pretending to play guitar like he used to, probably, in front of a mirror, and the audience are going ape shit and they are not applauding the band at all, they're applauding Eddie Jordan! A couple of thousand are on the floor and they are all doing this! I am dying in the meantime. What am I going to tell the manager, having brought the guy along, and he's now deflecting all the glory away from the band up to the box? There was a little bit of annoyance at the outset on the part of the band, but once they met Eddie and spoke with him for a while, I think they fully understood the charismatic qualities he was bringing to the whole thing. So they became friends, and I think subsequently the bastard ended up appearing in one of their videos or some such!'

He is never one to miss an opportunity, is he?

'I have to say, about his music, he is passionate. He absolutely loves the whole music merry-go-round, he is an absolute enthusi-ast. Marie takes it all with a pinch of salt, but Eddie loves it, he loves these gigs, he loves it backstage. He loves the feel of the whole thing, the whole backstage thing, that tension, if you like, that you get before a gig, which I would say is similar to a Grand Prix, but obviously not quite the same because they are going on stage, they are not putting their lives at risk, whereas the drivers, they are going out there themselves in a gladiatorial role.'

Eddie has made a lot of friends through music, hasn't he? Chris Rea, for example.

'I worked with Chris for a number of years. He was going through a hard time when I started working with him. He'd had some bereavements in the family and that, and when he came to Dublin to do his first gig he was decidedly depressed and thinking of chucking everything in. And the label he was with, in the UK, was pushing him in one direction, which he wasn't at all comfortable with. So we sat down and worked out a strategy that was quite different to that. And we put it in place in Ireland. It gave Chris back his stimulus for him to get on with his career, to grasp it. There were opportunities here, so the template we put together here in terms of getting Chris back on the road . . . Well, we asked the companies abroad to use the same sort of template and it worked, as we know, terribly well. He went on from success to success.

'When Chris changed labels, I kind of lost touch. We spoke from time to time, but then in 1991–92, when Eddie started in F1, our paths started crossing again because Chris and Eddie had created this tremendous friendship. Chris is an absolute realist when it comes to Formula One, whereas Eddie, at that stage, was still in the honeymoon period. It was dreamtime. And Chris would be there explaining things to Eddie. He would get firing on all cylinders and he would be there telling Eddie what to do. He'd say, "Nah. This is the way it is and you've gotta do this and you've gotta do that," and because Chris was such a great musician Eddie was actually listening to him! He would take on board what he said and go off and do things. Then, later, Eddie would ring and say, "What a tosser! What's he talking about? Let him stick to the music and I'll stick to the cars." But they do really have a tremendous degree of respect for each other, and I would go so far as to say it's a real close friendship there.

'Through contacts and other networking, if you like, Eddie has got so many friends. Do you remember the first Silverstone gigs he put on, where we borrowed Chris's back line, the amp and the drums and so on, and put them up on an old truck? Oh, Jesus. Chaos! There was Des Large on guitar . . . well, Des . . . he knows the first line of every song, so the trick was to ensure that they were popular songs we performed because once you started the first line the audience started singing and Des was off the hook. We were constantly trying to do that, after Silverstone, so that they were songs everybody absolutely knew. And the truth is, that is what really worked. There were a few other bands on, you know, who were playing with heads down looking at their navels. They were going down like a concrete Tiger Moth. We got up, not too terribly good at the old music stakes, but we gave it the lash. They knew all the material and the thing just cruised. I seem to recall at one of the last ones there were thousands of people there. If anyone was ever in absolute heaven, it was EJ when it was his turn to get up on drums and play away. It was fun, but, inevitably – and he would hate me for saying it – there had to be two kits of drums there. There had to be another drummer to keep time while Eddie was playing drums his own way!

'Eddie – he is the top wind-up man. He just loves to come in and craic. There are so many times, you know, with Eddie – you know how a room lights up when he comes in? He will always have a parting shot. "You tosser, you didn't get this", or something like that. It's all typical EJ strategy. You know, for him, attack is the greatest form of defence. But, honestly, he is absolutely loved over here in Ireland. And the extraordinary thing is that his musical tastes are all over the place in that there is not one type of music that it must be for Eddie. Eddie will listen to virtually anything. If it is good, he appreciates it, and I think people appreciate the fact that he appreciates what they are doing.

'You know, I am just in the middle of setting up an album with Finbar Fury from the Fury Brothers. His genre would be folk-ballad, but it was Eddie who sort of reintroduced me to the music. He plays at Eddie's Christmas party here each December, usually around 18 December, and every time you hear him, the hairs rise on the back of your neck! Eddie gets such a punch out of having a few people in who are brilliant at their craft, and sharing them with whoever is around. He wants great people in there to do these things, and he wants to share his sense of musical fun with everybody. As a person, overall, he is wonderfully generous of spirit. I am frightened to say it, but I owe him one for introducing me to Finbar.'

He is just one of those special people, isn't he?

'Absolutely. That energy in him is just so positive, and so fun-filled as well. The only person Eddie is in any awe of is his mother. He is afraid of her, and that's the way it should be. She is the boss, and I think it is great to see them together. She's great fun, and you see where it comes from. She's as sharp as a knife. Just like Eddie.'

Like Pennefather, Chris Rea is a Jordan fan and a music-lover. He was also, like Eddie, a late starter in his own career. He did not pick up a guitar until he was nineteen, but within three decades he was one of the most brilliant singer-songwriters in Britain and had sold more than twenty million records. Their friendship grew from an inauspicious start. 'I first met Eddie in 1983, but he doesn't remember it. I'd gone to watch his Formula Three team and I shook hands with him, but he was shaking hands with everybody. Somebody said, "This is Eddie Jordan," but he didn't even ask who I was, and then he was on to the next person,' Rea told Jonathan Thompson of the *Independent on Sunday* in a 'How We Met' feature. 'The next time we really touched flesh was in 1992 when he was having a terrible second year in Formula One. Yamaha had built what they were hoping was the ultimate road car and there was an opening for it in some grand mansion. He approached me and tried to sell me an idea that involved me giving him lots of money! We've been the best of friends ever since. We had a common bond. I was obsessed with motor racing and he was obsessed with the music business. I'd let him drum and he'd let me have a go in his Formula One car. I started going to the races with him. The idea of knowing somebody in Formula One was a complete turn-on for me. In those days, there was a great sense of achievement if the team got a championship point, and it felt exactly like being part of a big family.'

Rea's love of motor racing and his success in Ireland, which rekindled his career, gave Eddie another kind of life away from motor racing. He could feel some sense of personal fulfilment through his friendships, his family and his drumming. But, even at his lowest ebb, he never contemplated abandoning motor racing to revel in a musical lifestyle or a return to live in Dublin. He admitted he missed Ireland, especially Dublin, but when asked if he missed it sufficiently to contemplate going back, he had a typically quick reply. 'No, but only because I probably wouldn't have a liver left if I went back! The problem is that Dublin is a very fun place. They work very hard, they play very hard and there is always something going down, particularly if you are linked to the music business. The most vibrant business in Ireland is the film-making business. It is hugely successful. And the other big one, of course, is rock 'n' roll. We don't need to tell you the kind of movies they make in Ireland. There are some fantastic directors like a namesake of mine, Neil Jordan, who makes all these super movies. And then you just work your way through a long list of musicians.'

Dancing in the moonlight and tripping the light fantastic might have kept Eddie happy, maybe even sane, but it did not pay the bills. He still had a family at home in Oxford to think about and a Formula One racing team to run. And to his credit, albeit sometimes whistling in the dark, he got up, ran about and got on with it. By the end of January 1992, the jigsaw was falling into place and the new car for the new season, the Jordan Yamaha 192, was unveiled at the new factory, little more than a hundred yards from the front gates to Silverstone. Eddie had invested in the land and developed the headquarters during the hardest financial times of his life, somehow managing to juggle everything at once and keep his business in the air. The new factory had cost a reported £3 million to build, money that in the straitened times of 1991 was hard even to find. There were many deals to explain later on in life, but when the doors opened publicly on 22 January it was a day for celebrations and a day of special memories. The car was running and life looked a lot better than it had done at times earlier in the winter when another human tragedy had hit Eddie and the team.

Bosco Quinn was a very special kind of friend to Eddie, his family and his team. A slim young Irishman, bearded and a little earnest, he had known the Jordans a long time and had worked for Eddie both on the racing and the management side of Jordan Grand Prix. He was the man in charge of the creation and development of the new factory, and his work was almost finished, the place almost ready to be invaded by the team, when he was killed in a road accident in Blisworth, a nearby village. After a typically long day's work at Silverstone a week before Christmas 1991, he was heading home when his car was struck by another vehicle. He died almost immediately. Quinn had been team manager of the Formula Three team from 1987 to 1989 and had developed into the factory manager. He had been, in effect, Eddie's right-hand man in the run-up to Formula One. His departure, so tragic in the circumstances, was made worse for everyone by how much he was admired and loved within the team.

'He was a very, very special man,' said Marie Jordan. 'He was very religious and he felt very close to God. He felt that whatever job he was doing at any time he was doing because it was what God wanted him to do. And he was special. He would spend some time with me. He liked to play the violin and to talk, and if I baked a cake he liked to come round. He liked to come for dinner and he enjoyed a mug of coffee. He was, altogether, a very unusual man. He was very calm and very kind. When the new building was finished, the new Jordan headquarters, the job was done with Jordan. He knew it, and he was intending to leave. He felt it was over, and he liked his life to be complete in that kind of way. He knew it was his time to move on. He had talked of this just as it was finished. He would say that God had other work for him to do and he had to move on. But, when he died, he took everything with him, mentally. It was all in his head. He was the key man. He knew everything. He knew all about the whole business. He knew who did what, how much they were paid, the finances, and when he died everything had to be written down on paper. It was very difficult for Eddie and for everyone involved.'

Trevor Foster told David Tremayne, 'Funnily enough, he'd bought himself a genuine gypsy caravan at the beginning of 1991.

He wanted to stop [working] with us because he felt it wasn't really what he wanted to do, although he felt that he'd been aiming for it like Eddie had for all those years. He wanted to go off and trek around Europe. We persuaded him to stay for one more year and see how it went. I had several conversations with him at the end of 1991 when he said there were things he'd done that he'd wanted to do, and now he wanted to take time out and to travel. Tragically, then, he was killed. He was a great loss.'

More than a hundred media representatives from all over the world, including a large contingent of Japanese journalists, had descended on Silverstone and the new Jordan headquarters for the launch. The big story, for the daily reporters, was that the team had only one driver, the slightly built Italian Stefano Modena. Eddie said the second driver would be named within a matter of days. He was Mauricio Gugelmin of Brazil, a former Leyton House driver well known to Ian Phillips. The car, in green, cream and light brown livery, had a distinctive new name on it – Barclay, a cigarette brand familiar in Formula One. Technical director Gary Anderson, introduced by Jordan as 'a fellow paddy' from Coleraine, did his best to play the public relations role expected, but knew in his heart that things were not as they might have been. The big new Yamaha V12 engine had made life difficult when it came to designing the car. He had also decided to introduce a seven-speed semi-automatic gearbox. 'The gearbox is rare in Grand Prix racing,' explained the big Ulsterman. 'A number of design details were necessary, too, to accommodate the bigger engine . . . A clutch will always be required to get the car on the way, but the idea is to make it unnecessary when changing gear. As things stand, we can change gear in 0.1 of a second compared with 0.25 seconds last season. That is an appreciable advance.'

There was something apprehensive about Anderson's mood, and something equally woolly about Jordan's prognosis for the season ahead. 'Our objective is to consolidate on the fifth place last year,' he said. 'Any improvement on that will be a bonus.' The distinct lack of confidence was not due to modesty, it came from the knowledge that the car was not a perfect creation, rather a compromise created out of financial and technical necessity. Cash flow remained a problem. Sponsors of the right quality were difficult to find. The new Yamaha engine was bigger, heavier and less proven in terms of performance and reliability than its predecessor, the Ford Cosworth, and the introduction of a semi-automatic gearbox with seven gears, a design that had its source in motorcycle gear-changes, only added to the concerns about reliability. Eddie knew all of this and decided to work, work, work. The high hopes engendered by the excellent debut performance in 1991 were a heavy weight to bear.

The team's efforts to bring in an Irish sponsor were slow to find fruit. In a letter to the *Irish Times* in February 1992, a Mr E. Lyons of Kill in County Kildare had written about wasted opportunities after having watched the BBC television programme *Tomorrow's World*'s report on the new Jordan car. 'Sadly,' Mr Lyons wrote, 'it is no longer identifiable as the brainchild of an Irish team. The Irish logo is gone.' He explained that in 1991 the car had embodied the message that 'Irish entrepreneurial spirit and technological know-how is second to none'. He implored the Minister for Sport and others to 'wake up'.

The 'Ireland issue' was an important one to Eddie, but so was the survival of his team. The shamrock logo and the word 'Ireland' had to be erased from the car, he said, for commercial reasons. 'Even with free engines from Yamaha, our running costs this year will exceed £11 million,' he explained. 'We don't waste a penny. Apart from my 54 employees, there is the cost of travel, transporters, public relations work and running a factory to consider. I would love to have Ireland on the car, but it simply isn't possible. Our sponsors pay our bills. I'm Irish and proud of it, but the hard facts of life are that our country doesn't supply me with any sponsorship money, so my team's commercial department have taken the matter out of my hands. There are some great guys working hard in Ireland to get funding together and it would be wonderful if they were to be successful, not just from a financial standpoint but for our national prestige.' This was clearly a local difficulty Eddie was more than sensitive to, but space on the Jordan car could not be given away free of charge.

Happily, for everyone concerned at the time, an organisation called 'Racing for Ireland' raised £1 million to return the Irish identity to a prominent position around the cockpit of the car.

Ordinary members of the general public were encouraged to part with a tenner as an annual subscription for membership of the 'Formula One' club. It was the start of one of the most popular supporters clubs ever known in Grand Prix motor racing, and a considerable fillip to the team as Eddie put the finishing touches together on a car that had turned blue overnight thanks to the support of a new primary sponsor, Sasol, a South African petrochemical group, which had invested £6 million for a year's association with the team.

By the end of February, when Jordan and the other teams arrived at Kyalami, a dusty race circuit in the northern suburbs of Johannesburg, it was clear his second-season car was unlike his first. The drivers' line-up had changed, too, and the original 'small is beautiful' philosophy that had created the 'lean, mean and green machine' image had also been overhauled. 'Last year, our philosophy in designing and building the car was simple,' said Eddie, talking to reporters in the shade at the back of his garage. 'We used the best of what was available. We were customers. This year, we have to be different. The days of trying to be the best of the rest are over. We must now broaden the boundaries of technical excellence.' Warming to his theme, a frequent Eddie trait that has often prompted him to say more than he originally intended, he continued, 'If we are to close the gap on McLaren and Williams, we must develop new technical solutions, solutions exclusive to us. Solutions that will give us, and us alone, an edge. This path of developing our own technology will be difficult. There will be failures. But there is no other way to become a Grand Prix-winning team.' He added that he had high hopes of the partnership with Yamaha.

Nobody at the time could doubt his achievement in building a team. By 1992, he had done it, but it was just the start. Now came the even more formidable challenge of establishing the team, ensuring its future security and his peace of mind, and guiding it towards success on a consistent basis. At the car launch, Eddie had spoken of the passion and will to win that coursed throughout the team, and he mentioned, too, the lengths he had gone to in order to care for his staff – by installing a gymnasium, for example, in the new 48,000-square-foot factory. 'If you can't keep the body and mind healthy, all these other things I have put together just won't work,' he quipped. But this was only part of the reality. He had had little choice but to opt for Yamaha's offer of a supply of their factory engines, and all the sponsors he could get, including Sasol and Barclay. 'One side of my character radiates typical Irish eternal optimism,' said Eddie. 'The problem with reality is that you have to wake up in the morning and you appreciate how hard this F1 business really is.'

The 1992 season witnessed the growth of the Jordan team, but it also produced disappointment and failure on the circuit. The cars were forced into retirement more often than they delivered anything to celebrate, and Yamaha's and Jordan's reputations began to suffer. The V12 proved to be heavy and thirsty. It needed 44 gallons of fuel at the start of each race compared to the 38 needed by the Ford Cosworth V8. That additional weight helped turn Jordan's second season into one to forget on the track, but it was still a critical one in the team's development in other respects. The debts were controlled, the financial position was stabilised, the management was tightened. Jordan Grand Prix did not go out of business, as was once threatened, and plans for 1993 and beyond could be made with more certainty than before. It was an important season because it restabilised the whole team. That it was a poor year on paper, Modena scoring the team's only point of a long season in the final race in Adelaide on 8 November, merely summed up the fact that F1 was all about going the distance and surviving.

For 1993, Eddie showed again that he would not be backward in coming forward when it came to making changes. After the disappointments of his second year in Formula One, he switched from Yamaha to Hart for engines, a decision that took him from an internationally recognised manufacturer to a small English family business. But the man behind his new power supplier was no stranger to racing. He was Brian Hart, otherwise known around the paddocks of the world by his many friends and admirers as 'Jam Tart', a man determined to deliver everything the Jordan team needed to put their nightmares of 1992 behind them. Hart was aware that the Yamaha V12 had been too big, too long, too heavy, too complex, too inefficient and too bad to deserve any further time, and that Eddie had been placed under some pressure by Sasol and his most important technical man, Gary Anderson, to dump Yamaha and find a more modern, lighter and better engine. The choice boiled down to Hart and Cosworth, who had supplied the excellent HB engine in 1991, but this time Ford, who funded Cosworth, made it clear that exclusivity for the supply of their best engines would remain with Benetton. They also quoted a price that made the Hart option almost instantly more attractive. The decision was made swiftly – at Monza, Eddie and Ian Phillips had escaped from the paddock to ponder the situation under the shade of a tree, and within minutes Eddie had said, 'Let's just do it' – and this gave the team time to plan in advance.

In his book *Race Without End*, motor racing journalist and writer Maurice Hamilton traced the way in which the Hart engine deal was put together. Noting that the new Jordan Hart 193 car unveiled at the team launch on 15 January 1993 was completed during the night of 14 January, he wrote, 'Such a thing is almost expected. The contorted logic is that if a car is made ready with time to spare, then the team is clearly not trying hard enough. At Jordan, the effort is incessant. Drawing of the new car began the previous autumn as the 1992 season went into what was, for the team, its lingering death spasms. They couldn't be done with it quick enough. The scheme to use a Yamaha engine – chosen, among other reasons, because it cost nothing, as opposed to the £4.3 million bill which came with the off-the-shelf Ford Cosworth engine used in 1991 – foundered almost from the moment the Japanese V12 ran for the first time.'

Hamilton, like most close observers of the sport, knew that Hart was 'a racer', and therefore a man whose primary thoughts were not about commercial gain, but the sound of a high-revving engine and the thrill of competition on the track. 'Brian Hart mainlined on the sport from an early age,' he wrote. He was an engineer, a talented driver and a businessman whose first love was tuning engines to improve performance. He did not have the capital or the vast technological resources of a company like Yamaha, but he did have passion and a hands-on approach that meant he could dream, design and deliver faster than anyone else. When turbocharged engines were phased out of Formula One in

1986, Hart had pondered the challenge, again, of making his own engine. 'It finally came about because I recognised that the company needed its own product again. It's the only way you can survive at this level of racing. I bit the bullet and threw everything behind it, absolutely everything. The company funded the engine totally and it came perilously close to breaking the company.' More than £2 million was invested in the design and creation of prototypes before a suitable product was ready for sale, and one of the first interested purchasers was John Barnard, then working as chief designer for Ferrari. As Hamilton noted, it was like 'Gucci calling upon the advice of a seamstress in Southall'. In the end, the loss of face for the Italian team of becoming involved with a small specialist business instead of sorting out their problems in-house was the decisive factor.

In 1992, Hart was doing consultancy work for Yamaha, however, and it was during a routine visit to his premises at Harlow in Essex that Gary Anderson and Trevor Foster first gleaned any knowledge from the modest Hart about his three new V10 racing engines. 'They did not ask,' Hart recalled, 'and we knew they were in the first year of a four-year deal with Yamaha, so it never occurred to us that we could work together with the Hart engine. It wasn't until the Jordan/Yamaha situation deteriorated to the pretty desperate state it was come August 1992 that Jordan started asking about our engine.' The talks took three months to complete before agreements were signed. Four days later, in a rich irony, Hart received a call from McLaren International, the team that had won six world titles in the previous nine years. By then, it was too late. The engines were going to Eddie, the first test set for 17 November 1992, the Hart power unit going into a modified 1992 car. All went well enough to stimulate the optimism that spread through the team all winter. As Anderson told Hamilton, 'Y'see, Yamaha had the basic problem of not really understanding the fundamental needs of a racing engine. Brian understands.'

By the time he unveiled his new car, Jordan and his team were trying hard to stifle any suggestion of such optimism in their own ranks. It was difficult. The Hart engine proved capable of performing as its creator had promised, and it was extremely reliable. 'It's done more than ten Grands Prix in terms of distance during tests and, except for one small oil leak, it has run perfectly. The track has been damp a lot of the time here at Silverstone, but with this engine we have been considerably faster around the place than we were with Ford or with Yamaha,' said Eddie. 'Formula One was never meant to be easy. It's a tough, tough game. We now have two seasons behind us and we have learnt a lot. On that basis, I believe we are set for our best year. I will be disappointed if we cannot finish in the top three at least once or twice.'

All Eddie's qualities were never more valuable to the team than when he decided to sign a virtually unknown and inexperienced Rubens Barrichello to be his number two driver for 1993. The little Brazilian might have impressed by winning the 1992 British Formula Three Championship, and he might have brought with him a valuable £2 million in sponsorship from the Brazilian food firm Arisco, but he was only twenty years old. This was a perfect example of Eddie combining courage, far-sightedness and smart assessment of the talents available on the market in his management of the team. It left him with an even bigger problem, in some respects – who to recruit as his number one driver. Martin Brundle, Eddie's original Formula Three star a decade earlier, was the main target, but he decided against the job and went instead to Ligier. Briefly, there was an outside hope that the team could, unlikely as it sounded, secure the services of Ayrton Senna, who had visited the new Jordan headquarters in a social capacity after testing at Silverstone one summer's evening in June 1992 (he knew that McLaren's relationship with Honda was due to end that year). Eddie, seizing his opportunity that June evening, offered him a share of the team, emphasising that they intended to use the Hart engines the Brazilian had already experienced during his maiden F1 season with Toleman, in 1984. When the decision to go with Hart was taken, Senna remained interested, but in the end it was not to be, and he stayed at McLaren. Jordan signed instead the Italian Ivan Capelli, an old friend of Ian Phillips, for whom he had raced at Leyton House March before going to Ferrari. He had driven in 92 Grands Prix.

Unfortunately, Capelli's speed and determination were not what they once had been, and he was soon replaced by Thierry Boutsen, another veteran, who also struggled to revive his halcyon days. Thus, Eddie's selection of Barrichello turned out to be the first of a series of driver choices that persuaded him to confirm his own instinctive belief in giving youth a fling whenever possible. As a risk taker, it was his nature to avoid the obvious and the safe when choices had to be made, and he should have stuck with that philosophy for 1993, but at the end of the season he found the right pairing when Eddie Irvine was recruited. Irvine made a sensational debut in Japan on 25 October, partnering the man from São Paulo with such vim that their retention for 1994 was almost a foregone conclusion.

If the year as a whole was hardly a vintage one, with only three points collected, it was made memorable by that one afternoon, the day of the Japanese Grand Prix. Irvine, signed by Jordan at the end of the 'European' season (Emanuele Naspetti had driven in Portugal at the end of September), had done a quick test at Estoril, and was then put in the car for Japan and Australia. The Northern Irishman from Conlig in County Down knew the team well from his F3000 days, he knew Japan and he knew Suzuka. He had been racing in Japan for several years, earning half a million pounds annually, and had talked happily of staying. He also had decent local Japanese sponsors, and was blessed with an independent mind and a certainty as to his ability to produce a good, fast race in the penultimate round of what had turned out to be a frustrating season. When he stunned the team and most of the paddock by clocking the fifth best time in opening practice, it was clear something special was afoot. 'I reckon we'll be about tenth and twelfth,' said Hart.

In fact, Barrichello and Irvine soon found themselves eighth and ninth and in with good opportunities of scoring points. Later, Irvine was squeezed out of seventh by Derek Warwick. He took it in his stride, but was determined to make up for lost ground in the race. The race was run in dry and wet conditions that caused tactical mayhem for some teams and gave Irvine a perfect opportunity to make the most of his local expertise. At one stage, after being lapped by the leader, Ayrton Senna, he decided he had to re-pass him to maintain the ascendancy in his positional scrap with Damon Hill. Senna was furious. Later, in another incident,

Irvine bumped into the back of Warwick's Footwork Arrows car and the Englishman spun off. Barrichello came home fifth, Irvine sixth. It was an extraordinary result for Eddie Jordan and his team at the end of an amazing race, and Eddie enjoyed brief celebrations with his men before making a dash for the airport at Nagoya and an overnight flight to Australia and some sun, sea and relaxation.

What he did not know, as he fought through the dense Japanese traffic, was that an even bigger story was erupting inside the Jordan offices at the track. Senna, livid with Irvine's driving during the race and the way in which he passed him to unlap himself, marched into the Jordan team's pre-fabricated rooms to find Irvine surrounded by celebrating team-mates. After a verbal altercation laced with profanities and insults, Senna threw a left hook at the right side of Irvine's head. Irvine went down. The Brazilian was pulled away and removed, and as he clambered to his feet Irvine made a joke about making an insurance claim. After his momentous race, he had been right at the heart of an even more momentous news story that was put on the front pages of national daily newspapers all over the world. Eddie Jordan, meanwhile, cursed himself when he arrived in Port Douglas, Queensland for missing out on the biggest publicity opportunity for the team all year.

By the end of 1993, it was clear that Eddie had proved his team were in Formula One to stay. He had established his name, his personality and his value to the sport, he was winning the battle with his finances thanks to the support from his partners and sponsors, and he was emerging within the business of Grand Prix motor racing as a cult figure in his own right. His decision to host noisy, wild parties, disguised as musical concerts, in the paddock at Silverstone following the British Grands Prix in this period, as Pennefather described, was a masterstroke. Eddie's own love of music, and playing the drums, was well known, as was his equal fondness for a bit of a craic when possible, so it should have been no surprise to discover that he felt it was a great idea to shift his team's celebrations into a more public arena. In the summer of 1993, therefore, he decided to put on a real show at Silverstone. 'The original excuse was that it gave you somewhere to go without driving yourself mad sitting in a traffic queue somewhere,' he admitted. 'But, far better, we thought, to go berserk with some of the F1 "head-bangers" in the paddock, and it was left to me to put together the band that would entertain everyone after the race. The plan, I was told, was to have people like Des Large, Dave Pennefather, the bass player from the Blues Band and sundry other racing people, including me on drums, and to use gear kindly loaned to us by Chris Rea. The whole thing took place on the back of our articulated trailer, which we brought into the paddock on Sunday. It all went off in the end, but the organisation was only just on schedule! Anyway, it was a great opportunity to give all the teams and their staff a chance to socialise.'

That same weekend, at Silverstone, Eddie's team had started another mini-tradition by holding a factory clearance sale, selling all the odds and ends that were not needed any longer to fans who were keen to part with some money to support the team by obtaining a rare souvenir. 'I wasn't sure how it would work out, but I knew that whatever happened, it would be a nice way of keeping in touch with the racing enthusiasts, something I believe to be vitally important in all aspects of our sport,' Eddie said. 'Well, the queue began to form an hour and a half before we opened and the thing that surprised me the most was that all the more expensive items went.' His surprise was genuine, and reflected his equally genuine modesty. 'One of the first customers was Derek Daly,' said Eddie, still amazed. 'He went away with a nose cone and a rear wing. And he paid the full price, too. I don't think he ever paid me the full price for anything in his life before. I believe that living in the United States, where he is a television commentator, must have affected his sense of reason. He had the nose of the first car he ever raced, and he always wanted to have something from a Jordan because he said he felt a part of it all. I thought that was just a fancy plea for a discount at the time, but he was absolutely genuine and I was really touched by that. So was the team's bank balance at the time! In fact, when all is said and done, Derek was the first person ever to buy an ex-Jordan car. In the early 1970s, he bought my Lotus 61, paying £200 plus a Ford Anglia car. He took the Lotus straight to Mondello and, after a couple of laps, turned it over at the second corner. He never did get it home!'

The lively ending to the 1993 season was followed by a stable winter for the first time, the two drivers who had ended the previous year definitely staying for the next and the engine suppliers remaining the same. The continuation of Sasol's support for a third successive season was another reason for a greater sense of security and imminent success in the Jordan family's Oxford home. Eddie was optimistic, understandably, but with a driver as unpredictable and incident-prone as Irvine on board, he also had reasons to approach what lay ahead with some degree of trepidation. The car, the Jordan Hart 194, was launched on 11 January 1994 at Silverstone and prompted encouraging reactions from the drivers after the opening tests.

For Jordan, 1994 was a special and memorable year. The team rediscovered its form of 1991, made the most of the continuity and rode through some rough times to do so. The introduction of refuelling was the hot topic early in the season, but when Irvine was involved in a multiple collision midway through the season-opening Brazilian Grand Prix it was clear he had not shaken off his controversial tag. He was blamed for the accident, fined and banned for one race. When he went to Paris to appeal against his punishment, the ban was extended to three races, and Eddie had to find more than one replacement. But this was not all that happened in 1994. It was the year, too, of Imola, where Roland Ratzenberger and Ayrton Senna were killed after Barrichello had been involved in a huge accident; of a black-flag fiasco at Silverstone that led to a disqualification and a ban for Michael Schumacher; of a fire in the pit lane at Hockenheim involving Jos Verstappen and Benetton; and of an ugly ending to the championship when Schumacher and Damon Hill collided in Adelaide.

For Eddie and the Jordan team, however, the highlights were their first ever podium finish at the Pacific Grand Prix held in Aida, Japan, on 17 April, and a pole position, another first, at Spa Francorchamps at the end of August, where the team reacted with perfect timing to the conditions. Both feats were performed by Barrichello, a young man whose life had been turned upside down by Senna's death. Both signalled his growing maturity as a driver and a man, but also the team's maturity, too, in emerging from the early years of debt and self-doubt. It was in this period, the

Barrichello/Irvine era, that Jordan Grand Prix grew up and Eddie and his family really began to relax and enjoy the fruits of a good life. Chris Rea was one of the first to say so. As a close friend of Eddie, he knew what drove him and how much the podium in Japan meant to him. 'After that first podium, I went to a gift shop,' he recalled. 'I bought as many green candles as they had. Then, I bought miniature bottles of champagne, one for every member of the Jordan team – the mechanics, the lorry drivers, the lot. I laid the 52 bottles and the 52 candles out in the entrance to the Jordan headquarters and I got the security guard to light the candles when he arrived on Monday morning. The green candles have become a big thing now with the both of us, and when I was in hospital, he lit one for me.'

Sadly, in one way this progress brought its own casualties; at the end of the 1994 season, when the team's success earned them better opportunities with works engine suppliers, it was Brian Hart who suffered. Despite having played a prominent role in the team's resurgent run to fifth place in the 1994 constructors' championship with 28 points, his engines were replaced in the Jordan cars by those of the French manufacturer Peugeot. For Eddie, it meant a move into a bigger league altogether, with bigger budgets and greater opportunities for growth and progress. He had done this once before, with Yamaha, and paid for it, but this time he was confident it was the right move. Talking to Irish journalist Dermot Gilleece after a round of golf at Sotogrande, near his home in Spain, Eddie was warm in his praise for Ian Phillips for the way he had helped to keep their new deal a secret through the second half of 1994. 'In football terms, you could describe Ian as my assistant manager,' he said. 'His great talent is to keep me focused. I reckon I am a good ideas man, but I'm inclined to go off on tangents. He brings me back on line. And that's very important, because everything we do has to be right. At this level, and with so much money involved, you can't afford to make costly mistakes. It's not by accident that we are now being backed by the second largest car manufacturer in Europe, nor is it an accident that I have done a sponsorship deal with Total for next season.'

The deals were significant, not only for Hart, but also for Jordan, his team and his staff. By this time, it was clear he and

Phillips were proving highly successful at finding partners and sponsors, and that the profile of the Jordan team, not to mention the budget, was rising. Much of this was due to Eddie's own infectious Irishness. 'When I did my presentation to them, in the hope of clinching a deal for their engines, I raised a chuckle by insisting that I was not a "roast beef" [*un rosbif* being a colloquial French term for an Englishman]. I made it clear to them that I was Irish and that we shared the same Gallic blood. They loved that.' Peugeot had come to Jordan after a season with McLaren, who had signed with them when they found Jordan had reached Brian Hart quicker than they had. Like the Silverstone team, they were motivated to succeed.

'Our staffing levels haven't changed much,' said Eddie at the team's packed launch in the Jordan headquarters in late January 1995. 'And the philosophy remains the same – lean and green! We've got 69 people now, that's up from around 42 when we started. Compared to other teams, we are still only half as big. Last year, our budget was about £11 million including engines. This year, it will be around £13 to £14 million without the engine, but inclusive of a full test team.'

At the same occasion, he also revealed he had fended off approaches from others wishing to recruit Barrichello, who had borne up well through a difficult year in 1994. 'The death of Ayrton Senna was a terrible blow to him,' Eddie said. 'He was his mentor and his friend, as well as being the only true God to most Brazilians. He felt it, and he felt the pressures afterwards. But after all our talks and our contractual negotiations, he told me he would stay if I delivered an engine that was capable of winning. If the team is going to be successful, it has to lose this erroneous image that anything at Jordan is for sale. That might have been true in the early days, when we were struggling, but now this is a team that survives on its own initiatives. Hopefully, the days of developing young drivers and selling them on to finance the team have now gone. Now, if we have a driver with real talent, then every effort will be made to keep him here. We proved that fact twice, because apart from McLaren trying to buy Rubens, we also received a substantial offer from Frank Williams after the death of Senna.'

Referring to the parting from Brian Hart, Eddie said, 'To become champions, you have to have the best equipment, and while Brian Hart achieved a miracle on a limited budget for us in the past, now we have attracted the interest of motor manufacturers and we have to go this route. We were very fortunate to have contracts from two engine manufacturers on our desk and the promise of a third at a time when most people were finding it difficult to find one.'

The words, as always, flowed. But perhaps they flowed too easily this time, for by the end of 1995 Irvine had been 'sold' to Ferrari and Jordan Grand Prix had slipped from fifth to sixth in the constructors' standings. Sometimes, a few observers noted, it might be better if Eddie said less. But Eddie had always tempted providence, and he had never complained when the going got tough.

The highlight of the racing year was the result in Montreal, a city that has often been kind to the Jordan team. It is the place where the team won their first points in 1991, and in 1995, on 11 June, it saw Barrichello finish second and Irvine third, the team's best ever result, and on the same afternoon that another old favourite, Jean Alesi, finally secured his first and long-awaited Grand Prix win, for Ferrari. A similar, if different, pleasure came at Silverstone a month later where another former Jordan driver, Johnny Herbert, won his home Grand Prix, but the two Jordan men of 1995 were to suffer disappointments, too. For Barrichello, notably, it was a year of frustration. Little went right for him on a consistent basis, but with Peugeot in total support, Eddie was keen to re-sign both men for 1996. Indeed, an announcement was made, at the Portuguese Grand Prix in late September, that exactly that had been agreed. Five days later, Irvine was off.

'I've got mixed emotions about all of this,' said Jordan at the time, presumably after confirming that he and Jordan Grand Prix were to be the chief financial beneficiaries of the Irvine arrangement. 'I'm very sad to be losing Eddie, but I am absolutely delighted that he has been offered such a fantastic opportunity. I wouldn't dream of standing in his way, even though we've watched him develop into a very fine driver. However, despite having taken up our option on his services, there is a mechanism in his contract that allows the move to Ferrari and he goes there with all our very best wishes for the future.' Eddie then confirmed that Barrichello was to stay for a further two years, and within a matter of days he had agreed a deal with Martin Brundle to move at last from Ligier and race for Jordan Grand Prix.

'It all happened so quickly,' Eddie said. 'Sometimes I could hardly believe it all myself. Our feet had hardly touched the ground after coming back from Portugal, on the Sunday night after the race [24 September], only to turn around 24 hours later and fly to Lugano to finalise all the negotiations with Ferrari. The speed of it all was quite frightening. Eddie [Irvine] and I went to the Ferrari lawyers' office in Switzerland, looked through the contract, sorted out a few details and understood, more or less, where Eddie stood. The whole thing was done in a very friendly and pleasant way, and I have to say that Jean Todt and his people were very clear and correct in the way everything was handled. Eddie's manager, Mike Greasley, was recovering from illness and he wasn't able to be present, so I stood in as his substitute in order to help finalise negotiations and give Eddie whatever guidance I could. After that, the next thing I had to do was, having established that Martin Brundle was the ideal replacement, go out and sign him, and we did that pretty quickly too.'

Eddie's ability to add gloss to a story probably enabled him to glide serenely over a few sticky patches in this anecdote, which was narrated before the 1995 season ended in Adelaide where, in the last Australian Grand Prix to be held in South Australia, the Jordans suffered more ill fortune before rounding off the racing season with a team dinner. Eddie enjoyed that occasion greatly because, as he made sure everyone knew, Eddie Irvine had paid for it. Irvine's recollections, particularly of the details, do not coincide exactly with Jordan's, but the pair have always enjoyed differing over such matters. In his book *Green Races Red*, Irvine made it clear that he had 'signed a three-year contract with Jordan at the beginning of 1994', but had realised by the time he was 'halfway through 1995' that 'it was time to leave'. Irvine wrote that he 'told Eddie Jordan that if his team stayed as it was, I would not be driving for him the following year. My wages for 1996 were to be based on the results achieved in 1995, but my car kept breaking down, so on that basis the contract was totally unfair; I had missed out on prize money in 1995 and now it was going to affect my earnings in 1996. Of course, Eddie didn't agree. He said it was normal. There was to be no arguing with him. At that point, I decided to look elsewhere.'

Irvine stated that he had met Ferrari president Luca di Montezemolo earlier in 1995, and that this contact was followed up by his manager, Greasley, who spoke to Niki Lauda, then working for Ferrari as a special consultant. But when Lauda discovered not only that there was a buy-out clause in Irvine's contract with Jordan, but that it was for an exorbitant amount, he declared it 'ridiculous', and that seemed to be the end of that, according to Irvine. But Ferrari came back again in the autumn with another approach. 'I asked EJ if he could help me go to Ferrari,' Irvine wrote. 'He said he thought he could, meaning if the money was right anything was possible.' Within days, the deal was done. Estimations of the value of the compensation ranged from $4 million to $7 million, $5 million finally agreed upon by most speculators working in the media as the most likely figure. It was enough, whatever it was, to allow Eddie to sign Brundle within 24 hours for $2 million, and to purchase a wind tunnel and a seven-poster rig for another $2 million.

Irvine's departure to Ferrari ended the Barrichello/Irvine era, the growing-up period for the team, and ushered in an age of even bigger funding and the arrival of the team's first truly major title sponsor in Benson and Hedges. That meant that absolutely everything had to be bigger, better and faster, and that was a challenge the team tackled with relish, straining at the leash to break into the 'big four' and join the upper tiers of the motor racing establishment.

11. SOTOGRANDE

It is no wonder that Eddie needed a holiday home where he could lie down and sleep in the sun. Down at Sotogrande he can do that; there, he can spend good time with his wife Marie and children Zoe, Miki (Michele), Zak and Kyle and live a life his working week rarely allows him. 'As a father, well, he hasn't been available as much as he would have liked, but he is good with the kids,' said Marie. 'He spends time with them, as such. But it's not too easy. That's why we spend a lot of time in Spain, I think. The eldest of the girls [Zoe], she can be a bit of a one! You know, she'd have to come in at night at the right time. She'd come home and she'd say, "Hello, mum. I'm home." And then, she'd just go in her room and she'd be off, out of the window. I told Eddie, and he was up and out like a shot, at two o'clock in the morning. So then everyone was out looking for her . . .'

Not far north of the famous rock of Gibraltar, to the east of Algeciras where they used to make many of the old spaghetti westerns and to the west of the Costa del Sol, lies the small Spanish coastal town of Sotogrande. It is, unsurprisingly, a hot place, with sunshine virtually throughout the year and the western Mediterranean lapping its beaches. This is the part of Spain in which Eddie and Marie chose to buy land, create and build a holiday home, a place they have used frequently and which the whole of the Jordan family treat as a real home from home, a place to escape to where they can relax and be natural. It is where Eddie tops up his tan, where he disappears in his boat and where he and Marie can play golf with their friends. The children love to stay there for long spells, too. They have all 'lived' in Spain for long summers, picked up some Spanish and learnt how to have fun in the sunshine.

But it was not until Eddie's Formula One dream became firmly established in the mid-1990s that he could truly enjoy it himself. The critical deals – Jean Alesi joining Ferrari from Tyrrell in 1991, and Eddie Irvine following the same route in 1995 – were always identified as the ones that paid for his hobbies, his toys, his houses, his cars and his boats, but that would be a gross over-simplification. He just worked hard and enjoyed some of the rewards himself. When Irvine, in later years, poked fun at Eddie and suggested that it was his move to Ferrari that had paid for his latest Sunseeker boat, it was just that – fun. And there is nothing wrong with anyone enjoying life and spreading a few smiles around as he goes about it. Eddie had earned it. Yes, everyone said, he might have pulled a few deals out of thin air; yes, he might have blagged a few free rides and turned some profit on unlikely transactions; but he had done it all in his own way. His ability to make things happen simply bore fruit, sometimes in an orthodox business way, sometimes not. But Eddie's business has always been unorthodox, as anyone who has worked with him will testify.

When asked about memories of working with the man who has created more mirth in Formula One in the last decade than anyone else, virtually every past or present Jordan employee reacted with a smile and some affirmation of his charm and their loyalty. As a trickster, a tinker, a dealer, a rogue and a fixer, he has had no equal. Nor as a father, a leader, a husband and a friend. His style is warm and all-embracing. If you work for or become friends with Edmund Patrick Jordan, you become part of his life and he becomes part of yours. And this is why the word 'family' crops up so frequently in his conversations. His family includes his own wife and children, his mother, his extended family, his friends and his colleagues at Jordan Grand Prix and throughout motor racing. It is no wonder that some people find him hard to believe. He is larger than life. He has managed to find the Blarney stone, all right, and not only kiss it but swallow it whole.

It is no wonder that Eddie needed a holiday home where he could lie down and sleep in the sun. Down at Sotogrande he can do that; there, he can spend good time with his wife Marie and children Zoe, Miki (Michele), Zak and Kyle and live a life his working week rarely allows him. 'As a father, well, he hasn't been available as much as he would have liked, but he is good with the kids,' said Marie. 'He spends time with them, as such. But it's not too easy. That's why we spend a lot of time in Spain, I think. The eldest of the girls [Zoe], she can be a bit of a one! You know, she'd have to come in at night at the right time. She'd come home and she'd say, "Hello, mum. I'm home." And then, she'd just go in her room and she'd be off, out of the window. I told Eddie, and he was up and out like a shot, at two o'clock in the morning. So then everyone was out looking for her . . .'

This was the kind of family life Eddie could embrace more easily in Spain than in Oxford or London, where the Jordans bought a flat in the late 1990s. He would have appreciated the spirit in his daughter, too, given his own adventures as a younger man. It was the same when his third child and eldest son, Zak, caused some consternation while at preparatory school. His headmaster contacted Eddie to report that certain boys had been caught smoking. Eddie, a fitness enthusiast, a man who loves running and cycling, football and sailing, fresh air and life itself, was horrified. But Zak, the headmaster explained, was not one of the smokers. 'No, Mr Jordan. He was selling Benson and Hedges cigarettes to the boys at £3.50 a packet. Have you any idea where he might have got them from?' It was the best news wrapped in the worst possible way. His son was a chip off the old block, but it was not a smiling matter.

Another example of Zak's budding bid to become an entrepreneur before the age of consent came when he was found running his own unofficial sale in the street near the Jordan home in Oxford. According to one version of this tale, the Jordan parents were concerned about the whereabouts of their missing son 'and they eventually dragged it out of Kyle that Zak was around the corner. He had gone out on to the main road. They went to see, of course, and there is Zak and his mate from school and they've got half the contents of his dad's garage and are flogging spare parts to passers-by and people in cars. They're flagging down taxis and people in cars and flogging this stuff to them.' The father's reaction to this escapade is easy to guess.

As a family man, he is his own man, and he is loved for it. His work has made him less available, as Marie pointed out, but not unavailable, or elusive. 'He's been going away every weekend, or every other weekend, since I was little,' said Miki, his second daughter. 'So, I have not known anything different. People are always asking me how I feel about my dad being away so much, but it makes no difference to me. I was never really aware of anything different at all. Not until I went away to boarding school, where there were boys, and previously I had always gone to a girls' school. No one really knew what Formula One was before, unless they had a big brother, but when I started going to school with boys it changed and they were all watching it at weekends, and they got quite excited about who my dad was.

'But I've always known him as not exactly different but well known, especially when we go to Ireland. I feel Irish. Very Irish, completely Irish. But I know that I sound English because of my voice and the way I speak. I don't talk Irish, but I do use expressions they use sometimes, like "amn't" instead of "am not". I do that quite often. Then people look at me so I end up speaking like they do. I'm more likely to sound Irish at home. I never really do it much. Not even after a few drinks. I think then I am more likely to break into Spanish!

'I love Spain, even though my Spanish is not as good as it should be, and I love French, too. I was born in Brackley. Zoe was the only one of us born in Ireland. I was born in 1983, which I think was the year, the first year, of Eddie Jordan Racing – I think! Dad's life has never been peaceful. It's always hectic. We would always stay wherever we were and Dad would go off. Occasionally, Mum would go. And I used to get bored every Sunday because everyone used to come round and switch on the television and watch these cars going round which I absolutely hated. I used to go upstairs and play. I don't remember anything about his Formula One ambitions, not when I was small. When I was little, I wasn't interested at all and I just went out to play. Then, when I was about eleven, I began to follow it, and I've followed it all the way since then.

'We are a pretty close family, but I think we get on much better now I have been away to boarding school! Zoe, I think, is very like him. She has a quick-thinking mind. I am just the little angel, the good girl who never did anything wrong. Zak got into trouble for selling cigarettes at school, as you know! He also wanted to go to the tuck shop once and needed to find the keys, so he broke into a teacher's desk to get them! And he and his friend used to sell things by the side of the road, anything they could, to get money. Once, he sold a broken computer for two quid. Zak is also very, very good at maths. And Killer [Kyle] can sell anything. He is like Dad. He'll be a millionaire, or he'll go to jail. One of the two.'

Miki's love of her family and the family business saw her in May 2001, during her gap year between leaving Marlborough College and taking a place at Bristol to read French and European Studies, working for the team as a public relations assistant at the Monaco Grand Prix. It was, she acknowledged, not a bad 'holiday' job at all. 'Dad reminds us from time to time how lucky we are, and I can remember the times when it was not so good, and we were not here, in Formula One, or at the top,' she admitted. 'But Kyle can't. He can only remember us being at the top. I can see what has happened. I can see what Dad has done. The team owners, they all work so hard. Look at Frank Williams, too. I've got a lot of respect for him, for all of them really.' Talking about her father's character at home, she said, 'He's not a strong disciplinarian, not particularly, but one thing he doesn't like is a lot of noise. He needs his time away from it. That's when Mum locks him away in his room. He was always like that.

'We are lucky, really, aren't we? I can go back to Dublin quite a lot and I love it. I am very close to my cousins, and to Chloe my best friend. Des [Large] is a good friend of my dad's, and I know the story of their [Des and Marie's sister Ann's] marriage, but it has got told lots of different ways. I'm not so sure it's true, but I don't know – I've heard it so many ways. And my gran, Eileen, she is amazing – a nightmare, but we love her! That's how she is. She wouldn't be herself in any other way. Dad is just like her. I see her in him, him in her, all the time. And Zoe is exactly the same as well, but Dad can't see it. They have the same mannerisms. He puts his thumbs up and he moves his shoulders; Granny does just the same thing, and Zoe, but Dad refuses to admit he does it. We say, "Dad, Granny does that and you do it, too," but he won't agree.' Proudly, Miki admits that her middle name is Eileen, after her paternal grandmother in Dublin.

When talking about the childhood that might have been lost in a haze of Jordan business deals and mad pursuits of racing opportunities in all corners of the earth, Miki shows she has many rich and colourful memories. Indeed, the way she tells it, her father must either have had superhuman energy or have found a way of filling each day with 48 hours of life. 'I remember fun, going punting, in Oxford. And we usually used to have a picnic,' she said. 'He was good at punting. He loves anything to do with boats, anywhere. He loves sailing, in Spain. We have a small catamaran in Spain. Dad always used to take us out sailing in it, he loved it, and we all went out. He still does it. He'll take anyone who turns up out in it with him! He drags anyone, or anyone who will allow themselves to be dragged, out. He does it all the time. Even if Mum has already cooked dinner – it just doesn't matter. He always goes out.

'The boys went to Stowe and I went to Marlborough College. It's great fun there. Mum called it a year-long summer camp. I played a lot of sport, but I am not too competitive. I can lose, but Zoe can't lose. Even at Monopoly, or cards. Nothing. We play lots of cards. Mum usually wins. Dad loves to join in things. And, of course, he plays the spoons quite regularly. Especially when he gets bored. I play the spoons too! And the piano and the clarinet, but I'm not too musical.'

While Miki was enjoying her year out and waiting to take up a place at Bristol (UWE), her sister Zoe was studying business management at Newcastle with a view to moving into sports business and administration (she has been offered an internship with IMG). The boys remained at Stowe, where each summer Eddie and his gang revel at the British Grand Prix Summer Ball, and where, in 2002, he made one of his famous 'live' drumming appearances with the Stereophonics, one of his favourite bands. 'Zoe wants to be a football player manager, like an agent,' said Miki. 'Zoe is a pusher. She wants to do things her way and be there at the heart of everything and do the deals. She's just got an internship with IMG and she's very excited about that. Zak is doing his GCSEs and Kyle is at Stowe School too. Nobody wants to sit back. We all want careers. We all want our own lives. I want to achieve a lot, too, and to be self-sufficient. Maybe I am the most serious one in the family. I do a lot of watching and listening, but Zak is very self-contained and happy in his own company. We're all different. It's great being in a big family like this one.'

On one issue, Miki had no doubt: her mum was in charge of the family and the home. 'Yes, Dad can get frustrated when things don't work. Then he can get a bit angry. But he never takes it out on us. He just gets frustrated, sometimes disappointed, like when Zak sold those cigarettes, he had to tell him off, but I think behind it all he was saying, "Well, good boy!" He'd love us all to come home with As and then he'd be ecstatic, but he understands that we can't all be like that, and he likes us just to do our best. He helps us as much as he can! Still, Dad can rant and rave as much as he likes, but if Mum says no, then Mum says no. She runs the whole family. She's in charge. They're both great. When he's in a good mood, he's really infectious. It's because he's got something. He's charismatic, isn't he? I don't think there's anyone else in the whole world who gets away with it. He's got so many friends everywhere, yet all he ever does is shout abuse at them.

'He has tremendous energy. He is always doing things and going flat out. The only time you can tell he is tired is when he lies down and just goes to sleep. Straight away. Like that. Then you know. He never seems to have any trouble sleeping. With him, it's either full on or it's full off. There's no in between.'

When they were young children, said Miki, the family purse was controlled by Marie. Considering the unpredictable position of the Jordan team through much of that time, no wonder. 'Mum always handed out the pocket money,' she said. 'She controlled it. Dad had no clue how much we would need. We could all get round him. He is always like that. And he loves to have a party. At Christmas, every year, we have a big night. We usually go and hire a suite at one of the hotels in Dublin and it's a big party with family and friends and there are drinks and food and we all usually end up going out to a club. Everyone goes, all of us from my age up to Dad's age. We all go. It's really great fun.'

Miki, who would love to work in the team and travel the world as one of Formula One's top public and media relations managers, understood and appreciated what a blessed life her father and mother had given her in so many different ways, just as she understood and appreciated that it was impossible to consider Eddie giving up or slowing down. 'I can't imagine him easing off or giving up. What would he do? I can't imagine that Mum would cope with him around at home after half a year of it. What would he do with all that energy? How do you stop? Where am I and what am I doing? Just look at Gran! She is amazing. Isn't it great? She's amazing. She's got so many friends. Dad's like that, too, so secure and so energetic. Mum and Dad have never had rows at all, not behind closed doors or in front of us. They've had some arguments, but always in front of us. It's unusual, I know. I didn't realise it until I went to boarding school and then I found they all said "Well, my parents have split up" and "Mine are separated" and so on. And others said they wanted theirs to split up so that they would stop arguing, and then I came along and I was quite embarrassed because of mine being happy together. It's really funny, and fantastic. And it's strong. It gives everyone security.'

That family security is built now on their absences from one another as much as on their togetherness. 'We don't get together enough now, it's true,' said Miki. 'Just the holidays, and that's fantastic. And that's why the house in Spain is so good. We've all got friends there. And that's why when we won in Belgium in 1998 Dad had to get home and be with Mum and share the whole feeling and celebrate it.' And they had a fine time, too, back in Oxford, and later down by the beach in Sotogrande. But then, in Spain, in particular, the Jordan team has always known how to have a good time.

The Jordan 'family' has always been extensive, Irish and all-embracing; it is the good fortune, or otherwise, of all those to have been employed in any way by the man himself to have become part of it. One way or another, any former Jordan driver, mechanic, engineer, technician, truckie, secretary, salesman, executive or book-keeper has become, and has remained, one of the family. This is why Jean Alesi, Eddie Irvine, Damon Hill, Andrea de Cesaris and others visit the Jordan motor home whenever they are in the Formula One paddock. It is their version of Miki's home from home in Sotogrande. It has been that way since the start, since 1991, and before. It is why former Jordan folk love to join together and recall the old days. They worked for a man who was not afraid to be part of the team and part of the fun. He did not hide his mistakes, his buffoonery, his misery, his joy, his despair, his worries or his delight from anyone.

Louise Goodman joined the Jordan bandwagon in 1992 as the team's first full-time press officer. She succeeded Elizabeth Wright, who had worked for 7UP, and Mark Gallagher, a freelance who wrote the team's official news releases. Gallagher was not paid properly and often had to chase his employer for his money. Typically, he returned later to become one of the team's mainstays as head of marketing. When Goodman left, in 1997, to join ITV, she was replaced by Giselle Davies, who in turn moved on in 2002 to work for the International Olympic Committee. Helen Temple was promoted to Giselle's job in the realisation that the Jordan team provided its media manager with the best spotlight for career acceleration in Formula One. Not bad for a family with a bit of a wild reputation!

Drawn together over a glass of white wine at the 2002 Spanish Grand Prix, and joined by various others from Jordan's motley crew, staff and former staff alike were enlightening. When asked about her earliest memories of Eddie, Davies began, 'The first time I remember seeing, or meeting, Eddie was at Spa in 1996 when I was in a bus with Benetton, who I worked for, and we stopped to pick up this man who was standing, waving in the road. He jumped in the minibus with us and I just remember him talking a lot. He was very animated. We gave him a lift to the track and that was it. No more.'

Goodman: 'I was working with Jardine PR. Tony Jardine had told me that we were going to be doing the PR for a bloke called Eddie Jordan who had a Formula 3000 team. He came down to the office for a meeting and I can remember Tony had told me beforehand and given me this deep briefing, all about him. We were told to watch out for this guy. And I remember when Eddie came along to the office he had a conspiratorial way of talking to you, which you well know! He'd take you to one side. He has got that kind of "I need to talk, we need to talk" look about him when he wants to use it. I was told about "how committed he was going to be, how he would do this and that and the other, and this is how we are going to work together, it will be so wonderful". So, the funny thing about it was that everything Tony had told me he was going to do, he did. I was just watching him, smiling inwardly, and thinking, "Yep, Tony said you would say that! Yep, Tony said you would say that, too!"'

As with any Jordan family party, things soon got out of hand. Any hope of holding this group to a normal agenda for discussion was lost. As the wine flowed, the stories followed as quickly. They began in 1987, when Eddie won the F3000 title with Johnny Herbert and supporting sponsorship from Camel.

'I believe that was the year in which he bought a new motor home – well, actually a second-hand one,' Goodman recalled. 'I don't know what the payments were, but let's just say he bought it for ten grand and he spent three grand getting it painted. He then told R.J. Reynolds – or the aforementioned W. Duncan Lee – that it was the way things were done in Formula 3000 and it was the sponsors' motor home, and that he, Eddie, had bought it on their behalf! It had cost him sixty grand, he said, but he would give it to Duncan for fifteen in a good deal. And, he added, I did have it totally resprayed for you and that cost thirty grand too! So, what had basically cost Eddie around fifteen grand, he persuaded Duncan to pay forty or fifty for!' This was a typical tale of the early Jordan racing family. It summed up Eddie's attitude to money, sponsors and budgets, or at least hinted at how each was to be used. 'I don't seem to remember there being a massive amount of budget,' Goodman continued, recalling the F3000 days. 'It was a Camel promotional budget. Jordan, or EJR as it was then, were the only team I was dealing with. There were about six or eight Camel-sponsored F3000 drivers, so, really, he had nothing to do with that budget. It was different when I went to work for him later. Then, there was never any budget at all. I used to take the piss and say, "Look, I'm the only profit-making department in this company. You know I make you money!' And, you know, in my first year, he paid me about £13,000!'

So, why did you accept the job?

'I was sold to him. I was told I was going to work for him.'

You were sold?

'Yes, I was told by Tony Jardine. He called me into his office and he said, "You might need to move to Silverstone because you're going to work with Jordan." I said, "What do you mean?" and he said, "You're going to be Eddie Jordan's press officer." '

So, effectively, you were sold, like a piece of meat?

'Effectively, yes, but that wasn't EJ's fault.'

Were you happy with that?

'I didn't have much of a problem with it. Ian Phillips was there and I had been working with him at Leyton House March for two or three years. But it was a bit of a shock at first.'

And what happened when you got there?

'When I got there, it was in 1992. I was still actually paid by Tony then, but in 1993 I left Jardine PR and started working officially for Jordan. That's when I met up with EJ and I got £13,000.'

At this, Davies interjected. 'That's pretty good money for those days! Not so bad at all! When I joined, I had a conversation with Lou, and then I went and saw Eddie. I remember I said that I asked for X, and I can't remember exactly what it was. His voice dropped, and suddenly it felt as if I should have pitched a lot higher!'

Goodman: 'I honestly don't remember what Eddie paid me, but Sasol probably paid my wages, times three! They paid for my hotel rooms and they paid for my club class travel everywhere, despite the fact I always went economy. They paid for absolutely everything. Again, Eddie told them that that was the way it was done, despite the fact that I was employed by Jordan Grand Prix as their press officer! I just wish I'd had that much front.'

As things warmed up on this particular evening, some of the anecdotal material became as near the knuckle as Eddie's famous speeches to his sponsors. The following gives some insight into how he was perceived by his staff at various colourful moments during his career as a team owner.

Can you remember any mad anecdotes in the early years?

Goodman: 'In 1992, in particular, every time the car went out of the garage, the engine blew up. Sometimes it was not even out of the garage before it blew up! And do you remember Henny Collins' line to Eddie? [Henny and her colleague Chris Leese were in charge of the catering and the Jordan motor home operations in the early 1990s.] Well, you know what EJ is like – always making sexual advances to anything in a skirt?'

Davies: 'Oh, I think that's changed. Now he does that towards anything!'

Goodman: 'Well, Henny used to run the motor home here. And, once, in Brazil I think, EJ was sitting with Dave Price, and EJ was giving it all the usual "I know what you effing want, and it's in my trousers" and all that kind of stuff, which would normally have gone straight over the top of Henny's head. She would have just ignored it. But this time Henny turned round and delivered a mega line back, something like, "Eddie, I've already got one c*** in my knickers, why would I want another?'

Ian Phillips: 'Pricey got it immediately, in just a few seconds, and he was roaring with laughter, but EJ didn't. It took him a lot longer to get it!'

Goodman: 'I waited three years to use that line, because I thought it was so very good. And Eddie, he likes to repeat lines like that everywhere, all the time. He still goes around and tells everyone about it. And he is just the same. Today, if I am standing in my ITV gear and trying to look professional, waiting in line for an interview with somebody, he will come along and just burst out with all sorts of his favourite lines with sexual innuendos everywhere.'

It should be recorded that, by this stage, several bottles of wine were being enjoyed by the group sitting in the Spanish evening sunshine. The wine may well have loosened some inhibitions, prompting a stronger concentration of attention on the lighter side of Eddie's business.

Goodman: 'In 1993, there was no money, but it didn't stop us having a lot of fun. There would be a lot of banter going around the office. Then, it was just Ian, myself and Lindsay [Haylett, secretary to Eddie], all in one room with Trevor [Foster]. And EJ would be next door. He used to get on everyone's tits because he would come out, picking up bits of paper, and then every now and then Lindsay would say, "Push off, Eddie! If you want something to do go back into your office. I've got a pile of things in there, which you don't want to do, so go back and do those! Can't you see we're busy in here? Go on, off you go!" Eddie would just laugh, go and sit in his office, and now and again he'd stick his head round the door again and laugh.'

Phillips: 'He played golf, and he used to carry around those sticky notes, and when he had a good idea he would write on them and then leave them on everybody's desks.'

Goodman: 'And when it came to discussing a pay rise, first of all he would get personal and try to find out how much was in your bank account, and then he'd say what a great job you do, and how he wanted to do things right by you and so on, and then he'd get out a pen, suddenly, and he'd find a piece of paper, and he'd just write a figure down, and he would slide it across the table. I would cross it out and write a different figure. Then, he would cross it out and shove it back. And that was how salary negotiations were carried out!'

It was not uncommon, as it turned out during this evening of revelations, to hear that Eddie enjoyed mixing his business with his family life. He also liked to please his staff with helpful advice and good opportunities whenever he could.

Goodman: 'When we first moved into the new offices, there was a chap called Fergus, who had done all the interior design. In many ways, he was just like EJ in terms of his "financial Irishness", and, of course, he was another Dubliner. Fergus used to come up with these totally grand, impractical design schemes and it would cost an absolute fortune, and he and EJ used to have these massive rows. You could hear them. Eddie was screaming, "I'm not paying that effing price!" And then he'd go off and order all this expensive stuff from Italy. He had done a lot of work at their house, including installing a brand-new kitchen, which he had designed. And I had just moved up to Oxfordshire and I had a new place and I needed a new kitchen . . .'

At this point, during what has become a raucous and funny party with more people joining every few minutes, Mr Edmund Patrick Jordan himself joins in. His contributions, some risqué and some eloquent, have been edited from the passage, but removed for safe reading elsewhere in this book.

'Anyway,' Goodman continued, 'they were permanently trying to have each other over. Fergus was trying to whack a price on something and EJ was refusing to pay. It went on for ages. Fergus was fitting a new kitchen for him and I had just moved and I had no cooker, except for a baby Belling, and Eddie kept saying to me, "You can have our kitchen if you want it." So I said to Fergus that Eddie had offered me his kitchen and I asked him how much I should pay for it. So Fergus said to me, "I reckon you could get it for £500." I thought that sounded good. So, anyway, EJ calls me into his office and he says, "Lou, now about this kitchen, it's yours if you want to have it. If you want it, it's yours. Marie and I have discussed it." Well, Fergus was there and since I didn't have a clue how much it was worth, I asked Fergus again, knowing what he had said, and at this point I really had to stop myself from laughing. Suddenly, Eddie said, "Now, Fergus tells me I should charge you £1,000. But to you, Lou, I will give it away, for just £500. If you want it, it's yours." And I nearly broke up laughing because that's exactly what Fergus had told him to tell me! The funny thing then was that I pulled up outside and said to Fergus, "Cheers, mate, that was a good shout for me. It's a mega deal, what with the hob and the oven." And then he said to me, "What hob and oven? I'm having the hob and the oven! You're not supposed to have a hob and oven for £500!" And it was great, because I had them both over!'

It was a common theme, obviously, of the early Jordan Grand Prix years for each member of staff to enjoy every chance to pull a financial trick whenever possible.

Goodman: 'To be fair, Eddie also got me my central heating because he had been sponsored by a heating engineering company in the Johnny Herbert days. So, when I said to Eddie that I'd got no heater, Eddie said, "I'll tell you what, here's this chap, take him along to the test and I reckon he'll give you your central heating, radiators and boiler for free" – which he did!'

To avoid the whole conversation becoming a litany of Eddie's deals with suppliers, partners and friends, we begin talking about the serious subject of drivers, a subject that has always been close to his heart. Again, in a moment of truth, this discussion is ended abruptly.

Mark Gallagher: 'For Eddie, with drivers, it's like a lust affair. He has it with everyone, with all of them. It's full on for about five minutes and then that's it.'

Goodman: 'But some of them continue, like Jean [Alesi].'

No further reaction.

Davies: 'Really, the thing is that Eddie hates confrontation. Full stop. He just hates it. He just . . . when things get confrontational with drivers, that's when he passes the buck, or the shutters come down, or he gets all twitchy and funny. He can be all funny, and that's cool. Or he gets very serious and he talks to them. The big pep thing.'

Goodman: 'Oh, and what about the driver database? The great myth!'

Gallagher: 'Yes. He would be in a meeting and a name would crop up and he would say, "Oh, yes, we know about him. We've been following him since Formula Ford, year on year . . ." And it was probably just somebody he had read about in *Autosport*.'

Goodman: 'Or more likely it was someone who someone else had pointed out – probably Marie!'

Gallagher: 'And you know where he got that idea from? Dick Bennetts. I think Dick Bennetts did actually have a database.'

Goodman: 'But if Eddie did have a database, he would not have known what to do with it. He ranted and raved for ages about how he had to have a fax machine at home and it was very important that he had a fax machine. So, Lindsay organised for him to have a fax machine, and after a couple of weeks he was ranting again. "This effing fax machine doesn't work. It's ridiculous." Actually, it had just run out of paper. So what would he have done with a database?'

At this time, the author felt the conversation was drifting in a direction of amusing but not necessarily fair or accurate criticisms, reflecting too much the quantity of wine drunk – at Eddie's expense – and taking advantage of Eddie's easy-going nature towards his staff, perhaps due to his willingness always to give them a free hand. So, the partying participants were asked to highlight the qualities of their former or current employer.

In unison: 'Money.'

In unison (almost): 'Technophobia!'

Goodman: 'What about the time when he wanted to engineer the car at Spa? In the old days, in the old pits? Eddie was getting in everyone's way, and fussing around, and he wanted to do this and he wanted to do that. He ended up sending all the gear ratios rolling down the hill, down the pit lane, and it was just terrible. Disastrous. In the F3000 days.'

Gallagher: 'Another time was at the Brazilian Grand Prix this year [March 2002]. We had been poor all weekend and Sato was lapped by the Schumacher brothers. And the next thing, over the radio, the race engineer said, "Taku, try to stay with them!" And we were all thinking, you what? How can he? We've been two and half seconds slower than them all race, so how can he possibly stay with them? So I went down to Eddie's office on Monday and we were talking about the dismal performance at the weekend and I said to Eddie and [chief operating officer] John Putt, "And that stuff that comes off that engineering platform – I couldn't believe that somebody comes on the radio to Sato, halfway through the race, and says try to stay on the tail of Michael and Ralf. How effing naive is that?" And Eddie said, "I gave that instruction!"'

Wild laughter.

Gallagher (continuing): 'And it turns out he had told James Key [Sato's race engineer], "Tell him to stay with them," and James is young and naive himself, so he just said, "Oh, Taku, can you stay on their tail?"'

Goodman: 'But it wouldn't have been EJ who gave that instruction because EJ doesn't know how to use the radio. There was an occasion when he was going on at someone – I can't remember if it was John [Walton] or Gary [Anderson] – because Eddie wasn't happy with one of the drivers, and he was saying "tell him this and tell him that" and got "You effing tell him!" as a reply. So Eddie starts shouting "do this and do that" into the radio, and of course he hasn't pressed any of the buttons, but he thinks he's told the drivers what to do!'

Gallagher: 'Yes! And when we do garage tours, with guests, and we get asked if Eddie wears headphones, we always, just to be humorous, say, "Yes, of course he does, but he doesn't realise they were disconnected in 1993!"'

Warming to their mischievous work again, the group consume more wine. Eddie, having listened and grieved at his misfortunes and contributed his own (corroborating) versions of most of the stories, departs.

Gallagher: 'He was showing Sir Peter Bonfield, the chief executive of BT, and some other esteemed guests around the paddock at Monte Carlo three years ago, and he showed them the steering wheel in the car, and he is doing all the button malarkey, saying "this does that" and "that button says talk", but of course Eddie hasn't looked at a steering wheel in years! He wouldn't have a clue what was on it, but he comes through it and he talks about the levers on the back and gives a very practical description of a steering wheel. Then he refers to the carbon-fibre boss, which is a sort of collapsible bit in case you nut it, and he says, "This is the airbag." Sir Peter Bonfield and his guests may not know much about Formula One, but they have never, for sure, heard of an airbag in a Formula One car, so one of them bravely says, "I didn't know Formula One cars had airbags," and Eddie goes, "This has been developed exclusively for Jordan by British Aerospace." Sir Peter Bonfield says, "I thought British Aerospace sponsored McLaren," so Eddie says, "Yes, but they're only giving Ron money; they give us technology." And these poor people went away thinking "Wow! This is amazing!" and believing all these stories Eddie was telling them. Then he turns to me and says, "Is that all right? Was I right?" And I say, "No. It was bollocks." And he says, "But they won't know that. They don't know about it, do they?" And I say, "And you obviously don't know anything either!" '

By now, the examples of Eddie's alleged technophobia are running amok through the entire evening. It is an unstoppable flow of laughter. But Eddie is no longer there to stop it, join in with it or prevent it going on and on. And his wine (or more likely the wine supplied by one of his sponsors) is being enjoyed by everyone.

Goodman: 'I remember one time when we decided we would go out on the boat. We took the canvas off, and the entire thing was covered in salt. It obviously hadn't been washed down the last time it was used. It was down at the house in Spain, at Sotogrande. And it was when Eddie had just a small boat, a 25-footer, and it had a jet ski. There was myself and Rae [Feather, an Irish girl who worked in Formula One and was a friend of the family and team] and EJ and Zoe and Miki. So we got on the boat and all the girls wanted to go out on the jet ski, so we had to get the boat fuelled up. Then the jet ski broke or something, so Eddie tied them on the back and we went to the fuelling area, and after a lot of backing up and bashing into the jetty and reversing up again and bashing into it again we finally got the boat fuelled up. We had gone about 150 yards by this time and it had taken an hour and a half! Finally, we set off heading back out towards the beach, but we got halfway there when the boat stopped for some reason. So, there we all were with a broken-down jet ski being towed by a broken-down boat, and EJ didn't have a clue what to do with either of them. He ended up wading in and towing it all in behind us.'

After much laughter and tears, another question is asked to help move the conversation on. Why, after all this, do so many highly qualified, ambitious and capable people work for him?

Eric Silbermann: 'Can you imagine a group of us sitting around like this and talking about any other team owner in the same way?'

This comment by Silbermann, the paddock's most knowledgeable and most infamous gossip correspondent and reporter – he once suggested that working for Eddie Jordan in the 1990s was a bit like living through the sixties: if you can remember anything, you obviously weren't there – is taken to mean not only that Eddie Jordan is more interesting (or less dull) than the majority of other Formula One team owners, but also that everyone loves him. He is human. He enjoys laughter. He can laugh at himself and at his own expense.

Davies: 'I would say that he has an annoying habit of making you want to believe him! He has a habit of – how can I explain this? Well, you all know him well . . . it is a sort of heart and head thing. You are listening to him, and your head is saying this is all nonsense, it's not believable, but the other side of you is saying that it is believable, and you feel drawn by it all the time. It is the power he has over people. He has it over the team and he has it over all sorts of people, and he has the ability to make people do it, especially for him. It is not quite like bees around a honey pot, but it is like it once you see everyone jostling to be the one who curries the most favour with Eddie. And yet you hate yourself at the time because you don't want to care that much. At the end of the day, you know that he would drop you tomorrow . . . yet on the other hand he wouldn't quite. You know, also, that he wouldn't do that kind of thing. It's so strange. But he has certainly got a power.'

Gallagher: 'It has been explained scientifically to me by one of the consultants. You can either be conscious or unconscious in your life, competent or incompetent. And successful entrepreneurs fall into two categories: consciously competent, so they understand what they are good at, or unconsciously incompetent. In other words, they don't even realise they are incompetent, which gives them the bravado to keep on going for it, even though they don't realise it. You never get people who are consciously incompetent, because they are weak, and you certainly don't get successful people who are unconsciously competent, because they don't understand they are competent. So Eddie is here [he points to an extreme part of the room]. He is the unconsciously incompetent! And we are all trying to move him in this direction [he points again] so he is the consciously competent. But, of course, it is impossible.'

In yet another effort to re-focus the issues and bring the discussion back full circle, the author asked Davies why she decided to leave Benetton, the world champions, to join Jordan. She gave a succinct reply about cutbacks and opportunities. Then she added, 'So, I actually joined Jordan not really knowing much about Jordan beyond the team's image, which was friendly, open, all these things. It seemed to be the closest thing to Benetton's image at the time. It wasn't miles away in its approach, especially with the media, I thought. But I will always remember that when I joined Jordan, in one week I knew Eddie better than I had known Flavio [Briatore] in six months at Benetton! It was a totally different atmosphere in the team, totally different. As they were saying earlier, we sat upstairs outside his [Eddie's] office, and on the first day he came over, gave me a kiss and said, "Welcome to Jordan." He was always in and out of the office, there was banter, and you were right in there from day one. After one week, I felt like I had been there six months. It was completely different from Benetton, which was an office in a marketing department. Flavio was down the other end of the corridor, and he was governed by Patrizia [Spinelli, the head of communications at Benetton] anyway, but it was a very different atmosphere. I have never once regretted joining Jordan. Not once in all my time with the team.'

Goodman: 'When I left Jordan to work for ITV, I always said, "When you win a race, I want to get the first interview." We had this sort of banter, but when Jordan won at Spa, I was determined to get to Eddie first to say congratulations, and it was really bizarre because I can remember I really thought, "Hold on, I'm not a part of that any more, it is not actually my victory." It was sort of like my victory, but it wasn't my victory. It was really bizarre. Having waited for it for so long, it was a big moment, and I probably wouldn't have felt that at any other team, I don't think.'

Davies: 'Another thing about Eddie is that you always think you can change him. It is things like the language, the innuendo, as we were saying earlier. You just don't want to give up. You just keep thinking, "This is brilliant, and you could be so much more brilliant if this, that or the other happened." Always you are trying to make a little bit of a difference.'

So, for most of you, Jordan was a good career step?

Davies: 'At Jordan, it is nothing to do with how much you are getting paid or the fact that the team isn't the top one. It is all to do with the remit you get in the job you do. There's no doubt that the job I have done, in PR, I have been able to do a hundred times more effectively than I could ever have done in any other team in the pit lane. And that basically comes from Eddie himself. It goes to Mark and to Ian, but it is still the ethos of the company. If I was doing Ellen's [Kolby, press officer for McLaren International] job or Nav's [Sidhu, Jaguar] job, or any other job, it is not the same, and that was why it was a good career move. But I didn't analyse it as a career move at all because I wasn't looking for a career! That is not why I am here, but looking back, I wouldn't have got a job at the IOC, because although I might have been able to do a competent job in another team, I wouldn't have been able to make what I wanted out of it. If the McLaren job was available, I wouldn't want it.'

Goodman: 'It's all changed since my time. Ian and I used to work with each other and we'd say, "Did Eddie want to be rich today? Or famous today?" So we would know if we were going to have a busy day – and Eddie loves being famous. You would say to him, "I've got another interview," and he would say, "I'm not doing another effing interview, I've effing had it." Then he would have a big old rant, and ten minutes later he would come out and say, "Where's the effing so and so who wanted to speak to me?" He just loves the spotlight.'

Davies: 'If you are making him money, or you are making him famous, then he is happy. But you have to do it through gritted teeth and a lot of aggro sometimes.'

As the evening drew to an end, the wine supply slowing down, Goodman recalled more tales from the early days of Jordan in Formula One. In particular, she remembered the popular story of how Eddie Irvine's sensational drive in Japan in 1993 had been sponsored, and how the sponsorship had been demonstrated on the car. 'What funded Irve's debut in Japan was his backing from Cosmo, a Japanese fuel and lubricants company. But we still had Sasol funding at the time. So, with Irve having sponsorship from Cosmo, it was a total conflict. But Eddie came up with a scheme of actually putting Cosmo logos on his helmet and on his car in Japanese, so Sasol didn't know it was a rival fuel manufacturer. That was Eddie's idea. So, we ran Cosmo on the car, we ran two fuel manufacturers, and eventually Sasol twigged, but that was by the time we got to Australia and it was too late by then. The damage was done! We had got the money in the bank and we didn't care any more!' Jordan actually told Sasol that he had believed Cosmo to be a women's magazine.

This prompted talk of other short-term sponsorships, of which there were many in the early 1990s, when every deal was valuable to the team. Of some of the drivers employed, it was once said, 'We were left basically with a succession of paying drivers, all of whom were sweet blokes, but the appeal was not necessarily in their driving talent as much as in their bank balances.'

Goodman recalled, with some glee, 'Oh, yes! There were brown paper envelopes flying around in all directions in those days. In fact, Richard O'Driscoll [a former manager of Ireland's biggest bank who was appointed chief financial officer to the team by Eddie in 1992] used to purposefully watch the television to see what logos there were on the car at every race so that when he and Ian and EJ met on Monday morning he could say, "Right, there was a new logo, so where is the money for that?" And he would be met by these two schoolboys going, "What the f*** are you talking about?' And they would have their little divvy-up and it was in their back pockets! Or so we all believed!'

The party ended calmly and happily, long after Eddie himself had departed the Circuit de Catalunya for another engagement that evening. His comments, offered earlier on, did not add much more than colour to the stories, but he did reveal that, contrary to certain rumours, he had abandoned a ritual that had been attributed to him of always attempting to travel first class on British Airways, whether he was flying with an economy ticket in his pocket or not. Goodman had suggested that this kind of allegation, common in the paddock in the early 1990s, might have had some justification: 'Eddie used to pay for an economy seat, and we would get on the plane and we would all turn right, down to economy, but Eddie would go up to first class and he would plonk himself down in the first available seat. And there would be Ron Dennis and all these people, who had paid, and he would spend the entire flight saying, "Look at these people who've effing paid! Did you pay for that ticket? Hah!" And this worked fine until the time when they did a head count and Eddie, having done his usual trick, had to be escorted from first class down to economy.'

Eddie did not deny this final allegation. 'It was on the way to Canada,' he confirmed, 'and I had this unbelievable stroke. I was always last on the plane, always smartly dressed with a briefcase, and I always walked down there looking just it, you know. I never had my tickets on me, and if you go in last, there is nearly always an empty seat and you can take the empty seat. So you just look around and stretch for a couple of minutes, and you wait for the doors to close. The seat's empty, so you sit down and do the seat belt up. However, what she's talking about was the time when I went in and I sat down beside Herbie [Blash] and Herbie said, "I just don't know how you keep getting away with this." It was great, except this time, Herbie's mate was in the loo, and he never told me. The whole place was chock-a-block, I sat down, and then I heard the loo door, but still I didn't pay any attention. Then this guy is talking to me. And then, I think, they ask for my ticket, and I'm going through all my pockets like this and that and so on. Anyway, to cut a long story short, they got me! They caught me, and they marched me down to economy. And I got such a slagging! They were all waiting for this to happen, the whole plane. All of them going back to London! The whole way, everyone just howled with laughter.'

It wasn't the first time Eddie had supplied a laugh, being such a self-effacing and generous character, and it most certainly will not be the last. Not for nothing is he regarded as the funniest, most human and best-loved team owner in Formula One.

12. SPA FRANCORCHAMPS II

The circumstances of the victory, the drama of the race and the background not only to the weekend but to the years leading up to the Belgian Grand Prix of 1998 contributed to the emotional groundswell that swept through the paddock that evening. Team orders had been issued requesting Ralf Schumacher not to fight Hill for the victory in the closing stages of a dramatic rain-hit contest that had seen Michael Schumacher depart angrily after a collision between his Ferrari and David Coulthard's McLaren Mercedes-Benz in the blinding spray. This had soured the young German's feelings. But nothing could hold back the tide of delight that filled Jordan, Hill and the rest as they sped into one of the most extraordinary aftermaths of any Grand Prix.

Only a handful of modern Formula One circuits stir the blood in any special way. Monaco, for obvious reasons, is one. It is extraordinary that cars pushed by more than 800 horsepower can be guided through the steel barriers of that unforgiving street circuit with such finesse and grace. Monza, set among the pastures of a former royal park north of Milan where tradition and the raw passion and power of Italian motor sport are in the air, is another. The Spa Francorchamps circuit in Belgium, where a purpose-built section of racing asphalt has been added to the traditional country roads amid the sweeping pines of the Ardennes forest, is certainly a third. To some drivers, it is the only real remaining test of their manhood in an age when Formula One's arenas have been redesigned to become entertainment facilities, neutered sporting environments for a motor racing public that has little taste for the politically incorrect risks of the old days, when blood flowed on the tracks, black headlines covered front pages and the stench of death lured people to the greatest races on earth.

Eddie Jordan has seen it all. He has lost friends, been in big accidents, watched helplessly as his own drivers have danced into eternity, and suffered on the sidelines as a team owner while events beyond his control have unfolded. He has known all the drama of the business, and on a regular basis he has returned to Spa Francorchamps to experience more of it. It is an annual race, of course, but it is also a special date in the calendar. It is the weekend when the 'silly season' often takes its final spin, when drivers are transferred or signed or retire or do something mad. It is the weekend when great men do great things, too, such as winning exciting races in appallingly difficult conditions, with blinding spray, virtually zero visibility and high tension all around them. It is also the place where Michael Schumacher made his Jordan debut, in 1991; where Rubens Barrichello delivered the team's first pole position, in 1994; where Ferrari's first approaches to Irvine and his manager Mike Greasley were made; where Giancarlo Fisichella finished a wonderful second, in 1997 (when Damon Hill was made increasingly aware, too, of Jordan's interest in recruiting him); and where, in 1998, Hill delivered Jordan from his long wait for victory by scoring the team's first triumph in a magnificent, memorable one-two ahead of Ralf Schumacher. No wonder, then, that when 'Spa' is mentioned in Eddie's presence, it triggers all kinds of emotions and warm memories of historic moments.

But Eddie is not the only one. Anyone who was there that late August weekend in 1998 will recall the emotional rollercoaster of Jordan's first win. It was a triumph shared by the paddock, by his friends from all around the world, by Irishmen in every bar on earth, and by anyone who had worked for the team. There were tears and hugs and drinks and toasts and wild signals from fans and people who had no reason to be delighted, but were, because Jordan was the team for everyone. Eddie celebrated with a jumping, dancing, demented jig that summed up his Irish mood, one that was, thankfully, caught by television for posterity. Hill also jumped, star-shaped, arms and legs akimbo, joyously, in a fashion that recalled Michael Schumacher's famous punch-the-air skipping exhibition of fitness and youth, but also delivered an ironic commentary on Hill's own embarrassed and pink-faced early appearance on the Spa Francorchamps podium when he was rising to his personal zenith with the Williams team.

The Belgian win was the result of more than Hill's arrival and Benson and Hedges sponsorship money, however. It was the culmination of a decade of hard work, Eddie's personal sacrifices, the genius of Gary Anderson and the contributions of many other men in many other jobs. That is why it mattered. Most people who knew about motor racing and who knew about Formula One realised it was a special hour when Eddie Jordan won his first Grand Prix. Just imagine how those who had been part of the team felt when they heard the news, but were absent from the party. Men like Gary Anderson, who deserved to share the moment. Women like Louise Goodman, who had been tempted away by television after several years' service in Eddie's offices. It was a victory that signalled, finally, that after successive years of progress in 1996 and 1997, the team had finally grown up. It opened floodgates of emotions, yet after all the years, the months, the days and nights, and the hours Anderson had given to Jordan Grand Prix, he was not there when it mattered. The growth of the team, the growth of the budget, the changing management structure and the political strains that went with all this had combined with his own unwillingness to take a rest when he most needed one to leave him tired and ill. He had developed a small stomach ulcer; aware of this, Eddie had persuaded him to miss a few races in order to recover from the minor surgery that was necessary before embarking again on preparations for the 1999 season. Mike Gascoyne had been recruited to strengthen the technical team's organisation and to relieve the pressure on Anderson; in some eyes, he made a critical difference to the team's performance that day. Eddie Jordan had tried to contact Anderson to tell him about the famous win, but he learnt the details only when he was contacted by mobile phone by the senior race mechanic Andy Stevenson from the Plain Vent restaurant, up the hills near the track. 'He's choked, completely choked,' reported Stevenson, who, like others who were there that night, had been with Jordan since the early days, having joined in 1987. That was why grown men hugged that day. It had been such a long time coming.

Anderson would have enjoyed the celebration party, too, and so would Eddie, had he had the time in his busy schedule. As it was, once the realisation that a Jordan car had won a Grand Prix at the 127th attempt had sunk in and he had recovered from a rare moment of stunned silence, he had to face the media, cope with literally hundreds of calls and plan how to get home and share the magical moment with his long-suffering family.

The circumstances of the victory, the drama of the race and the background not only to the weekend but to the years leading up to the Belgian Grand Prix of 1998 contributed to the emotional groundswell that swept through the paddock that evening. Team orders had been issued requesting Ralf Schumacher not to fight Hill for the victory in the closing stages of a dramatic rain-hit contest that had seen Michael Schumacher depart angrily after a collision between his Ferrari and David Coulthard's McLaren Mercedes-Benz in the blinding spray. This had soured the young German's feelings. But nothing could hold back the tide of delight that filled Jordan, Hill and the rest as they sped into one of the most extraordinary aftermaths of any Grand Prix.

Sadly, no Irish national anthem was played when Eddie stood with his drivers and third-placed old favourite Jean Alesi on the victors' podium. If that was a cause for minor concern (and it was), Eddie was not going to allow it to spoil his triumphant day. After receiving the winner's trophy, he stepped forward and mouthed to the hundred-strong Jordan staff – many of whom had come out especially from the factory that weekend on a trip planned by Eddie – that it was for them as much as for him or anyone else. When the drivers reached the media centre for the post-race news conference, they were greeted by a standing ovation – a rarity in itself that spoke volumes. Bernie Ecclestone telephoned Eddie and told him, 'Jesus, Jordan, you'll be unbearable now.' After making a heartfelt speech to his team and hundreds of onlookers who seemed to have joined them for the night, Eddie Jordan had to find a way home after he and Ian Phillips missed their flight from Brussels and ended up flying back to Kidlington airport near Oxford in a plane scrambled from Jersey by his good friend Brian de Zille under lights switched on by the local airport manager by special request, following a phone call made by Eddie's personal assistant Lindsay Haylett. It was an amazing end to an amazing day, the first and best victory in the life of Jordan Grand Prix and Eddie Jordan.

Many things had changed after Eddie Irvine's move to Ferrari during the winter of 1995–96, before the sport returned to life at the season-opening Australian Grand Prix in Melbourne on 10 March, among them the introduction of a major sponsor in Benson and Hedges, paying a reported £15 million per year; the recruitment of the vastly experienced Martin Brundle, at 36 a veteran of 142 Grands Prix, to partner the São Paulo-born Rubens

Barrichello; and a Peugeot engine package that was proving more reliable than in a highly disappointing campaign in 1995, one pock-marked by retirements and failures. The bigger budget brought with it a bigger team and a bigger set of ambitions, including the establishment of a test team that gave Jordan their most comprehensive pre-season preparation to date. Yet in spite of all this, and Eddie's determination to succeed, he worked at playing down too many high hopes in the build-up to the opening race. 'Everybody here is so upbeat at the moment that my main concern is to damp down enthusiasm,' he said on the eve of the Australian race. 'I have always taken the view that the public's level of expectation is too high, and now I have the same problem with my own staff. It must have a lot to do with our encouraging testing in Estoril last month.'

His sense of trepidation about 1996 proved well founded. As many around him talked of aiming at a top-four finish, winning a race and taking regular podium appearances, Eddie sensed something else afoot, but still did his usual best to keep plenty of positive momentum moving behind the team. 'I think our big hope has to be to pick up points this year from what may prove to be a struggling Ferrari team – which wouldn't be too bad, considering their budget of £100 million and staff of 500 compared with our staff of 85 and a budget that is less than a third of theirs.' Those with sensors who detected someone 'getting his excuses in first' could be forgiven for thinking like that, because Jordan were never able to live up to their potential in 1996. The critics, of course, were quick to point at the team owner himself. He was told that Brundle was not in the tradition of fast, young and hungry drivers Jordan were known for introducing, and that he had begun to lose focus, to step back too far, and to enjoy life too much and too often. Given an opportunity to answer some of the critics who were sniping at his recruitment of Brundle, Eddie hit back before the racing even began in Melbourne. 'We were rubbished by some people for taking on Martin. We are, after all, supposed to be the team that gives young drivers a chance, but we can't be a kindergarten all our lives and we were, perhaps, missing something last year. I think it may have been the kind of experience he can bring. Last year, Rubens was too busy vying with Irvine, looking after number one, to make enough real progress. Martin will help Rubens to develop and bring him on.'

This kind of criticism was hardly fair, but it continued. Early in 1996, Eddie hosted a British media lunch at the Jordan factory only to find that the stories that emanated from it were less positive than in the past. This was another side-effect of his team's growing maturity; by joining the bigger teams with major title sponsors, factory engines and experienced drivers, he was moving into a different league on and off the track. It was noted by *F1 News* in late February that Eddie regarded Irvine's move to Ferrari as a considerable windfall for himself and the team. 'The other day, I was asked who our main sponsor was,' Jordan was quoted as saying. 'And so I told them. It's Luca – Luca di Montezemolo of Ferrari. Not only did I sell him Irvine, but Alesi was one of mine as well.' In the same magazine, it was also noted that Eddie had 'recently become the proud owner of a Sunseeker yacht – second-hand I hasten to add'. It was suggested by the columnist that the boat should be called *Irvine I Love You* or *The Todt Windfall*, two obvious references to the Ferrari money paid to release Irvine from his Jordan contract.

But such stuff was only a trifling irritation to Eddie as the season began. Like everyone, he was hopeful, and he had placed much faith in Brundle. In his pre-season column in the same magazine, he wrote: 'Along with our new title sponsor comes a brand new livery and a new identity. It's a fairly tall order to change the team's colours in such a short space of time [the new colour for the cars, aptly, was gold], but somehow we've managed it. So, now, we not only have the most distinctive cars in the pit lane, we also have the longest title: Benson and Hedges Total Jordan Peugeot is the new official name of the team.' Eddie also welcomed Brundle back to the team, noting that he had enjoyed success when racing for a team sponsored by another cigarette brand, Silk Cut, also owned by the Benson and Hedges parent company Gallaher Limited.

It all seemed to be going almost too well before the opening race. Jordan had come of age, shed their green coat and taken delivery of a new golden one. Eddie even admitted things were changing, that philosophies were being reconsidered. 'We have really had to rethink our attitude and our approach. We found out just how tough it is to break into the top group of teams and there is no question about it now – the pressure is on us to deliver this season. But I feel we are ready to do it. We have learnt, developed and moved on to do this the right way. Now, we have the funding and the organisation. We know we have to win our first race this year – and I believe we will. We have done everything but win a race up to this point. We've made the podium, had second and third in one race and pushed well, but it is the toughest thing to make that next big step. We have found out the hard way that it takes time. That is why we have reassessed things.'

Jordan's anxiety to deliver a win to satisfy his sponsors was understandable given that Jackie Stewart, one of the most respected figures in British motor racing and a three-times drivers' world champion, had announced that he was bringing his team to Formula One in 1997. Just as Jordan entered Formula One in 1991 with Ford engines, so too did Stewart, but his agreement with the American manufacturer was not for a customer supply. It was a fully supported long-term partnership. Eddie welcomed his imminent arrival with a warning. 'It's good for Formula One to have someone of Jackie's stature coming in, and I am sure he'll put together a good package, but it is unrealistic to expect him to start winning straight away. He'll find Formula One is a very different world to anything else he's done.'

The much-awaited win didn't look like coming at Albert Park when Brundle was involved in a multiple collision at the start of the race. Not only was the incident one of the most spectacular airborne accidents of modern times (Johnny Herbert described seeing Brundle's car literally flying over him as reminiscent of the film *Top Gun*), Brundle was also greeted soon afterwards by the news that his father had died. In these circumstances, of course, Eddie's deep sense of humanity rises to the surface of his ebullient personality, and this was, no doubt, a source of strength for his experienced driver during the weeks and months that followed. Jordan had known Brundle's father well for many years, and this, too, helped him assist the driver in his recovery from the devastating news that must have cast a shadow across his mind, however bravely and professionally he continued to drive and race in Brazil and Argentina.

The results that followed were decent enough, but as the season unfolded it became increasingly clear that the car had problems, and that these were exacerbated by the infancy of the team's relationship with Peugeot. Eddie admitted to growing pains in mid-July, but added, 'when we ultimately come on song, we will be a very tough force'. Unfortunately, he and his most trusted team members had underestimated the disruption caused by the team's growth to close to a hundred staff by the end of July and the demands made on everyone involved, particularly the team management, in retaining control of the entire business and its strategy at the same time as racing. Still, it signalled that the team was progressing, as Jordan had said at the start of the year, and it was therefore shedding a lot of its old habits as the sponsors, notably Benson and Hedges, pushed for a less hand-to-mouth way of doing business and a better return on their investment.

Ian Phillips hinted at much of this when he revealed, during an interview in the summer of 1996, that it was becoming increasingly difficult to match the happy-go-lucky lean-and-green team with these new demands from a corporate partner. 'Everyone knows that Eddie, for a period of about twelve minutes, is the most effective, brilliant salesman you are ever likely to meet,' he said. 'He is not a con man, not at all, because he believes genuinely that he can deliver everything he says. And at a Grand Prix he can charm the pants off five hundred people in the Paddock Club. Most people call us Laurel and Hardy when we work together. This is because Eddie will come up with the wonderful, innovative sales pitch and then, at a certain time, he'll come to a halt – often if he receives a nudge from me under the table! Then it's my job to add all the practical information. I guess it is a sort of double act, but the inspiration always comes from Eddie.

'The other thing we have going for us is a tremendous public following for the team, especially considering that we don't have a pile of wins or championships to our name. Of course, we want people to come and visit us at our factory and to be involved with Jordan at other events. We take our car and our team and we go out to the people. We are not elitist. Perhaps there is too much elitism in Formula One. But you can go a long way with the strategy of keeping the sponsors happy, even seven days a week, and I hope we never lose that. But at the end of the day, the reason we are all passionately involved in this game is because we want to win, and of course the sponsors want to be associated with the winners.

'We started in 1991 as total privateers, at the depth of probably the biggest recession for fifty years, and we have built up since then with a very solid platform of achievement during difficult times. But that honeymoon period must be over now. The pressure is on for us. We don't want to be known as one of the teams that make up the numbers. We are trying to convince our sponsors that with serious investment we can buy the drivers that are going to win the world championship. We have Peugeot, who are very close to having the best engines in Formula One, and we are investing in our own resources to make sure we've got a car that is capable of matching the best. The final element is drivers. And, of course, you can't achieve anything without money.'

This truism of Formula One was to echo resoundingly during the next few years as Jordan Grand Prix climbed to a peak of achievement in the late 1990s, acquired the big-name drivers Phillips referred to, and finally won some races and ran among the championship contenders. It was, however, only a plateau, and it was followed by a decline that spread with the recession at the start of the new millennium. But in the bright English summer days of July 1996, the prospects looked alluring as sponsors were drawn to the ever busy, ever-colourful, headline-snatching Jordan team. For example, in the run-up to the 'home' Grand Prix at Silverstone, a sponsorship deal with G de Z Capital worth £2.5 million was announced at a typically unusual and eye-catching launch at the Jordan headquarters where Brundle posed as a snooker player and a real snooker player, world champion Stephen Hendry, posed as a racing driver. It was backing like this from a friend like Brian de Zille, whose plane was to fly Eddie home from Spa Francorchamps in 1998, that was so typical of the time for his team. If anyone knew where and how to do a sponsorship deal, it was Eddie and Ian.

'G de Z Capital is a young and exciting new venture and as such it fits perfectly into our sponsorship profile,' said Jordan at the time. 'From a personal point of view, it is an association which has a special appeal because, as a lover of all sports, I am pleased to be involved with something that not only benefits Jordan, but also links us with world-class sportsmen [G de Z was also sponsoring a stable of thirteen snooker and golf players].' Within hours of this launch, Eddie was invited to London to host a live phone-in by BBC Radio Five. It was called the 'Eddie Jordan Grand Prix Evening' and, once he'd overcome his own apprehension, it turned into a huge success. 'You may not have realised this, but talking seems to come quite naturally to me,' he quipped afterwards. 'If things get really bad, I could always turn to broadcasting . . . The time flew by and the banter and repartee were tremendous. We even had David Coulthard calling in from Monaco. I certainly hope the BBC paid for the call because I didn't let David get a word in edgeways!'

It was not long before Coulthard's name was added to the list of established drivers in whom Jordan Grand Prix were interested. The rest of the list included Damon Hill, then pushing for the world championship with Williams Renault, Jean Alesi and, unexpectedly, Nigel Mansell. The speculation had started in the middle of the season when it became clear that both Brundle and Barrichello were labouring at times to deliver the kind of impressive consistency required. More than this, however, the title sponsors, Benson and Hedges, wanted a big name to attract even more publicity and greater success. 'I've always rated Damon,' said Eddie when probed on the subject. 'Increasingly so in the last couple of years. Apart from Barcelona, you'd have to say he has been in outstanding form this year. He drove for a Formula 3000 team Jordan ran in 1991. It was a difficult year for him, but he just slogged away at it. That's what I like about him. I think he's never really been given the credit he deserves. After all, he's had a rough ride. Remember, when he started racing with Williams in 1993 he was still a novice, but he helped Alain Prost take the championship when he didn't pass him – or wasn't allowed to pass him, for various reasons. When he was able to go on to win, he did. At the moment, I don't think we have a big enough budget to go for Damon, but it would depend on how much money he wanted. He has certainly proved that if we gave him a car that's capable of pole position, then he can go on and win the races.'

No one was in much doubt come August 1996 that Eddie and his team were in the throes of a serious growing-up exercise, but that did not stop them enjoying life as they went along. When the circus flew to Budapest for the Hungarian Grand Prix, held outside the capital city at the nearby Hungaroring, the Jordan team made the most of the opportunity to 'explore' the old city on the Danube and make a note of appropriate watering holes. One of these, the Irish pub and restaurant known as Becketts, quickly became a home from home for the team and their followers. It had been opened a few years previously with patronage from the Jordan boys and had, since then, added to its reputation with music and live bands. Predictably enough, too, the music was perfectly in tune with Eddie's tastes and he was able to enjoy a session on the drums while Phillips, a regular patron, made the most of his personal weakness for music from the 1960s. 'Most of us didn't recognise any of it at all,' said Eddie. 'But it's different for Ian as he is of a certain age, and he was really happy.'

At this time, Eddie was also being drawn into the politics of the administration of Formula One as speculation built up about the future direction of the sport following various disputes over aspects of the Concorde Agreement, a binding document that is the 'rule book' of the F1 business. These disputes centred on the share of the growing television and commercial revenue generated by Bernie Ecclestone's interests, but Eddie, a solid supporter of Ecclestone, made it clear that he felt there was nothing to worry about. In his view, Ecclestone, the former president of the Formula One Constructors' Association (FOCA), the organisation that had been used to work on behalf of the teams in all talks about the sport, was an entrepreneur like himself and had been the man who had taken all the big risks in building the sport and investing his own capital in new digital television technology in his modern role as the head of all the commercial companies that held long-term rights to exploit F1's potential. 'For me,' said Eddie, in September 1996, 'all this talk of trouble suggesting that Grand Prix racing is about to collapse in a heap is very wide of the mark. The Concorde Agreement is a document which sets out the basic rules about how the sport is run, and the current version expires soon. Along with the rest of the teams, Jordan has been presented with a proposal for the next version, and after a few changes had been made I was happy to sign it, but a few other names chose not to do so. As a team owner, you have to do the best thing for your own team and negotiate as hard as you can for the rights you are due. There has been some debate over the sums accrued from television rights, but as far as I'm concerned Bernie Ecclestone took the risks early on when setting up the various deals and I am happy with the way things are being run. He has done a job nobody else could have done. Not just for the teams, but for motor racing in general.'

In September, during the Italian Grand Prix at Monza, it was announced that Hill would be leaving Williams at the end of the season, so it was natural for speculation about his future to intensify and for Jordan to be at the forefront of all the stories. The team's progress by then had been, as Eddie put it, 'pretty erratic', the pressure from Benson and Hedges rising in line with the general levels of frustration felt at the fact that a sequence of good results remained just around the corner. It was timely, therefore, that both drivers finished in the points in Italy on a weekend when their futures, and that of the team, were under scrutiny. And Monza, as everyone knew, is a place where deals are often done; sure enough, just a few weeks later, Eddie was smiling broadly as he confirmed that not only would his team be retaining its sponsorship from Benson and Hedges for 1997, Ralf Schumacher, the younger brother of Michael, would be joining them too. At that stage, Ralf was graduating from winning the Formula Nippon Championship in Japan after an impressive earlier career in Formula Three. He was, therefore, a Formula One rookie, but at 21 he was regarded as a new boy with great prospects. Indeed, after an impressive test with McLaren he was seen as a driver with the potential to follow in his brother's illustrious footsteps. Hill's future was decided when he chose to decline Eddie's offer, this time around at least, and instead join Tom Walkinshaw's Arrows team. 'We made an offer for Damon,' Eddie confirmed, 'once we knew exactly what was going on at Williams, but there were certain points which, at the end of the day, we had difficulty agreeing upon, and then the negotiations began to drag. Usually in Formula One, if things don't happen quickly, they don't happen at all.' The positive announcements concerning the team's future plans were made in Estoril at the time of the Portuguese Grand Prix, where Peter Veen and Nigel Northridge, the managing director and marketing director respectively of Gallaher Ltd, were among the team's most important guests.

After another points-scoring result in Japan had secured fifth place, again, in the championship, Eddie was able to relax and digest the implications of a difficult year fraught with internal political struggles, some personal recriminations, much frustration and many disappointments. A bright start in new golden colours had been followed by a gradual decline just as the rising pressure from the team's backers intensified. It was, therefore, a watershed year, a season when the team had to work diligently to complete a painful transformation that was not always easy for everyone to accept.

Gary Anderson, for example, was sometimes at loggerheads with the new ways in which things were done; in mid-season, as some critics suggested the team was experiencing a kind of crisis and as Brundle battled to regain his confidence in a car that was reluctant to provide any rear-end grip, he was given an enforced holiday. He had been in the middle of everything in the team for so long that he could not always, as the expression goes, see the wood for the trees. 'When you get additional funding, as we did then, it doesn't help immediately,' said Trevor Foster, the team's race director that year. 'A lot of the things you need, like machinery, have a three- or four-month lead time before they become useful. It all takes time to sort out. I think we were probably better prepared for the first few races than we had ever been, but there were lots of other people struggling, and when they all got their act together we were pushed back. We weren't really able to respond fast enough. When Gary went on holiday, around the time of the British Grand Prix, we had to look very closely at the whole operation. Gary had been to virtually every race and every test for five years and he'd never had a decent holiday at all. We wanted him to stand back, take time away from the factory and clear his mind. He had to release his grip, at least a little, because the whole operation was so much bigger than it had been at the start. We had to restructure, and when he returned he was calmer and had some good ideas.' Anderson had initially felt that the way things were done, the way in which Eddie had effectively ordered him to go on holiday, was wrong. 'At the time, I resented it, and I resented it for a while afterwards,' he explained. 'When I look back, I still think it was done wrongly, but it probably wasn't the wrong thing to do. It did help me focus on what I needed to do, what I needed to concentrate on, and it helped a lot of the people involved to realise that what we were attempting to achieve, to build up a successful Grand Prix team, was not easy.'

By the end of the season, it was also clear that Barrichello's form and relationship with the team were in decline; it was the end of a cycle for him, and it coincided with the team's growth and Anderson's holiday, an event that was at the very apex of a season of change. 'Gary had always been there for me in the previous two years,' said Barrichello. 'When he went, I felt a little isolated. I felt left on one side.' In fact, under pressure from sponsors who were looking for success, and therefore a change in outlook, Eddie had performed the difficult task of making each individual, including his drivers, aware of the new expectations. 'Eddie Jordan can be very supportive when he wants to be, but he can also be very depressing when he wants to be,' said Barrichello in an interview with David Tremayne at the end of 1996. 'From the middle of this year, I just didn't have the support I needed . . . The whole circus was not making me feel good and I started thinking it was right for me to move on. I considered a change, a big change, to go to America, but in the end I received another offer, from Stewart, and it was too good to turn down.'

As a transitional year came to an end, Eddie decided to hire Giancarlo Fisichella, 24, as the young Ralf Schumacher's partner after talks with Martin Brundle had, reportedly, broken down. Fisichella had signed a long-term agreement with Benetton chief Flavio Briatore, but was 'loaned' to Jordan for two years. There were some raised eyebrows, but news of the complete change of line-up was welcomed by Anderson and supported by Benson and Hedges. The team had a fresh all-yellow image and a German-Italian driver pairing that was attractive to the international media. Both were regarded as young and fast, but also inexperienced and reckless. Many pundits suggested it had been foolhardy to dispense so abruptly with Brundle, who had shown signs towards the end of 1996 that he retained all the necessary pace and commitment to do a very satisfactory job in Formula One. But Eddie had other ideas in mind and, understanding the needs of his sponsors, weighed up a variety of options including a return to competition by the 1992 world champion Nigel Mansell.

In December 1996, Mansell, then aged 43, flew to Barcelona and tested for two days with the team alongside many of the other regular drivers. It was a clever public relations exercise that helped the driver erase the memory of his desultory departure from Formula One in 1995 when he abandoned his McLaren Mercedes-Benz car at the same Circuit de Catalunya, and it also provided Jordan with a sizeable level of media interest at a time of the year when most people have forgotten all about Formula One. Eddie flew to Barcelona to attend a news conference alongside Mansell, the pair of them reminiscing about some of their greatest golf matches and old racing days, and generally providing much slapstick entertainment. In a more serious moment, Jordan said, 'I felt it was an honour, a great honour. The Jordan team has come of age now. Nigel and I go back a long way and he has been a great ambassador for the sport, here in Europe, the States and worldwide, and I felt proud and honoured that he should fly here to drive a Jordan. But Nigel has total belief in himself and in his own talent, and the thing that has really impressed me the most was that after just three laps you could see he had come here to make a point and to go quick. It is what I will remember most, because when he did his time I was not prepared for it at all.' It was the last time Mansell would drive a contemporary Formula One car in earnest.

If it was purely a publicity stunt, it worked. But Eddie was not going to let on. More serious matters were in progress as he and the team prepared for their golden era under the Benson and Hedges banner, principally the harnessing of the talents of two fast and furious young drivers into a formidable team effort that would, eventually, build the momentum for sustained success. Certainly, Benson and Hedges were keen to exploit the two opportunities that lay in front of them: the team's increasing competitiveness and the image that went with that, and the marketing skills of Formula One's greatest salesman, Eddie Jordan.

In his early years, Eddie had once said, 'The day I have a big launch in a big London hotel is the day Jordan loses its small feel. It's the day Jordan goes corporate.' Some in Ireland said that Jordan had actually sold out and 'gone corporate' when the shamrock logo disappeared in 1992, but when, in February 1997, the new line-up, new colours and new identity of the team were launched at the Hilton Hotel in Park Lane, London, there were no arguments. Any resemblances to the old and homely lean-and-mean machine were lost in clouds of dry ice and dancing models. The appearance of the car was the first sign that things had changed; the metamorphosis that had taken place slowly through 1996 had been completed under the darkness of winter. The cars, the symbols of the team and of Eddie's ambitions, had been turned into lethal-looking reptiles thanks to the imagination of the Benson and Hedges creative team, who had also enjoyed a joke at Eddie's expense during the consultation process before the designs were endorsed and introduced.

This launch of a race-winning and potentially championship-winning package demonstrated that in 1997 Eddie was intent on going places with his team, and on shaking off his image as a lucky wheeler-dealer born with the gift of the gab. Early in the year, as points were accumulated slowly and surely but not with the spectacular level of success everyone involved yearned for, he admitted, 'I'm still getting people going on about my being able to sell sand to the Arabs, and I'm not sure that it comes across the right way. There is a fine line between being a bit of a wide boy and a wheeler-dealer, and certainly a con man wouldn't get away with it in this business. We are the only private team to have survived in the last eight, nine or ten years, and sixteen out of seventeen of those that have come in have failed. The reality is that if being a wheeler-dealer is what it takes to succeed, then I've done a good job. But I'm very twitchy about this Jack the Lad image. The argument seems to be that you've got to be surly to be serious in this business, but I don't see why there should be that sort of connection at all. My view is very clear. If I can generate a nice atmosphere here while I'm doing the job, then that is great. It's easier when you've got two go-ahead young drivers who look good and are "on the case" and the team has a very youthful image. I like that.'

Eddie was also prepared to concede that the team had been through some difficult times during which he, personally, had shouldered a lot of the problems and the pressures. 'Yes, sure, there were big pressures on me then, but in Formula One I think you've always got them. But you have to hide them. You can never let the doubts become transparent. If you do that, it will infiltrate the whole team. Any slight chink in the armour, with regard to self-doubt, can become devastating. It's like a bush fire. So you make sure it doesn't even start.' He admitted, too, that he had struggled with the realisation that changes were necessary. 'I had always said that there were certain things that were dear to me – not letting the team grow too much, not losing the family flavour, not letting it grow over a hundred people. Well, I must say that was all probably down to ignorance. I have to admit that. We are now well past a hundred people and I think that was necessary because as a team we had to make the jump. We had to move forward to that position where we were attacking from the front of the race. These two youngsters [Schumacher and Fisichella] will bring fireworks with them, I know that. Sometimes it won't be too pleasant, sometimes it will be.'

He was right. It was a year of excitement, with clashes and collisions and disagreements and plenty of drama, highlighted by the efforts of the two drivers to deliver the team's first elusive and long-awaited victory and the signature, in the end, of Damon Hill on a contract to join Jordan Grand Prix for 1998. It was a year, too, that saw the team reach the hundred Grands Prix mark, in Argentina in April, where Schumacher ran Fisichella off the road on the way to a podium finish. 'They are like two young dogs living in the same garden who mark out their territory all the time,' said Eddie. 'They are not experienced, but they are making fantastic progress.' The pugnacious pair provided great entertainment and endorsed a general view that the team was ready to secure its first win, but it proved to be more elusive than anyone expected, the German Grand Prix on 27 July perhaps offering the best example of the bad luck that seemed to dog them at vital moments. In this instance at Hockenheim, Fisichella had looked certain of second place when his car suffered a puncture at 180mph; he had qualified on the front row, only two hundredths of a second off pole, and had in fact led 90 per cent of the way. It was a bitterly disappointing end to a typical Jordan weekend blotted further by the unexpected announcement from Benetton team chief Flavio Briatore that Fischella would be moving back to race for his Enstone-based outfit for 1998. Eddie professed surprise at the news. But, as always, his mind was planning months, if not years, ahead of all that. He had been ruminating all year on his options for taking another step forward to match the expectations of his partners and backers.

As the team grew, as budgets expanded and as expectations rose, so Eddie became a rich man. His family enjoyed the benefits. The lifestyle that had once seen Marie worrying over income from the lodgers had been transformed into a more carefree and comfortable existence, their time divided between their homes in England and Spain. Social, sporting and entertainment engagements filled their diaries. At the Monaco Grand Prix, for example, where once Eddie and Marie had changed into their evening dress after showering on the beach, they were now staying in the best hotels and dining at restaurants such as La Chaumière, high up on the Corniche, where they exchanged jokes with Hollywood film stars such as Geena Davis. Life was sweet. A wind tunnel, at nearby Brackley, was added to the team's resources, and a new sponsor, Mastercard, joined Benson and Hedges in support of the team's burgeoning ambitions. This feel-good factor was reflected in the line-up for the post-British Grand Prix party when performers of high reputation such as Chris de Burgh, Jamiroquai and friends from Queen, Level 42 and Pink Floyd joined Eddie and Damon Hill, complete with guitar, on stage. Afterwards, as always, he was drawn away by the sun and the sea and took his family with him on the boat to Sardinia, where they encountered many other familiar Formula One people including Fisichella, Walkinshaw, Ecclestone and Briatore. It was there, apparently and unbeknown to Eddie, that Briatore was completing his plans to recall Fischella.

Over this issue, Eddie had in effect been caught out at his own game of managing drivers and controlling their careers. Or so it seemed. The dispute over who should have Fisichella as a racing driver in 1998 ended up in the High Court in London, where the ruling went Briatore's way, as he had signed Fisichella under a long-term contract to Benetton; still, Jordan were awarded more than £1.25 million in compensation for losing the second year of a two-year loan deal.

But that summer of 1997 was a curious one in Formula One. Many of the top team principals, the top drivers and others appeared to be spending a lot of time floating around the Mediterranean on holiday, exchanging pleasantries and negotiating deals that were to change the face of the sport yet again. Damon Hill, unhappy at Arrows, was at the heart of much of the speculation, and he held what turned out to be fruitless talks with Ron Dennis at his holiday home near Cannes about a possible move to McLaren. Eddie maintained a dignified silence but kept a close eye on the situation. He observed, 'I wouldn't be surprised if Ron found that Mercedes-Benz were less than impressed by his failure to sign Hill, bearing in mind that, as far as I understand it, Mercedes set out a wish list which bore the names of Michael Schumacher, Ralf Schumacher and Damon Hill. And none of them is on board for 1998. Obviously, I don't know the full facts, but it seemed to me that Dennis offered Hill so little money that he didn't want him to take it. It seems strange to me that the man who told me he was dictating the driver market has actually been forced to keep the same two drivers he had before.'

By the end of August, Eddie knew he was in a difficult position. Still refusing, on the surface at least, to accept that Briatore and Benetton had any right to sign Fisichella, he launched a protective action. Fisichella continued his impressive but unpredictable form and was second in the Belgian Grand Prix. He made it clear that he would prefer to stay with Jordan, but admitted he was under a long-term management contract with Briatore. When it became inevitable that Fischella was going to Benetton, Eddie intensified his search for a replacement and his pursuit of Hill. It had been and continued to be a long and often frustrating stalking process, but in the end it paid off when, by a stroke of luck, Hill retired early from the Italian Grand Prix at Monza on 7 September and needed a lift home.

'With both Arrows out before the finish, Tom [Walkinshaw] had made a hurried departure in the hope that he might get to see his latest acquisition, Gloucester Rugby Club, produce a better result than his F1 team had managed,' Eddie wrote in his regular column in *F1 News*. 'In his rush to get back to England, Tom had left his driver [Hill] behind, which turned out to be a bit of a careless move in the light of what happened next. It so happened that Ian Phillips, David Marren, Gary Anderson, our technical director, and Nigel Northridge, the sales and marketing director of Benson and Hedges, were also on Brian de Zille's plane, which we use for travelling to races in Europe. When we got on board, Damon was already tucked away at the back, so I don't know who was hijacking whom! All I do know is that by the time we got to Kidlington, the guts of a deal had been thrashed out. Damon spoke about various aspects with Gary and then talked to Nigel and me about matters I understand better than technical matters and are closer to my heart.' The deal was subsequently confirmed after an all-night session at Gallaher's offices in Weybridge where the same group plus Hill's solicitor Michael Breen met to discuss remuneration, terms and conditions. Hill was excited by the prospect of joining the Jordan team again, and also by the prospect of his car being powered by Mugen-Honda engines, Eddie having signed a two-year deal with the Japanese company to succeed Peugeot as engine suppliers (Peugeot switched their attentions to the new Prost Grand Prix team). The 1996 world champion was seen as a man of great talent, achievement, stature and experience who would help Ralf Schumacher develop and offer Jordan their best opportunity of winning a Grand Prix. The foresight proved correct, but it was not easily achieved.

To those who suggested that he had had to eat some humble pie to achieve his ambition in signing Hill, who had turned him down the previous year, Eddie replied, 'No, that didn't even come into it. In F1, things change so dramatically and quickly. It is all about being alert and taking the best opportunity when it comes along. The dialogue we had with Damon never really stopped. The fact that he lived in Dublin helped because we met socially, a little, and sometimes we played a bit of rock 'n' roll together. And there has always been an element of us saying to him, "Come on,

Damon, when are you coming back on board again?" We desperately needed a driver who was going to steer us to winning races. We have hired him for two years to win races and to win championships. No other reason. We are in a position where we have a huge new dawn in front of us now.'

Hill used the announcement of his intention to leave Arrows and sign for Jordan to explain why he had left Williams after his 1996 championship-winning season. 'People said I was sacked by Williams because I asked for too much money,' he said. 'Was I hell! I was sacked because they wanted a BMW engine and I had to make way for Frentzen.'

Due to his contract with Arrows, it was some time before Hill was free to drive a Jordan car. When he first tested one, in Barcelona, it was already the final week of January 1998. He was 37 years old and he had been out of a Formula One car for 87 days. He pronounced the car 'fantastic', but swiftly revised that opinion as time went by and the initial euphoria of simply sitting in the cockpit of a racing car wore off. He had spent some time in the build-up period practising left-foot braking by going karting outdoors in difficult conditions – Hill had always driven with three pedals, but the Jordan offered just two – and he was delighted with the sensation. But serious study of the times clocked by the team's rivals disturbed his optimism as testing progressed. Hard work was required by everyone to turn great promise into great results.

At the team's launch at the Royal Albert Hall in London, Hill looked delighted to be back in the limelight with a publicity-conscious team that attracted plenty of mass media coverage. He laughed freely, made jokes, bantered with his employer and exuded the kind of ease and confidence that made anyone in the team who needed a shot of motivation feel better. Asked how his new boss was behaving, he said, 'EJ's like a cat on a hot tin roof right now. He's completely berserk. Really. But every successful organisation needs a dynamo and he is the dynamo in this organisation.' The upbeat mood spread through the team. But Hill was also careful to add some more deliberate comments about changes of engine supplier always bringing problems to teams and the need for a period of patient consolidation. 'We'll be extremely lucky if things run completely smoothly,' he said. 'We've got only a limited amount of testing between now and the first race.'

Unsettled weather was the chief problem in the run-up to the first race in Melbourne where the 1996 world champion was due to make his debut in the Benson and Hedges Jordan Mugen-Honda 198, an event anticipated by the team owner every bit as much as anyone else. The team knew it, and could not quell the optimism that rose like a tide. The prospect of a first win hovered in every mind. Race director Trevor Foster tried to be realistic and keep things in perspective, telling *Autosport*, 'There are no threats, but we are steadily running out of excuses as a team, aren't we? There is always one you can find, but at the end of the day we've probably worked through most of them. Last year, it was that the car was good enough to win several races but we had a pair of inexperienced drivers. Now we don't have that excuse. So, what's the next one going to be? The bottom line, in my book, is that we have to perform. We have the resources and now we've got to do it. That's it.'

Sylvester Stallone, the Hollywood film star, was in Australia for the race, studying Formula One preparatory to playing a role in a film about the sport. He had been before and he knew the characters. When asked why he was there, he revealed his knowledge when he quipped, 'I'm an Eddie Jordan groupie!' Eddie himself, his star rising, the economy strong, his team favoured for at least a win, was involved in many media and entertainment activities. His busy life was becoming ever more hectic, seemingly heading towards chaos, but somehow he always retained control of his own destiny as the round of appearances, parties, promotions and new deals filled his every waking hour. A television company from Britain was filming his year and the highlights of the team's season in a documentary. In this, he revealed that he could still remember his first car vividly. 'It was a Morris Minor. ZU 484. In black. I hardly slept at night and had to wake up to check it was still there.' His mother Eileen was also interviewed. She was filmed telling Eddie it was time he removed his facial hair. 'It's time to get rid of them,' she ordered. 'They look like a black mark on your face. Even on the golf course they'll say get rid of those sideburns.' The whole family was becoming embroiled in the development of Eddie's own celebrity as Formula One gained a greater and greater hold on international sport.

At that opening race in Australia, Hill finished eighth, 4.2 seconds behind the Williams of Jacques Villeneuve, who was fifth, but a lap down on the victorious McLarens. If Eddie was not delighted with the result, he was pleased with Hill's attitude. 'I was impressed with him,' he said. 'He was very professional in his approach, and what I liked the most was that when he came in after the race he admitted it had taken him until half-distance to really get up to speed. If we can run with the speed he had in the second part of that race, then we should have no problems – except with the McLarens, of course.' Two races later, Eddie had to revise his thinking. In Buenos Aires on 12 April, Hill showed his frustration, kicking his car and throwing his helmet across the team garage, a display of ill-tempered petulance that reflected how things had gone in the three lacklustre season-opening races. 'When you are not on the pace, there is concern, of course,' he said. 'The reality is that we have had some very bad races. Can I see us getting out of it? Of course I can. There is a problem, and when you have a problem, firstly you must address it, and then you have to rectify it. But you also have to have faith in the people who brought you to where you are.'

Gary Anderson was not impressed and suggested that more was expected from Hill. 'I thought Damon would drive us on a bit more,' he said. 'I know he's trying to do this left-foot braking and so on, but it doesn't really matter to us whether he does or not. If he's not comfortable with it, then he shouldn't do it.' Hill wanted to persevere with the technique, believing it would bring longer-term rewards, and deflected the implied criticisms. 'It's down to Eddie and Gary to improve the team position. I can contribute what I can as a driver, with my experience, but I can't tell them how it's done. I'm not a designer, or a team owner.' He said he retained his optimism and his motivation. 'We can still make in-roads, but it is not easy. This team doesn't have the capacity of some of the others, but it does a very good job with what it has.' A podium finish, he added, was a realistic objective.

But it was clear as the first half of the season unfolded that 1998 was to be no easier in many ways than 1997. For Eddie, grappling with the need to provide sound management but at the same time tied emotionally to his old team within the bigger structure, the situation clearly needed careful thought and tough decisions. It was a state of affairs brought to a head by a dreadful performance on 24 May at the Monaco Grand Prix, where Eddie had taken his whole family as guests to enjoy the most glittering and famous event in world motor sport. The Manchester United footballer Ryan Giggs was also a Jordan team guest and had to witness a weekend that saw Hill qualify fifteenth and Schumacher sixteenth, then finish eighth and retired respectively; it ended with Eddie close to a rage of anger and frustration. The whole Jordan bandwagon was rocking, but not with the music this time. Instead, it was rocking on its foundations as everyone within began the kind of political infighting that can quickly lead to destruction. 'Pretty appalling, really . . . disastrous,' was Eddie's summary immediately afterwards. Later, he added, 'It is going from bad to worse. I have learnt how to endure serious amounts of pain. There will be some changes. Some may be radical. But there are no quick fixes. The easiest thing to do is to sack the boss, but that's not easy, because it's me. I suppose you can say sack the designer, but Gary Anderson has built stunning cars in the past and I am confident that this is conceptually a good car. It is not a question of taking a guillotine and chopping half the team's heads off. But speed counts, and it is speed that wins races.'

Within days, Mike Gascoyne, then working for the Tyrrell team as deputy technical director, was approached to join the team and Gary Anderson, the Jordan technical director, was withdrawn from duties at the next two races in order to work on 'a major quest for performance' from the car. The reshuffle pushed Anderson away from the kind of direct day-to-day, hands-on involvement in everything, a role he loved, but instead made him a technical overseer with supervisory responsibilities. Anderson, again, was not happy, but he decided to tackle the problem of improving the car's performance with great urgency and instituted more than eighty changes in all areas of the competitive package in the weeks that followed before, finally, he chose to leave. It was typical of the way Formula One worked that it was Gascoyne, not Anderson, who was credited with the upswing in performance that followed, beginning when Schumacher finished sixth at the British Grand Prix at Silverstone, and typical of Anderson's luck that he was no longer around when the team delivered their maiden win.

Indeed, in the eight opening races of the season, the team had scored zero points; but in the second eight, when Anderson worked on strategy prior to his departure and Gascoyne worked on the finer points of the car, the team collected points in seven races. The result was a total of 34 points and fourth place in the constructors' championship, not to mention that famous one-two in Spa Francorchamps, the circuit that lies at the heart of so many famous Jordan exploits. Even in advance of his team's historic first triumph there, Eddie was being asked frequently about his prospects and feelings. 'We always seem to get the rub of the green there,' he replied, before reeling off favourable results at the Belgian circuit. He said he had feelings about the place – and he was right. Nobody, surely, could have predicted that after all they had been through, Hill and Schumacher would reel off a one-two as they did. Only the absence of Anderson and the Irish anthem, and the unexpected arrival of Michael Schumacher at the team motor home in order to protest after his brother had obeyed orders and finished second, did anything to mar an otherwise perfect day in the Ardennes.

'I like this,' said Eddie afterwards, in one of the hundreds of interviews he faced in Belgium that Sunday, then back in England the following day. 'I like it so much I want to do it again!' He had been congratulated by Bernie Ecclestone, Tom Walkinshaw, Ron Dennis, David Richards and the rest within minutes of his Irish jig in the pit lane, and he had responded with uncharacteristic bemusement. He could barely take it all in at the time, but his long-held and stubborn dream of a race win had finally come about at last.

He conceded, however, that he had enjoyed some luck in a race that had to be restarted, which gave Hill a reprieve as he had made a mess of his first start. Mika Hakkinen's tangle with Michael Schumacher had helped, too, as had Coulthard's spin and subsequent role in a collision with Michael Schumacher's Ferrari. Hill admitted that he was lucky, too. He said that after one deployment of the safety car during the race, he had been worried about being involved in a collision with his own team-mate if they raced for glory in the perilous conditions. 'Ralf was on my tail,' Hill recalled, 'and at the same time my wife was on the phone to Michael Breen [Hill's lawyer and agent] asking him to plead with somebody to stop the race because she had seen enough. She was on holiday in Spain and by this point she was a nervous wreck, not because I was winning, but because of all the accidents. My fear was that Ralf, who was suing Jordan for the right to leave the team for Williams, would feel under no obligation to obey team orders.' Hill decided to remind the team to ask Eddie to make a decision, and he duly did so. It was a decision that was perfect for everyone except the young Schumacher, whose disappointment at a lost opportunity to take a maiden F1 win was written across his face even on the podium at the end.

In the interviews that followed that race, Eddie revealed also that he had made a modest bet with a Swiss journalist that a Jordan car would win, and that he'd been given odds of 10–1. The winnings went towards paying for the parties. He also took his chance to put the record straight on various other issues, and joked at how expensive it would be to him in bonuses. 'It would have been cheaper for the company if they had both crashed,' he said. 'But this is the most pleasurable money we'll ever have to pay out.' Then, when asked about his alleged reluctance to invest sufficiently heavily in the team, he retorted strongly. 'You mean skimming off money on the side? I find that very irritating, to be honest. The problem is that we get a disproportionate amount of coverage for the results that we've had, but that's the way we operate. Having said that, I would safely say there is no team in F1 which spends its money as cleverly and as prudently as we do.'

For that famous Belgian race, Eddie had also shown his generous side, in recognition of the long hours and hard work put in by his staff. The factory had been running with non-stop twelve-hour shifts to achieve the many changes required to bring the massive performance improvements delivered from Silverstone onwards. Revised engines, new tyres, improvements on the car and various other ideas had been utilised to ensure that the opening six months of 1998 were banished from the memory. 'We did a deal because they'd worked so long and so hard,' he said. 'I said that anyone who wanted to go to Spa would be taken over by bus, stay in a hotel, have free meals, transfers to the circuit and tickets for the race, but had to wear and carry a flag and be part of the action. It cost a token twenty quid. We had two busloads there in all, a hundred people, and they had a fantastic weekend. You should have seen the state of them afterwards on the Monday morning.'

The win in Belgium was followed by a disgruntled Ralf Schumacher's departure for Williams and Heinz-Harald Frentzen's move in the other direction. The transfer signalled that the Jordan team was now truly part of the big time, that the world championship was a more realistic ambition, as Eddie claimed – the Jordan team now had two winners in the driving seats – but also that nothing would ever be quite the same again. Anderson had gone, not bitterly, but sadly, his friendship with Eddie surviving the new power politics that went with big teams in Formula One. 'It was just one of those things, those kinds of situations, where the time to leave was right,' he reflected. 'There were things I just couldn't argue with Eddie about because of our friendship. Probably we were too good friends and that made it very difficult. Not everyone could understand that. There was a lot of back-stabbing going on and I didn't like it. It just got worse and worse.' His departure gave Anderson an opportunity to ask people to look more closely at 1996 and the performance of the Peugeot engines. At the time, when he was given an enforced break, it was perceived that the Jordan car was in need of an overhaul. 'Peugeot was God's gift, wasn't it?' he said, his eyes twinkling. 'As far as they were concerned their engine was the best in the pit lane. Well, you look at it now. Three years on, their best results in all that time have still come from us.'

Eddie, of course, had other things on his mind. He was in the throes of his next business coup. By November 1998, he had accomplished it by selling an equity partnership in Jordan Grand Prix to the American investment group Warburg Pincus. It provided him with a reported personal capital investment of £40 million and gave the team the security it required, but without changing much more than the management's modus operandi.

Eddie remained in control while Warburg Pincus held shares as an investor. 'It was a tough decision, as I had heard so many horror stories about investor relationships with teams,' he said, 'but in order to win the world championship, I felt we had to change. I had just turned fifty, too, so I felt it was the right time. Warburg Pincus turned out to be an absolute dream to work with – they didn't know much about motor racing, but they trusted us and they allowed us to get on with the running of the company.'

By January 1999, there was no doubt that Eddie had decided to relax and enjoy his new status as a multi-millionaire owner of a Grand Prix team who could afford to luxuriate in the fun of being a celebrity. When *Autosport* threw a surprise party for him to mark his team's success and breakthrough maiden victory, he flew back to Birmingham to attend at the National Exhibition Centre from a holiday in Portugal. 'I was told I should get back to Britain for something important,' he said. 'But this doesn't look much like a sponsorship deal!' Nobody minded the quips or the jokes. Eddie was no longer a laughing matter. He was a Grand Prix-winning team owner with substantial sponsors and very substantial backing. But he was still keen to be involved in all the fun going and took a full part in the penalty shoot-out in which he competed against the television chef Gary Rhodes, Coventry City football manager Gordon Strachan, *Sky Sports* presenter Richard Keys, *Big Breakfast* presenter Melanie Sykes and *Top Gear* presenter Tiff Needell. Predictably, there was plenty of fun, featuring wind-ups of Eddie with Damon Hill, Martin Donnelly and Dave Price taking part as old times were recalled and success toasted. People from far and wide came to join in and pay tribute to the success he had enjoyed. 'Back in 1970,' Eddie told them all, 'I was doing Formula Ford and towing a car by a piece of rope. They were the most unbelievable and difficult days of my life. You don't forget them. It is a wonderful sport which has been very kind to us all.'

Partying was just part of the scene for the newly successful Jordan team. Shortly before Christmas, Eddie flew to Dublin for a champagne reception to launch a book called *Against the Odds: Jordan's Drive to Win*. It was the story of the 1998 season, and it had been written by Maurice Hamilton, the Northern Irish journalist and writer whose flair and insights guaranteed a fine product. The Jordan name on the cover alone was hope of commercial success. In fact, a signing session the pair had been involved in during the day at a Dublin bookstore had been such an outstanding success that every book on the premises had been sold. At the reception in the evening, friends and family turned out in force, together with Damon Hill, winner of that famous race in Spa. It was a night to remember, finished off with the sight of Eddie and Damon heading into the Playwright Pub, down in Blackrock, where they gave a spirited mini-concert for the regulars.

For a time, of course, it must have seemed to Eddie as if the world were smiling on him. He had found security and success in one swoop, it appeared, and when the new season began and Heinz-Harald Frentzen delivered second place in his maiden Formula One outing for the team, on 6 March 1999 at Albert Park in Melbourne, the positive vibe spread rapidly through the entire team. Frentzen had shown a steely self-confidence in the build-up period and did not want to be meekly overshadowed by Hill. In the race, his car had developed an electronic problem that had reduced the power, but he still performed excellently to secure six points in the first car developed by Mike Gascoyne, who had picked up the reins in a dignified and responsible fashion following Anderson's departure and subsequent decision to join the new Stewart team. Hill, unfortunately, crashed out on the opening lap after a collision with Jarno Trulli's Prost. It was not an omen, but it did seem to be a sign of what lay ahead in a year when Frentzen rose and shone as Hill seemed to decline and lose his dazzle.

Unfortunately for Eddie, he was too busy to notice. His life, which had revolved around his team for so long, was embracing broader aims and activities. He spent time building new ventures associated with the development of the Jordan brand, he developed his standing as a celebrity. He was in Spain, or London, or Dublin, or Oxford, or in meetings around Europe, but he was still, albeit to a lesser and lesser degree, in control of the team that had carried him to a position from which he could develop his dream. On Monday, 22 March, for example, he returned to Silverstone, but with a very 'saddle sore' backside following the unique experience of riding a bike for three days, for charity, between the Dead Sea and the Red Sea, from Jordan to Israel. He had joined fifty other cyclists, including his wife Marie, in an effort to raise money for Cancer and Leukaemia in Children (CLIC), a charity in which Marie was involved. Other cyclists included Angie Rutherford, wife of the musician Mike Rutherford, and the dress designer David Emmanuel, but there were also many less well known participants from all walks of life, including doctors, nurses and labourers.

'I joined them in Petra [in Jordan] on the Wednesday, just for the last few days,' Eddie explained. 'It was just over a week after the Australian Grand Prix. Of course, it was not what I am used to doing, but it was great because it was something special and something I would not normally do at all. It was very fierce work in the heat and I must say it was just an amazing experience. We cycled through some of the most dramatic scenery you can imagine. We endured a sandstorm, and though I only did half the journey because of my work commitments, which had kept me in the UK beforehand, I certainly got a taste of it. It was an emotional experience. We saw nothing but hot sun and Bedouin tribes. And, for me, for a man the wrong side of fifty, I have to say the physical demands were intense. The sand ripped me apart. I had no idea of what it would be like. But there was a great feeling of euphoria in the group and it was a tremendous thing to be involved in. One man had spent ten years in prison and he said that the experience had totally opened his eyes and changed his life. That was the most important message of the week, I think.'

This kind of diversion, or alternative involvement, became an increasingly frequent part of Eddie's life. As his team appeared to settle into its new role as one of the leading contenders in the pit lane and paddock, he was busy with his work as the Irish Ambassador for Sport and Tourism, or attending rock concerts or racecourses, both those where his own horses were running and others, or planning brand development built around the Jordan name, to take in clothing, drinks and other merchandised goods. His appointment as the sporting ambassador, however, caused a few problems because many health department officials and anti-smoking lobbyists were outraged that the Irish government should pay him £100,000 to take the position when he was the head of an operation funded by Benson and Hedges. Eddie, however, received staunch support from the Irish sports minister Jim McDaid as the controversy raged. For a time, though, it seemed that Formula One was providing him with an escape to reality from an alternative public life that was swirling like the Irish Sea.

It was a welcome escape in more ways than one. Frentzen's second place behind Eddie Irvine's Ferrari in Melbourne had thrilled Eddie, but Hill had had a disappointing weekend. Eddie noted this when he remarked, 'It's a pity Damon could not have joined Frentzen on the podium. He had a bit of an off weekend. I feel Damon goes better when he is slightly aggravated. He was in very relaxed and confident form in Melbourne and the weekend didn't work out for him.' Hill was beginning to show signs that the total dedication and inner commitment that had carried him to the world championship was deserting him. Trouble lay ahead, but Eddie did not pick up the early warning signals in a season when Frentzen's form turned him and the team into front-runners.

As the team's form and fortunes rose, as Eddie's fame and celebrity gathered him greater and greater publicity, and as Frentzen emerged as a possible challenger for the drivers' championship with famous victories for the team in France and Italy along with a string of other impressive results, Hill slowly drifted into the shadows. By mid-season, when Frentzen, still sore and slightly injured after a high-speed accident in Canada, won in the rain at Magny-Cours, the problem became apparent and Hill began speaking openly about retirement. There was talk of him walking away and missing the British Grand Prix at Silverstone because he did not feel mentally prepared to do the job any longer. Eddie understood the turmoil facing the former world champion and said, quite simply, that he would not make him race for the team against his will. 'The business of human relations is a funny thing,' he remarked. 'Well, funny is not perhaps the right word to use when the going gets tough, but certainly working relationships are very interesting, and sometimes intriguing.'

After that Magny-Cours race on 27 June, Eddie was full of admiration for his German driver. 'Like the team, Heinz-Harald has matured a lot, and we have now won two of the last eleven races [across 1998 and 1999],' he said. 'And we are learning all the time. H-H is giving us his input and leadership.' He recalled the team's launch, at the Royal Albert Hall in London, when Frentzen picked up his microphone during the interviews to remind the media he was there and that the team was not going to be a one-man show built around Hill. 'Some said that was a bit arrogant, but you need that kind of self-confidence and presence to succeed at the top in any sport,' said Eddie. 'And there is no doubt that Heinz-Harald has got it. The result in France was just further proof of what he is made of. He is a very talented, very brave and really nice guy. He was right to say "Look at me!", and now we can all see why. But it was a shame that Damon was not able to match him.' In Eddie's opinion, Heinz-Harald had walked into the Jordan team, taken a look, liked what he saw and enjoyed himself. He praised him for his maturity and his cool attitude, his dry humour and his rapport with the technicians. He also noted that Frentzen had thrown a party, a rock 'n' roll night, at the Monaco Grand Prix for the whole team. It was an evening to which even Hirotoshi Honda and his wife were invited, and he performed a song that was memorable, though not as memorable as that performed by a professional female singer of voluptuous proportions who danced on top of the tables. 'She was adequately dressed,' said Eddie. 'Just about.' It was the way of things for the team in 1999, as it peaked and plateau'd, riding a wave of success with Frentzen while at the same time sharing Hill's frustrated and ultimately disappointing season. He finally bowed out of the business after a sad showing in Suzuka on the last day of October. 'He drove well at Silverstone for us,' Eddie said. 'He scored some points, but, on reflection, I dare say that was the time to stop.'

At Monza, where Frentzen won again to give Jordan their third victory in little more than a year, Eddie staked £2,000 at 14–1 on his own man to beat Mika Hakkinen and win the Italian Grand Prix. When Hakkinen crashed out of the race, Frentzen went on to collect the ten points for victory, and Eddie took home a cool £28,000. This was a typical example of his foresight and his courage in backing a hunch. By the same token, when it came to signing drivers, he had had winners and losers. Hill had given him his first win, but was a dismal disappointment the following year. To replace him, Eddie went for a fast young Italian with a decent record and big potential – Jarno Trulli. Eddie believed that Trulli, a former karting world champion, would have the hunger to push Frentzen, who had finished third in the 1999 drivers' championship, to even greater heights, and that in turn this momentum would allow the Jordan team to rise further up the constructors' table (they finished third in 1999 behind Ferrari and McLaren). Frentzen was 32 years old, Trulli 25. On paper, it was a good combination.

'I believe we can make second place and we certainly intend to give Ferrari and McLaren a run for their money,' Eddie confirmed at the pre-2000 season launch, this time held at the Theatre Royal in London. 'It would be a disaster, I think, if we cannot go on as we have done. At our first launch [in 1991] we had eleven people, or something like that, and one of them asked me why I was bothering! Today, we have a thousand people here – and that is a measure of how far we have come. We are very close to the pinnacle now and we will keep striving until we reach our target.' His speech, as rich in promises as language, as usual, had come after he was briefly rendered wordless by the unexpected (for him) arrival on stage of Michael Aspel with the red book that indicated Eddie was to be the subject of a *This Is Your Life* programme. It was a very amusing show.

Before that, however, Eddie concentrated on his team and his new driver line-up. Trulli, he said, was a future star. 'I had him signed up before his sensational drive at the Nürburgring [in the European Grand Prix on 26 September 1999], where he hung on for second. He has real speed and he doesn't block people. Only time will tell, but I think he is the right guy. I am excited about him because he has the blend I feel is necessary to achieve success. He has a beautiful manner, but also that touch of arrogance in that he doesn't hold back when he thinks things are not right.' He also revealed that he had learnt from some of his earlier experiences and would never again throw two young 'tigers' in together, as he'd done with Ralf Schumacher and Giancarlo Fisichella. 'That was suicidal,' he admitted. 'One of them could, and should, have won in Argentina in 1997, had they not run into each other. Everybody pointed at me and said, "I told you – you were mad to do that," but that did not daunt me. I would make those kinds of decisions again, but for now, this time, this is a new dawn and a new year and we have to get on with the blend we have.'

On reflection, that razzmatazz in the Theatre Royal – when Aspel sauntered on to the stage and Jordan became a red-book victim, when he talked so confidently of challenging and breaking the duopoly of Ferrari and McLaren, when he stood high with the backing of Warburg Pincus and Benson and Hedges and increased support from Mugen-Honda and the best season of his life in Formula One behind him – represented the zenith in terms of the team's realistic expectations. The bubble was so big at the turn of the century, it seemed fit to burst; in the end, it went down slowly. It was not clear then, in those dark winter days of 2000, but the Mugen-Honda engine was past its peak. So was the world economy. Uncertainties were creeping into key decision-makers' minds. The golden dream, born in green, paid for by Benson and Hedges and ushered into reality by Damon Hill and Heinz-Harald Frentzen during two memorable years, was destined to fade.

13. LONDON

The passing of the Hill era eased that pressure and left Marie with a lifestyle she could hardly have imagined when she had first bumped into Eddie Jordan in Leopardstown in 1977. Her neighbours at their new London apartment, bought for a reported £2 million, in The Bromptons, where the Brompton Hospital previously stood, included Jackie and Helen Stewart. Other well-known people hoping to purchase another flat in the building included Madonna, the American pop singer, and her British husband Guy Ritchie. It was a chic property purchased in a chic part of London, and Marie and Eddie were happy to enjoy it. They felt they had earned it, and they had. It was satisfying, too, for many around them who had seen the sacrifices they had made in the past.

When the team flew to Melbourne for the opening race of the 2000 season, expectations were high. Eddie had great faith in his driver pairing, the engine supplied power, the team was seasoned, strong and competitive, and the budget was, reportedly, the best it had ever been. The acrimony associated with Hill's limp final half season in Formula One, during which he struggled to find the heart needed for his driving as he and Eddie disagreed over the terms of his retirement, was forgotten now. The arrival of Deutsche Post as a secondary sponsor to Benson and Hedges encouraged some pundits to claim the gross budget had exceeded $100 million for the first time. This was calculated as comprising nearly $60 million in direct sponsorship deals, $28 million from trade and technical support, and $17.5 million from other sources, chiefly the television and prize money contributions earned from the Formula One commercial operation. It was a far cry from the situation a decade earlier when Gary Anderson was building the team's first car on a budget of little more than $1.5 million. Now, the drivers were being paid to drive, albeit for less money than Eddie had been required to find for the fees that attracted Hill to run alongside Ralf Schumacher and Frentzen in 1998 and 1999. Thanks to the work of chief financial officer Richard O'Driscoll, a career banker who had joined Jordan in 1992, the business was in sound shape and being cleverly run by a man known deservedly as the best deal-maker in Formula One. But it was the final flush of a boom. The arrival of the car manufacturers, armed with plans for their own series, at a time when the world economy was receding was not good news. Costs steadily escalated, and more and more people became concerned.

On arrival in Victoria for the race weekend at Albert Park, of course, all in the world seemed well. The skies were Australian blue and the future looked bright. But the result was a disappointment, a 'zero points' finish that should have flashed a warning of what lay ahead. Frentzen was running second, but had to retire with a hydraulics failure; Trulli, on his Jordan debut, was aiming at third place but was stopped by an engine failure. The dream start to the year did not materialise. The Mugen-Honda engine, a powerful unit respected by everyone, was heavier than many rivals'. Improvements were promised, but for the team this meant waiting, hoping, depending on events in the future, not running aggressively with total confidence right from the start. 'The reason I am happy to continue with the engine we have this year is that I really want to have a crack at the championship,' Eddie told the *Sunday Telegraph*. 'That may prove wide of the mark, but who knows? This time last year, nobody gave us a chance, but Frentzen was up there. I know there will be disappointments along the road, but we can bounce back.'

By the late spring of 2000, the Jordan Grand Prix factory was bursting at the seams in more ways than one. The number of employed staff had exceeded two hundred, forcing Eddie to backtrack again on an old jocular promise he had made to sack himself if he ever hired more than a hundred people. He had handled the Deutsche Post deal himself and delivered it in rapid time so, given the new age in which the team found itself, he could hardly be considered vulnerable. The deal had been done in December 1999, and it impressed many knowledgeable observers in its speed and magnitude. For Eddie, personally, it meant he could relax properly at Christmas and take some time off. He had a choice of places to go: Sotogrande, in the off season, Dublin, Oxford or London, where Eddie and Marie were spending more and more time. Life was good. The children were in excellent schools, the team was running well and making money and the future appeared equally attractive. 'That Christmas was a good one,' said Eddie. 'In years gone by, I had spent much of the holiday on the phone, chasing and chatting, never ceasing the search for money we needed for the following season. But then, for the first time in my company's history, we had our entire technical and commercial programme fully secured before the festivities began. We had done all sorts of deals in the past, and carried on up to February. If we went to the Monaco Grand Prix, we'd be flexible and offer sponsorship on an eighteen-month basis to make sure we brought people in. But by Christmas 1999, we had been able to lay down a different set of long-term plans. We had cash in hand. The figures were boldly linked in the metaphorical ledger rather than scribbled in pencil with caution!'

The changes brought about by success, progress and much bigger and better sponsorship deals had brought greater pressures, too, of course. During what the Jordans later loosely described as the 'Damon Hill time', they'd had more publicity than was normally desirable, even by Eddie's standards. 'It was when we got Damon Hill in the team that we got all the big publicity and it changed,' said Marie. 'It made me feel more nervous. It was more difficult for the children, too, even just going to school. There were so many people who wanted to talk about Damon, pro- or anti- or whatever. We had a few problems. We had to have some extra security and so on. We had extra cameras and things like that. I phoned the insurance company.'

The passing of the Hill era eased that pressure and left Marie with a lifestyle she could hardly have imagined when she had first bumped into Eddie Jordan in Leopardstown in 1977. Her neighbours at their new London apartment, bought for a reported £2 million, in The Bromptons, where the Brompton Hospital previously stood, included Jackie and Helen Stewart. Other well-known people hoping to purchase another flat in the building included Madonna, the American pop singer, and her British husband Guy Ritchie. It was a chic property purchased in a chic part of London, and Marie and Eddie were happy to enjoy it. They felt they had earned it, and they had. It was satisfying, too, for many around them who had seen the sacrifices they had made in the past.

'I know how much Eddie has given to achieve all of this and what we put on the line at different times,' said Marie. 'But we have had a strong relationship all the way through and it has helped us. I think we're actually very compatible. We simply get on with our lives and meet in the middle. I think my stable upbringing probably helped. My father was in the civil service and we all went to normal schools and took our month-long holidays and everything was always the same. Our parents never argued. I think it was different for Eddie. His family are more volatile, but they are very close, too. Life with Eddie has meant understanding that and the nature of his business. I might, quite suddenly, be expected to go with him on a last-minute business trip to Spain and he'll just ask if I can be ready for 10 a.m. And that's it. You never know what's next. I always say to the kids that they should get things done while their time is free because God knows what tomorrow will bring.'

For the 2000 season, neither Marie nor Eddie had a clear idea of what lay ahead. Eddie knew his business was booming, but he did not know if this would produce the kind of results on the track he wanted. He was still desperately keen to keep the numbers down and to retain as much hands-on control of things as he could, but he knew it was becoming more difficult. 'Headcount is a particular issue for me,' he told *F1 Racing*'s Peter Windsor. 'I'm very keen that the team's layer of middle management is as small as possible because I don't like layers of reporting. I like the people who make the decisions to have a direct link with the people who action them. I don't want too many intermediaries.' He explained, too, that he preferred to have the designs of everything for the cars done in-house so that prototypes were produced in-house, only the mass manufacture done outside. This, said Eddie, kept the team as lean and flexible as possible and avoided the risk of holidays and suchlike interfering with demands for production. He confirmed also that Jordan had a contract with Mugen for both 2000 and 2001 and that he welcomed the pressure of competing with the new British American Racing (BAR) team that had arrived in Formula One with a Honda works engine deal. 'The team has a big heart, a tough soul, and we ain't going to get screwed over very easily,' he said. 'When we need to fight, we'll stand up and fight because we know how difficult it was to get here. Anything we've got, we've paid for. We've learnt by making mistakes. We've got nothing for free.'

Eddie has always had great admiration for the achievements of Frank Williams and Ron Dennis, in their different ways, with their teams. But he chose to attempt to proceed by a different route. He did not tie himself to a particular manufacturer, but sold a large stake in his business to an investor. 'My feeling is that a major manufacturer would slow the business down,' he said. 'Our company needs to move with the ease of a speedboat, not a ship. I need to move and attack things.' These were the type of comments that made him increasingly famous as a good man for a quote. Bold, dramatic and colourful remarks were Eddie's stock in trade. He was becoming a kind of Irish icon, too, as David Vivian described him in *GP2000*. 'Right now, Eddie Jordan has image to burn. He's as Irish as Guinness and twice as fashionable. Among fellow Formula One team bosses, he gleams like a lump of Kryptonite in a murky sea mist. Only Jackie Stewart's canny wee Scot "schtick" suggests similar accessibility and warmth. Ron and Frank simply look too serious, are too serious, and, as far as anyone knows, have never been remotely as daring in the facial hair department.'

More than anything else, Eddie was excited by the prospect of seeing what Frentzen could do in his team with a decent budget. 'I don't think you could be as happy with a team member as I am with Heinz-Harald,' he said. 'He is a joy to work with. What he has brought to the team is amazing.' Frentzen, in these happy days, was as delighted as his employer. 'Nearly ten years ago, I was the wrong man for Eddie, but now I think we have both changed. Eddie has learnt how to survive in F1, and I have learnt this too.'

Alas, this beautiful state of bonhomie was not to last for ever. As the 2000 season progressed, it turned from being a year of high promise into a year of disappointment and, ultimately, transition and change. The changes began, perhaps, with the realisation that the Mugen-Honda was too heavy to work competitively any longer – or, maybe, with the knowledge that Mike Gascoyne had been offered a job by Renault and had decided to take it and leave Jordan after only a short period as technical director. Still, Eddie had been aware, from the results, that it was only a matter of time before he started to implement a few changes of his own. He had been talking to different people about new engines. Then, one midweek night in the early part of the summer, he took a flight to Tokyo and, during the days that followed, finalised a deal that was to make Jordan one of the two fully works-supported Honda-powered teams in Formula One from 2001 onwards. Not long afterwards, on 28 June, a meeting was held in the headquarters of the rival British American Racing (BAR) team and chief designer Malcolm Oastler explained that Honda were no longer going to give BAR an exclusive supply of engines. The supply was to be shared – with Eddie Jordan. BAR had believed they had a three-year exclusive deal, but Honda, and EJ, had moved the goalposts.

Eddie had boarded his plane, however, to the unnerving sight of several senior executives from British American Tobacco sitting nearby. Moreover, among the throng flying to Tokyo was another extremely well-known Formula One face – his old adversary and rival Flavio Briatore. Naturally, the Italian team chief wanted to know where Eddie was heading and why. It was a delicate question, of course, and one that was therefore answered adroitly with a suggestion that he was visiting Bridgestone. Flavio was not convinced. Later on during that trip, after the meeting, Eddie was in a club in Tokyo called the One Eyed Snake with Briatore. It was a social evening they had planned together, as Eddie recalled. 'I had just had the meeting of my life and Flavio was being very generous with the champagne, but I couldn't tell him, or anyone! I was thinking that if he really knew what I was doing in Japan, drinking his champagne ... But Flavio is smart. When the deal was announced, at the French Grand Prix [at the beginning of July], he came up to me and he said, "Now I know why you were in such good form that night in Tokyo!" He was right. I wanted to stay up all night the way I felt – and I did.'

For the Jordan team, it was a great move and great news. The old and heavy Mugen-Honda engine had not been through a development phase and had been costing the team something in the region of £5 million per year, but the Honda deal would guarantee the team a free supply of engines. 'I suppose you could say that this is the most important and significant event in the history of Jordan Grand Prix,' said Eddie. 'I am absolutely delighted. We will be building an all-new car next year and I believe we now have all the components we need to do the job.' The deal had been swiftly executed from start to finish. 'I was talking to a number of other manufacturers aside from Honda; they came in late in the day,' explained Eddie. 'The deal happened so quickly. I didn't believe it was going to happen. I've only got a number of years that I can continue to do this and I was prepared to risk everything. Luckily, it paid off.' He confirmed he had also held talks with Audi, General Motors and Toyota.

As this deal was done, and as Mike Gascoyne confirmed he had signed for Renault then disappeared on a period of extended gardening leave, Eddie was performing a precarious balancing act. He kept confidence intact, maintained the momentum of the team and at the same time continued his own high-profile gamut of publicity stunts. The team was still growing in the belief that it was laying the foundations for an all-out assault on the championship, and on 3 September, in a feast of madcap motor racing entertainment, Eddie and his men threw a public party at Donington Park complete with a performance by Eddie himself, on stage, with Thin Lizzy and Westlife, during a concert in the evening. Music, as always, was there in his life at all times. More than fifteen thousand people turned up to join the celebrations of Jordan Grand Prix's tenth birthday, old stars and new mingling with the crowd on a perfect afternoon. John Watson came back for a run in the old 191 he had tested at Silverstone back in 1990. So, too, did Andrea de Cesaris, and, of course, the current drivers. There were autographs stands, meet-the-team sessions and Guinness in the Irish village. 'Other than Ferrari, Jordan is the only other people's team,' said Eddie. 'Today is about fun, but there's a serious side to it as well, and that is that we have had enormous support from the fans and we need to give something back to them.' At the time, after a mediocre season by Jordan standards, the team were fifth in the constructors' championship and Frentzen and Trulli were ninth and tenth in the drivers' standings. Cynics began to suggest that Eddie sounded dangerously like someone who was beginning to believe his own publicity.

That season, Eddie was also involved in a lot of the political machinations swirling around the sport. He attended a meeting at which Ron Dennis of McLaren International and Frank Williams of Williams Grand Prix attempted to unseat Max Mosley as president of the sport's ruling body, the Fédération Internationale de l'Automobile (FIA). They contended that he meddled too much in the running of Formula One. Indeed, only days before the Jordan party at Donington, there had been a confrontational meeting at the Hilton Hotel at Heathrow airport, where Mosley, in an adroit move, crushed the possibility of rebellious talk before it had grown into serious revolt. The problems, as the team owners saw it, centred on issues such as the deteriorating quality of the 'show', the amount of time wasted in trying to understand a vague set of technical and sporting rules, and, particularly, electronics in motor racing, tobacco advertising and sponsorship, and the simple fact that when a majority of the teams agreed on an issue their views could be, and were, overlooked and ignored by Mosley and the ruling body. The rebellion might have been still born, but its causes were later to be considered and dealt with by Mosley in his own way and in his own time.

All such talk of political chicanery and plots for the future were swept away, however, on 10 September, when fire marshal Paolo Ghislimberti was killed by flying debris following an accident involving both Jordan drivers at the Italian Grand Prix. Frentzen, approaching the second chicane, was caught out by the deceleration of Rubens Barrichello's Ferrari, could not avoid clipping the back of the Ferrari and then, in turn, his team-mate Trulli's Jordan. This accident triggered a multiple collision in which debris flew in all directions. The luckless Ghislimberti was struck and died after receiving emergency medical treatment at the side of the track. Frentzen was shattered by the news of the marshal's death. Barrichello, in a typically passionate outburst, heaped the blame on Frentzen, but later, when he had cooled down, modified his words. It was, for Eddie Jordan, a salutary reminder that motor racing is a dangerous affair and not to be treated lightly.

Less than a month later, after this public catastrophe for Formula One, Eddie was informed that his post as sporting ambassador for Ireland was not to be continued for a second term. The decision was reached after a year of controversy sparked by the Jordan team's involvement in Formula One and, of course, with tobacco sponsors. The row over Eddie's role and the £100,000 allocated for him to perform it continued to arouse widespread criticism in the Irish media and became something of a *cause célèbre*. When he was appointed, Eddie had said, 'I can understand the concern, but I do not see any merit in it whatsoever. I'm Irish, I'm enormously proud to be Irish. The team is sponsored by a tobacco company, but I cannot possibly see where the connection is, apart from maybe Eddie Jordan and the Jordan company is the same thing – and clearly it is not.' The row simmered on and opened up old disputes within Irish politics about earlier grants made to the Jordan team to promote Ireland. Eddie's popularity was put under the microscope; even his decision to apply for a coat of arms featuring four bezants, or gold coins, became a minor controversy. Sensibly, he eased himself gently out of the glare of the Irish political limelight at the end of the year.

The peak of Eddie's popularity, marked by the appearance of Michael Aspel and his red book at the team launch, had not been followed by a new peak for the team. From a ground-breaking third in the championship in 1999, Jordan slipped to sixth in 2000. Podiums and points became less and less frequent. Eddie, deeply disappointed with his team's mediocrity, remained philosophical and pinned his future hopes on the works engines deal with Honda. 'At the beginning of the year, you could see that Formula One was changing, and changing quite dramatically,' he explained. 'You could see that the emergence of the manufacturer engine teams across the board would provide a significantly higher level of competition. BMW, Toyota, Renault and Mercedes . . . their demand for success is much higher than that of a very capable customer supplier like Mugen or Supertec. It all changed. For us, having a customer engine from Mugen left us with a massive uphill battle. When we decided not to renew our option with Mugen, in Monaco in June, it was a brave move, but it was the right one. We were rapidly repaid by landing Honda.'

Still, having rejected one offer from Honda, who were interested in buying his team in 1998, Eddie was wary of encouraging the new philosophy that suggested a manufacturer-led championship was the right future for Formula One. 'I think equity participation is fine. It's a good thing for the manufacturers to have a handle on certain controls of the marketing mix in F1. It gives them an opportunity to sell more products. But I'm old fashioned in that I believe it must be conducted through the teams. We are the people who will be there on wet days and dry days in fifty years' time. F1 has stood the scrutiny of time for the past half century, and the teams and Bernie Ecclestone are the fibre of what has made F1 strong. Manufacturer equity participation is fine through the way Mercedes has done it at McLaren, but what I am nervous about is manufacturers taking over whole teams, such as Ford has done with Stewart. What if the results are not what they want ten years down the line, and the marketers feel the programme has run its course? I want guarantees to make sure that the team itself is left intact when they leave, that it is handed over in good and proper working order. The team owners were the ones who took the intensive risks to start with. That doesn't give us the divine right to total access to the sport, but historically we are the bedrock of the whole show.'

By the end of the first year of the new millennium, the mood of high confidence was deflating slightly, but not enough to show. Eddie, who had been voted Ireland's Entrepreneur of the Year 2000, embarked on a hectic round of golf appearances and matches, including one at St Andrews, where he accepted an invitation from Colin Montgomerie to play for the benefit of the British Lung Foundation, one at Sunningdale for team sponsors Scania, and one for Cancer and Leukaemia in Childhood. Eddie also visited the Southampton Boat Show and purchased a new Sunseeker 105 yacht. 'I wanted to get a bigger boat before the children fled the nest, as it makes a great base for us to spend time together,' he said.

For 2001, his priorities were clear. The team needed to regain its position in the top three, or better, and the momentum that had lifted the team from among the also-rans to a place amid the front-runners had to be regenerated on a consistent basis. The doubters had to be banished. The old spirit of the original Jordan team had to be fanned back into flames. The whispering campaign started by those who had left the Jordan team to work elsewhere had to be silenced. To begin with, Eddie cancelled the team's

Christmas party, an unexpected action that was to send shock waves through the factory. At the team's launch in January, Eddie talked about these issues and urged a revival of the team's old fighting spirit. The team used a video that highlighted the work done by the unsung heroes back at the factory, the people who never, or very rarely, attend the races. The departures of former technical director Mike Gascoyne and chief designer Mark Smith were forgotten. The team regrouped around its leader and its core philosophy.

'We restructured the management, added nearly fifty people to the workforce and witnessed the team gelling together into a committed and dedicated team, probably the best Jordan has ever fielded,' Eddie said. 'I felt that to face the challenge of the years ahead, we had to grow the company in every direction. It was not easy, but at that time I had never felt so confident.' Both Frentzen and Trulli seemed to be happy with the progress made over the winter and impressed by the bold manner in which Eddie was approaching the season. 'We should start now where we finished the 1999 season off, but do more of a complete job,' said Frentzen. 'I am going to help the team achieve this.' There were more positive comments, too, from Trulli, but the bottom line, as Eddie expressed it, was that this was the big chance for him and for Jordan Grand Prix.

To replace his lost technical staff, he had recruited Eghbal Hamidy, an aerodynamics specialist who had been successful at Williams, Stewart and Arrows, and in his management reorganisation he had brought in a new chief executive, John Putt, effectively moving old friend and original team member Trevor Foster to a different, lesser position. 'If we blow it this time, you can blame us alone,' said Eddie. 'We'll never get this kind of opportunity again. That's it.' As famous for his verbal hoop-la at pre-season launches as he is for his noise on stage at rock concerts, Eddie knew his comments would go on the record to be used against him. But he knew, too, that they had been every year for a decade. He could live with that. He had the ability to talk his way in and out of trouble. 'This is the realisation of a dream,' he went on, referring to Honda's involvement. 'It represents a total commitment to winning the world championship. Honda has an unrivalled success story in Formula One and we have been given the awesome responsibility of adding to that record.'

Just as awesome, to those in their wake, was the strength of the Ferrari and McLaren operations. As Eddie saw it, they probably felt they only had to worry about each other. In Melbourne, however, in March 2001, Heinz-Harald Frentzen said he felt the Honda-powered Jordan was the team's best car. Then he qualified fourth on the grid and finished fifth in the race. Not bad for starters, with a new car-engine package. 'As I said during last season, be very careful when you write us off,' said Eddie. 'You do it at your own peril. That is not just me being cocky. But I love it when people slag me off, because it tempts me to try harder. I said to the guys at the end of last season that we had to learn by our mistakes and ignore what the press were saying about the staff changes. I just wanted them to do a good car, get some good results, and the ones that have gone and left the team will be the ones who are the losers.' In general, Eddie and the majority of his team were also unconcerned by any comparisons with the performances of BAR, because they did not see the all-Honda battle as anything like as significant as their own effort to climb into the leading bunch again.

According to one unconfirmed report, published that April, the gross budget for the team was $172 million, which included nearly $100 million dollars in trade support, nearly all of it from Honda. The same publication, *EuroBusiness* magazine, also suggested that the team's preparations had been hindered by 'private and unattributable bad-mouthing from ex-staffers who claim that since venture capitalists Warburg Pincus took a stake in the team there has been too much of a bottom-line focus and not enough spent on the team'. Eddie responded to this by saying, 'We wouldn't be alive without my favourite subject, which is money. We have asked our sponsors to really dig deep this year because we have never had a bigger demand for research and development, and for testing.'

At this time, Frentzen believed all was well. He had started the season solidly, if not sensationally, and he believed he had earned respect from all around him. In an interview with *F1 Racing* magazine in May, he said, 'When I joined Jordan, I knew this

Formula One business more thoroughly [after being with Williams]. Both Sir Frank Williams and Eddie Jordan are very strong characters, and in the end they have to make very tough decisions. Sometimes you think they've made an illogical decision, but it's only because of the need of the team. They have so many people in the factory, so much responsibility, that they have to make tough decisions sometimes. So, I understood when they [Williams] said that they didn't want me as a driver. I knew it wasn't a successful time for them, back then, but I also knew what I had learnt. If I were to join Williams now, I would know how to handle the situation. I wouldn't be afraid to go back to Williams now.'

Two top-six finishes in Australia and Malaysia were followed, in Frentzen's sequence of results, by a run of poor form that tested his and the team's patience and faith. Eddie stood by him, in public at least, for most of the first half of the year. 'I can't remember a time when I have enjoyed two drivers like I have these two,' he said. 'Jarno learns from Heinz, and they are easy together, but they are also pushy and they want more. Jarno definitely has that killer instinct. I think Heinz has quite a bit left to give. I have no doubt whatsoever that if I was to give Heinz or Jarno the right car they could get the job done. Ralf Schumacher is a fantastic driver, but either of my current drivers could do the same as him.'

Such comments might have been composed to haunt Eddie, given what was to happen in the middle of the season. Frentzen's performances had not been as scintillating as expected, the team's form was nothing like as flamboyant as Eddie had hoped, and the results were not good and did not look like improving. It was a continuation, in reality, of the underlying decline that had characterised much of 2000, and to make matters worse Eddie was facing the likelihood of having to pay out around £7 million to Frentzen in the eighteen-month period to the end of 2002 for what he considered might be a negligible level of commitment and performance. Eddie, therefore, decided he needed to act fast. He had given Frentzen the support he craved after his departure from Williams and had helped to transform him from a dispirited shadow of the driver he once had been into a dashing race-winner who delivered two victories to the Jordan team in 1999. He had maintained that support and he had kept the warmth apparent in public. But, gradually, almost insidiously, frustration had crept into his feelings, doubts into his thoughts. He did not want to end up, as he felt he had in 1998, paying top money to a driver who was doing little more than going through the motions.

'Did I know about that? Oh, yes, I did!' declared Marie when asked about her memories of Eddie's collapsing relationship with Frentzen in early and mid-2001. 'Having been bitten by Damon the year before – you know, when he called him "the highest paid taxi driver" in the world – well, I know Eddie didn't want to get caught like that again. I know that the Germans wrote that [Frentzen] didn't know [about his dismissal] until just before the German Grand Prix. Well, I knew the Monday week before that, which was when [Eddie] told him. So, maybe he was just saving face. But, you know, that was the story that was never printed. Eddie Irvine said it in a column he did, and he got it right. He said Eddie had been bitten by Damon Hill the year before so he wasn't going to let it happen again. But it didn't get written by anybody else, anywhere.'

The sacking of Heinz-Harald Frentzen caused a furore when it became public knowledge on Wednesday, 25 July, just four days before the German Grand Prix, his home race. A fax had, however, been sent to his home in Monte Carlo on Tuesday, 17 July. It told him the team was terminating his contract with immediate effect. But the team did not issue a news release or any public statements on the subject until the following week, and this delay was the cause of much of the confusion and controversy. Jordan had lost faith in Frentzen during the course of a poor run of unproductive results after his sixth-place finish at Imola on 15 April. Equally, Frentzen had lost his belief in the team. When he was dismissed, his father Harald told the *Sun* in London that someone in the Jordan team had been 'pressing buttons' to sabotage his son's car and that this was the cause of all the technical faults that had undermined his season. It was a bizarre and outrageous allegation. Various conspiracy theories were quickly published, some of them merely claiming that Frentzen was a victim of Jordan's misplaced decision and wrong opinions, others suggesting that a desire to be rid of the German in a carefully prepared swap deal with Prost, for the release of his old friend Jean Alesi, was at the heart of it all. This, it was suggested, would have pleased Alesi, who was growing tired of the disappointments of racing for the under-funded French team, and who was a former Jordan protégé, of course, and it would have pleased Frentzen, too, who was equally disappointed with the chronic lack of reliability he was suffering with Jordan. Approaches, it was reported, were made to Alesi long before matters came to a head, but Eddie had not been able to persuade Alain Prost to release him.

The key to the whole episode was the weekend of the British Grand Prix, 14–15 July, when Frentzen finished seventh and, not for the first time, blamed his result on the car and its set-up, citing understeer and lack of downforce as the main problems. An investigation at the Jordan factory on the Monday after the Grand Prix revealed that the telemetry taken from Frentzen's car did not support one of his claims, which was that the launch control system had malfunctioned. At the same time, Alesi received a fax at his family home at Avignon. It told him Prost had fined him for his public criticism of the French team following the French Grand Prix on 1 July. Alesi, who had not been paid his 2001 retainer, was very upset by the letter and, it is believed, felt this was the end of his relationship with the Prost team. When Eddie learnt of Alesi's position and his feelings, he made it very clear he wanted him to replace Frentzen. Talks began, but the entire episode was complicated by the Frenchman's need to gain his release from his contract with Prost. Having held long discussions with Frentzen during the Silverstone weekend, Eddie and the team decided to withdraw him from testing at Monza the following week and to send Ricardo Zonta instead. This prompted a furore in the German media, who mistakenly believed he had failed to show up.

With Frentzen sacked, Eddie needed a replacement driver for Hockenheim, but with Alesi struggling to extricate himself from his Prost contract, Zonta was called up to race instead. That weekend in Germany turned into a very unpleasant experience as Frentzen's fans turned on the Jordan team. Offensive banners, criticism from all quarters and open dissent in certain parts of the team made life difficult; for Prost, the revelation that Alesi was set to leave for Jordan was an added shock. He and his former team-mate, and friend, were eventually separated by the Contracts Recognition Board on 1 August, on which date Alesi became a free agent. Within a week he had been fitted for a seat, had had his photograph taken in Jordan overalls, and had been confirmed as a Jordan driver until the end of the year.

Briefly, in the post-Frentzen excitement, high hopes were rekindled, but not even someone as naturally charismatic and fast as Alesi could help turn the tide. It was not a year to remember, other than for a successful appeal against Trulli's exclusion from fourth place at September's United States Grand Prix, which belatedly lifted the team up to fifth, ahead of Honda-powered rivals BAR. Yet even the success of that appeal was due as much to the incompetence of the race stewards as anything else; also, by the time it took place, Trulli was on his way to Renault in an exchange that saw the popular Giancarlo Fisichella returning to Jordan as the 2002 team leader in another Briatore-inspired swap deal. Fisichella's team-mate for 2002 was, appropriately, revealed in Japan. He was the 2001 British Formula Three champion Takuma Sato, a cheerful and enthusiastic driver who was introduced as a future world champion by Eddie to the Formula One media in Suzuka at the season-ending Japanese Grand Prix. This time, with all due respect to Sato, the claims were taken with a pinch of salt, since that same weekend it was Eddie who was telling anyone who would listen that Formula One was facing a recession that would hurt everyone. He was right.

14. ANALIVIA AND *THE SNAPPER*

His house at Sotogrande, facing the sunshine and the African tribal beats, is a sprawling family villa he has called Analivia. It is named after the character in James Joyce's *Ulysses* who represents the river Liffey, the thread of water and life that flows through the heart of Dublin and out to the Irish Sea. It is a name that evokes those parts of Eddie's life that are rarely noticed, seen or understood in his life as Formula One team owner and popular lifestyle celebrity, but it is a part of him that is as sincere and genuine as his love of his family and his ambition to succeed. His boat, *The Snapper*, a sleek Sunseeker 105, is one of his most proud possessions. Its name helps to sum up the other half of this complex and multi-faceted man. If Analivia is the woman of Edna O'Brien's Ireland – the river, the womb, the cave, the cow, the sow, the bride, the harlot – then *The Snapper* is the escapist, the racer, the entrepreneur, the risk-taker, the speedster and the celebrity. One is a river, the other is an ocean. One is home, the other is away.

When Eddie was growing up in Ireland, he was always close to the sea. He loved it. He would gaze into it, play on the beach, listen to the swell and go swimming. He would look out across it to the far horizon and dream. He would listen to music to the sounds of his sea, and go out in boats with laughing friends. He had fun by the sea, he relaxed to the sound of the crashing waves, he felt at home. His special kinship with the Irish Sea, and later with all seas and oceans, was part of his childhood, and it has stayed in him. It is the main reason he needed to buy a house away from the hustle and bustle of his working life, away from the big cities and their hassles, down in the south of Spain; it is the main reason, too, that he had to buy a boat and sail away. He needed to escape, he needed to breathe sea air.

His house at Sotogrande, facing the sunshine and the African tribal beats, is a sprawling family villa he has called Analivia. It is named after the character in James Joyce's *Ulysses* who represents the river Liffey, the thread of water and life that flows through the heart of Dublin and out to the Irish Sea. It is a name that evokes those parts of Eddie's life that are rarely noticed, seen or understood in his life as Formula One team owner and popular lifestyle celebrity, but it is a part of him that is as sincere and genuine as his love of his family and his ambition to succeed. His boat, *The Snapper*, a sleek Sunseeker 105, is one of his most proud possessions. Its name helps to sum up the other half of this complex and multi-faceted man. If Analivia is the woman of Edna O'Brien's Ireland – the river, the womb, the cave, the cow, the sow, the bride, the harlot – then *The Snapper* is the escapist, the racer, the entrepreneur, the risk-taker, the speedster and the celebrity. One is a river, the other is an ocean. One is home, the other is away.

Eddie Jordan, of course, is all of these things. But on some days he is none of them. He is a man who loves all other human beings, but he can be an irascible and awkward sod at times. He is an employer who has earned deep loyalty and love from his staff and friends, but who is forgetful and has the attention span of a gnat, according to those who know these things well. His grasp of the past, in terms of recording events, dates, places and times, is vague, but his visions of the future are glorious and colourful and rousing. He is a sportsman and a gambler and a musician and a deal-maker and a leader and a father and a husband and a lover and a sailor and a showman. He likes to make things happen, to overcome challenges, to tease and to tempt and to provoke and to match-make and to laugh and to cry, but most of all, he loves to be loved.

When Frentzen was sacked on the eve of the German Grand Prix, in the middle of the 2001 season, Eddie knew he had lost a lot of admirers. He had taken a tough decision, one of the most difficult of his life, on the eve of the driver's home race. He had upset Frentzen, a man he had admired greatly and treated as a friend. He had upset his family, his friends and his fans. He knew this would create a reaction, particularly among the many Germans who attended the race weekend. But he was surprised at the venom and range of the backlash, and when it came, it hurt him. 'I expected some stick, but not all of that,' he said. 'They were vicious towards me. The attacks from the Germans, in particular, were hurtful. It was very unpleasant for me.' He knew, too, that the German public would not understand, or consider, that it was Eddie who had introduced Michael Schumacher and his brother Ralf to the sport – the former at a time when Germany had virtually no Formula One traditions at all – and that he had worked hard with Frentzen to find a way of resolving their problems. 'We had a huge difference of opinion in how the team should go forward, and as the gap between us widened, I realised it was inevitable that we should separate. In the end, I did give him a chance to race for us in the German Grand Prix, but he turned me down. It was hard for me because I really liked him. He is a very nice man. He was third in the championship for us in 1999 with two wins, but in this business, you just can't allow your heart to rule your head.' Eddie had experienced one disappointing ending of a relationship with a driver with Damon Hill, and did not want another. This episode, the 'Frentzen Affair' as it was later dubbed, showed he was capable of taking the steely decisions when required even if they seemed to go against his very nature. It proved, too, that he really is a man of many parts.

When Eddie was interviewed by Andrew Longmore for the *Independent on Sunday* in March 2000, he was asked to be introspective and to talk about himself. Longmore wrote that Frentzen had described Eddie as a 'man who can open a barrel', meaning that he was a man who made things happen. It was a complimentary description from someone who at the time was working closely with him. Talking about himself, Eddie said he was often thought of as an actor, but suggested that was only a part of him. 'People say I act all the time, but it's not true,' he explained. 'That thing down there with Johnny [Dumfries, a former driver, with whom he was filming a documentary] I found difficult. In a minute, I've got to read a statement about the team for a sponsor. They've given me the text. I'd rather skim over that and ad lib it. I'd never make a great newsreader, but I do make a great bullshitter!' That final remark was half-joke and half-truism. 'I understand the buzz the drivers get in this game because I've tasted some of it myself, though not at the same level,' he continued. 'But, to me, doing the deal, making it happen, and making it successful, that is by far the biggest buzz in this business. The business side is probably the one that needs me the most.' When asked if there were, in fact, two Eddie Jordans and not merely one, he went on, 'Well, there's one who desperately feels he missed out on a life in music. That one is very musical and very Irish. They go hand in hand, those two. But then there's the one who likes surfing the market and looking for companies who might burst on to the scene and who loves the intrigue and the analysis. Should we cash in? Should we be in stocks? What's happening? What's the perception? That's the punter side of me, I suppose, the one you find at Cheltenham, or at Windsor on a

Monday evening. I don't know where the horse part of me comes in. Maybe, in fact, there are four Eddie Jordans!'

Pinning down just one of these Eddies is no easy task. He is a whirlwind of humanity. He loves the energy of cities as much as the unpredictable peace, or storms, of the sea. That, he has said, is why he has his apartment in London, his house in Spain and his boat. He has dreams, too, that fill him with as much delight as his financial worries in the past have torn his nerves to shreds. 'I adore skiing,' he said of his passion for escaping to Courchevel. 'I never have enough time for it. And I have a vision that I must sail the Atlantic. I would love to take a year off, sail round the world and visit the places I want to visit and take it nice and slowly and stress-free. I am in love with the sea.'

In Ireland, he is adored for his achievements, for his success in putting Ireland on the global sporting map with a smile and a sense of purpose. He is respected, enjoyed and admired, but always treated as one of them. He is not put on a faraway pedestal and made untouchable. And this guy next door is as bad-tempered as the rest. He cannot hide it. His blow-ups, when they come, are legendary. It is his very good fortune that he is married to a placid, even-tempered and intelligent woman who can let such moods pass. 'It just washes over me,' said Marie. 'If he's having a paddy, I look at him and I think, "What's happening here?" I find it very strange. Like, one moment he's normal and the next he's kind of lost it. I just don't get involved. I never take it to heart because it is never directed at me, and in ten minutes, usually, it is all forgotten.' Marie's influence on Eddie was also important during their most stressful times when he came home depressed about their situation. 'If you're having a bad year, the pressure can just pile up. The morale of the team gets lower and lower. It can affect everybody. When the kids were younger and we had had a bad day, Eddie would come home and we would change into playing "happy families" for the afternoon and forget about motor racing. We'd discuss what the children were doing and we'd use our minds on the positive sides of life – like how lucky we were to have a family to be with on a Sunday afternoon. And when Eddie was very stressed during the really bad times, we used to tuck him up in bed with all the newspapers and just keep taking him cups of tea.'

Those, of course, were the blackest days of the early 1990s when there was not enough money coming in and too much going out. 'We were working on credit,' said Eddie. 'We would wait to order items on the first day of each month, thus winning that month and a further thirty days before the money was due. One of the most difficult things at the end of the month would be looking at how much we had available and establishing how far the bank would let us go. Then we'd decide how many of the bills we could pay. Everyone received his money eventually. I'm proud of the fact that we never went bankrupt and restarted under a different name, even though such an easy option was favoured by many companies who left their creditors high and dry.'

This is the character of the man shining through, whatever the weather. This is why Eddie is as welcome to stand shoulder to shoulder with anyone in a Dublin pub as to walk through the front door of any bank in London. This is why he has so many friends and so few enemies. He has done it all, including, as he revealed in one of his many unguarded moments, 'everything you can do when you stay in Monte Carlo' after using a boat, for the first time, to accommodate and entertain the team's sponsors. 'I have experienced everything there now, from a tent to a caravan. I've even been one of four in a twin-bedded room when I shared once with Martin Donnelly, Mark Blundell and Johnny Herbert!'

It is undeniable that Eddie is a man of wide experience and many interests. He loves his music and his sport. Since he first came to England, he has become an ardent Coventry City fan and a shareholder in Glasgow Celtic. His introduction to Coventry, and English football, came through a friendship with a great motor racing fan, Harvey Pallett, the owner of a small pub in Ireland, the chairman of Nuneaton Borough and the vice-president of Coventry City. 'He was a huge man who used to like drinking pints,' said Eddie. 'Apart from being a wealthy builder, he also used to breed donkeys. He was a bit of a character to say the least. If there wasn't a race, and it was a Saturday, he used to take me with him to Coventry. That's how my association began. It never occurred to me for a minute to support anyone else. I follow Oxford United, too, because I live in Oxford, but my allegiance to Coventry has stayed strong.' His love of sport is likely also to see Eddie at golf or horse racing events. He loves them all, just as he loves to socialise and wheel and deal with people.

Every year, once the Formula One season is over, he is involved in all kinds of charity activities, partying and promotional work on top of his normal role at the head of Jordan Grand Prix. He hosts a great Christmas party, too, in Dublin, an event that is famous in the city for bringing together people from all walks of Eddie's life – his family, his friends, his business associates and all the people in Dublin he has shared his life with down the years. His family Christmas is another story, of course, as he maintains the traditions in his own home. 'Of course, for the family, it is the perfect time to get together,' he said. 'We have a rota where we either stay at home, go to Ireland or take in a bit of skiing or sailing. I am in the happy position where we can now afford to make that choice, but even when times were tough, the Jordan family Christmas was never quiet. In Ireland, as you would expect, there is a different structure and style to Christmas. At some point, all the furniture will be pushed to one side and you do your party piece, be it singing, playing a game, telling a story, juggling or whatever. My mother has always got up and done "The Walls of Limerick", which is a lively little dance! If we are in England, we invite the family across to us. We'll have a barrel of Guinness on tap all day and everyone has a good drink. There'll be brown bread and smoked salmon to tide the party through until the early evening, and then we'll sit down to eat. It's always an open house, providing you like Guinness.'

The Christmas of 2001 was celebrated as raucously as ever, despite Eddie knowing that he was facing a much more difficult year ahead in 2002. The problems caused by the worldwide recession and the shock of the events in New York on 11 September had taken their toll. The budgets for the Jordan Grand Prix team were hit. Benson and Hedges wanted to reduce their commitment. Eddie sensed the changes and prepared himself for a different kind of future, at least in the short term. He talked of the coming problems in terms of his team and Formula One as a whole. He warned paddock and public alike. When Prost Grand Prix collapsed before the new season began, there were heads nodding in agreement. But Eddie kept his sense of fun and carried on wheeling and dealing and juggling. New sponsors came in,

DHL and Virgin Mobile among them. His new band, V10 – Jonathan Perkins, vocals and keyboard; Jimmy Taylor, guitar and backing vocals; Matt Exelby, guitar and vocals; Peter Noone, bass; Chris Thomas, E-bow and keyboards; Keith Prior, percussion; and Eddie Jordan, drums – performed creditably at the Royal Albert Hall where the Formula One-supported Stars and Guitars concert in aid of the Brain and Spine Foundation took place in February 2002. Their cover of David Bowie's song 'Heroes' almost brought the house down, and the performance earned V10 a further booking in Monte Carlo during the Monaco Grand Prix. Eddie was also given a chance, which he took up, to join the Stereophonics in performance at the British Grand Prix Ball at Stowe.

The thrill of performing on stage with established bands was always a delight to him. Music and dance have always been part of his was of life, after all, merging with his interests in words, writing and being at the heart of any good fun that was around and available. Just ask Des Large. He has been around, close to Eddie, from the start of his meteoric rise from bank clerk to Formula One team owner and he and Eddie are linked by marriage to the McCarthy sisters Ann and Marie. 'I first met him in 1977 and Eddie was on crutches,' he recalled with a laugh. 'I was doing a bit of rallying and he was doing stuff at Mondello Park. After that, I was playing in a band and Eddie came to the gigs. I was the guitarist in the band and he always had this great interest in music. We were called The Good Times! Well, Eddie then proceeded to become a pseudo-journalist for a magazine called *Hot Press*, I think, and Ken Ryan (the late Ken Ryan, a Dublin journalist) was involved in this. And Eddie found that having a press card was a very useful thing because it helped to get him into a lot of gigs and that kind of thing. So I got to know him that way.' Des's recollections of Eddie 'working' as a journalist with a press card that enabled him to write music columns are supported by many others, notably David Marren, who has rediscovered some of the original Jordan jottings in print. Large, however, got to know Eddie much better as time went on and has remained a very close friend ever since.

'He started to date my sister on a few occasions,' he added. 'Not Marie or Ann, but Gill! There is a very funny story about one

Christmas, when Eddie came to our house. We were good Protestants, you know, in Dublin, which was a bit unusual, but Eddie, to impress my mother, he said he was a Jew! And, he said, he went to Sandford Park, one of the local schools. He was done up to the nines in a blue velvet suit and took my sister off to a party. Well, subsequently, my sister went out with Derek Daly for a couple of years in England. But it was almost scandalous, the idea of Eddie trying to impress my parents by saying he was a Jew! He'd try to get away with anything. Then we moved on and I became more friendly with Eddie. I was involved with a company called P. O'Reilly and we were doing various sponsorship deals and we sponsored Derek Daly. Eddie, as he does, befriends anyone he thinks there might be a few shillings in and so we became quite good friends! We gave him a few bob for tyres and stuff like that you know. Those were the Mondello days really when Eddie was doing Atlantic. Well, then I had a marriage break-up and Eddie proceeded to introduce me to Ann, in Mondello.

'The true story – and Eddie doesn't like it to be told too much – is, in fact, not quite the way most people have heard it. Eddie always tells it as if he charged me for introducing me to Ann. Three hundred pounds, I think it was. That's about right. But in actual fact, I had put him in as a sort of auctioneer to help to sell my first house and this was actually a payment for that. But I told him I wouldn't be paying him. I was messing him around. Then, I told him that if he got me a date with this lovely lady then I would pay him the money that was due. And that's the truth. He sold my house. So it was his fee for that. I did pay him, but he always said it was for the introduction to Ann! I remember telling this one at the warm-up for *This is Your Life* and Eddie leaned over and he said: "Jesus, Des. That makes me sound like a pimp! We'd better drop that one a bit."

'Later on, I moved in with Eddie when he lived in a very small house in Dublin and we were dating the two girls and Eddie was selling his cars outside the front door. We were living together for a brief time while I was trying to purchase another house. Were we a deadly duo? Yes, it was a bit like that. I was best man at his wedding, and the interesting thing about that was that all he wanted to do, as I recall, was go for pints, before the wedding, in

Terenure, which is where Marie grew up. I think it was called
Floods and the reception was at a place called Lamb Doyles, and
I was best man, I think, because I organised the band –
and Eddie, of course, had to play at his own drums at his own
wedding!

'And then, of course, he moved to England soon after that. I
think it is probably correct that it was the first time Marie heard
him on drums. I knew he could play. I had seen him get up and
he had played with us and I was quite surprised how good he was
and that he could do it. Well, Ann and I got married the following
year, in Towcester. It was organised by Eddie. We married there
and he hosted the party after the wedding at his house in 'Little
London' which was their first house over there, a tiny little place,
but great fun. We were thinking he was going to come with us on
the first night of our honeymoon, but in the end he didn't.

'Then, of course, Eddie did his F3 and all of that and then the
gigs started at the British Grands Prix in the days when it was just
a field really. He said to me, in 1991, this is our home and our
home Grand Prix and we should have a bit of a party afterwards.
So, he went off and got a trailer with gear on it and we had a great
bash that night. Dave Pennefather was there – and he was a
drummer, too. Dave was drumming first and Eddie got up and it
grew, and grew, and we had people like Chris De Burgh playing.
The first ones were the best. They were magical. With Damon
(Hill) and the rest of them. Fantastic. Great fun.

'He is an incredible matchmaker. Anyone who works with him,
especially girls, will tell you he is always trying to match them up
with different people and he certainly matched me up with a good
'un. He is a great friend, too, absolutely. There have been times
when I've needed him and times when he has confided in me as
well; both family and business. He has been a super friend. Our
kids are all very close and his lads come over here and my young
fellows go over with them, and they all go to Spain together.

'The great beauty of the two girls, Marie and Ann, is that they
are so laid back. Nothing bothers them at all. I can tell you if
Eddie was married to a different woman, I am not sure they would
be still together because he is so go, go, go all the time. She just
says 'well, Eddie, you just go off if you want to.' There is one story

too about Miki: she had a little too much cider at one of the parties after the Grand Prix and I was left to look after her. I brought her home and then Eddie blamed me for getting her into a state, while he was practising signing his autographs!

'But the wonderful thing about him has always been that nothing was too big for him. To go rallying, or racing, or do something . . . If he didn't have the money, he could go out and sell a few cars. There was this time when he did the Galway Rally. I think it was 1978 and he bought this Triumph 2.5 pi. And he bought it, I think, two days before the rally and he took it down to Galway and it had no sump guard on it. So he proceeded to take a manhole cover off the road, a square one, and welded it onto the front of the car in the car park. The job was done by a guy called Liam Nevan. There was a bunch of lads did some work for Eddie including Martin McCarthy and a fellah called David Meek, and they looked after his engine at Mondello and so on, but they were down in Galway that weekend. And they proceeded, as I said, to weld the manhole cover to the front of this Triumph. He did the rally. And he sold the car the following Wednesday after the rally.'

Like all Dubliners, Des loves the annual Jordan Christmas party. 'The big Christmas party is in the Berkley Court Hotel and it's so nice because it's not all business people,' he said. 'Yes, there'll be Dermot Desmond there, but there'll be local people you wouldn't see from one year to the other and it's guys like David Meek and Liam Nevan and people he more or less grew up with in those days. But they are super nights. He throws a great party and he always has music at it, too. He has become quite fond of a guy called Finbar Fury who was part of the Fury Brothers and Finbar always plays the whistle. Eddie has invited him back in his house for St Patrick's Day parties in the UK, too. The parties are great and Eddie usually brings a driver over and so on if he can.'

Marren, another Dubliner of a later vintage, but a man who has spent much time close to Eddie, has similarly colourful memories and anecdotes of their times together. He recalled the magazine, edited by Ken Ryan, in which Jordan the journalist enjoyed writing reviews of music in Dublin. 'Ken Ryan used to edit a magazine called *Scene*,' said Marren. 'And one of the columnists was Jordash. It was one Eddie Jordan, who didn't get paid any cash, but who would manage to get all the latest releases and his job was to review them. He reviewed music. Truly. And I tell you what, a couple of years ago, when I was working for Marlboro, I took a whole bunch of Irish journalists with me to one of the Grands Prix and Ken Ryan was there.

'He was in his white cap (a Ryan hallmark) and he said to me "wait till I show you something . . . I've just moved house!" He had gone through some old boxes and he pulled out copies of the magazine. And so we read aloud Eddie's reviews of various albums and various artistes! It was great. And Eddie had a laugh and a half, too, and I think Ken might have even left copies of the magazines with him. I suppose it was all part of his time in Dublin and his great fascination with music. He was so big into it. He had a huge collection. And the thing is, even today, he's still into seeking out and listening to and watching all sorts of obscure bands that nobody's ever heard of, or haven't made it yet. He's completely consumed by it.'

Marren first met Jordan in the late 1970s. 'He was driving, I think, for Derek McMahon and I think he did a Formula Atlantic race at Phoenix Park. They called it the Dublin Grand Prix at the time. I think it was the last tobacco-sponsored race in Ireland because there was a bit of flack with the Department of Health afterwards. But Eddie was bedecked in his Marlboro World Championship Team gear and, you know, some other stuff! I was still at university and in my spare time I used to act as a "stringer" and write about motor racing. It meant that I was able to enjoy my hobby even though I wasn't competing, but I was passionately into motor racing and I was able to claw back some of the costs.

'One of the things about Eddie that I love is that he flies the Irish flag. He is passionately Irish and he loves all things Irish. I suppose, when you grow up in Ireland, anybody who has any success becomes British. But not Eddie. Even now, with the team, the fact is that he has it registered as an Irish team. And, the first time they won a Grand Prix, in Belgium, they didn't have a proper national anthem for Ireland. So, Eddie went away and he got a copy of the anthem that he keeps with him now.'

Marren became more closely involved with Jordan through working for Benson and Hedges. 'Half-way through 1996, Nigel

Northridge told me he thought they were not really getting enough out of it and he asked me to join the team,' he said. 'After a few more conversations, I went down to Weybridge to meet him and his team and I put an idea to them and we decided to carry it through. So, I really got involved full time from the start of 1997. I tell you, one of the more interesting ones was the very first meeting we had at Silverstone, where I was sort of in charge of the sponsorship, and we had all these flashy ideas about putting up a new image.

'You know the kind of thing: but how do you do things that are not quite the norm in Formula One? We were talking about livery. We were doing silly things, like introducing characters and creatures and whatever. That year, we introduced the snake. But Eddie, he was throwing all of his toys out of the car, he was going absolutely mad. He absolutely did not want a snake on the car. I said: "It's not his call. The contract clearly states that the livery is down to us. So, we'll determine it." Eddie was there, on the factory floor, pacing up and down, and Nigel and Barry Jenner, who was his right-hand man. They came in and Eddie said "I don't give a f***. Tell them to stick their f***ing contract up their ****!" I wasn't quite sure if he was joking, but the thing is, he persisted with this thing to the point that I thought "He's serious!" So, I managed to get Nigel and Barry out from the factory floor.

'We were looking at a mocked-up version of what the livery would look like and I guess it was in late January or whatever. I remember Ralf (Schumacher) was around because I think he was doing some sort of seat fitting at the time. It was the start of 1997. The one thing we wanted to do was to change the colours to yellow because gold is such an unworkable colour on television. So, we're on the factory floor, and I think this thing is going horribly wrong. This is my first job. This is my first day, really, as man in the middle between them, and Jordan is going beserk. So, I'm talking to Ian (Phillips). Ian's pleading with Eddie. He's saying: Eddie, this is not the time, nor the place, for this. We've got the sponsors here. You're having a nervous breakdown. But Eddie was adamant. Eventually, I got them out of the way. This was at midday. At six o'clock, I had to say "Nigel, Barry, leave." They were so shocked. They'd never seen behaviour like this before, especially when they were the ones paying the money.

'They were used to getting involved in cricket or golf. It was their event. They were very much in control. All of a sudden, they had this guy who was going ballistic. I stayed there and by then I was feeling a little shell-shocked myself by what was going on. What had I let myself in for? I've known Eddie, this is the funny thing, for a long time. We did all the Formula 3000 time together. I went up to Eddie at nine o'clock and he was in his room and he said: "I've just wrecked the contract." Too f***ing right! I said. How am I going to apologize? You've just wrecked the contract and we had this all day long. That was typical Eddie.

'But also it set the tone for the year because I found myself in this sort of strange position where whilst I was a friend of his, I also had to work the other side of the fence because the people I was representing were Benson and Hedges. And some people thought this was going to compromise my role. In fact, I was lucky enough, maybe because I've got a fiery Irish temperament as well, but I'd end up standing, shouting and roaring at Eddie. I'd give him as much as was giving me. And in the end, there was sort of a mutual respect.'

Marren's arrival with Benson and Hedges brought a new professionalism to Jordan Grand Prix in 1997. 'I think that one of the things was that there was a culture in the team where, in the old days, they would try to do every little deal going. And what we were saying was hang on a minute; we've got to do this properly. You've got a potentially big sponsor here and you've got to respect that. You've got to change your whole attitude. It didn't happen immediately. There was an awful lot of grating, but at the end of the day it happened. He was the consummate professional and he put on a different persona when he had to. And Nigel was never really aware of what was going on in the sparks behind the scenes. But in the end, he turned round, and was man enough to say, you know, I think you were right: we've got to start looking at the bigger picture.

'The way they had been doing these sorts of one-race deals was actually compromising everybody in the end. It was such a short-term thing. They would accuse us of over stepping the mark sometimes. I mean, for example, we would talk about things like "well, Eddie, what are you doing about finding drivers for tomorrow?" Or "Have we got a scholarship programme?" And then there was his famous line: "You stick to selling effing cigarettes and we'll run the race team."'

One of the results of Eddie's blind fit of anger about the cars' livery was that Marren and his men decided to gain revenge. 'We decided that we were going to stitch him up, big time,' he explained. 'And what we did was this: we wanted to go through the livery that we were proposing for the following seasons, so we got Eddie down to our offices in London, and Ian came, and we decided that now, as we've got our British driver (Damon Hill) and a German (Ralf Schumacher), the theme of the next campaign is going to be the Battle of Britain! So we brought out some graphics. We've still got them somewhere and they are hilarious. On Damon's car, we had the RAF circles on the side and his overalls were camouflage-coloured. And, the London Rowing Club oars that Damon has on his helmet were painted in as bombs. Ralf had swastikas painted on his car. So, Eddie's looking at this and he's scribbling away furiously. Ian, for a split second, was horrified. Then, he realised there were a few people smirking and he knew it was something funny. But Eddie was completely focused on the presentation and on what we were doing. We were holding the real presentation back! And Eddie said: "I never doubted, for a second, the creativity within this agency, but I have one or two very serious concerns – one of which is that we've got a Japanese engine supplier and . . .' We had also given Ralf's helmet a World War One spike on top. And Eddie said: "What, in Jesus' name, is that?" Eddie, we said, we have thought about that. We think that could be the radio monitor! It was hilarious. He was completely taken in until we all collapsed with laughter – and it was a great way to get our own back for his behaviour the previous year.'

Like all the Irishmen around Eddie Jordan, in one way or another, David Marren became a close friend. He was part of the team. He became a part of the family, as did so many. One non-Irishman adopted by the Jordan team was Paul Jordan, who shared a surname, but was not a relative. Paul began working for Eddie in the 1980s at Silverstone, fulfilling a wide range of jobs for him. He recalled the episode when Eddie won sponsorship from Camel and how the motor home was resprayed from blue to yellow and back again each year at the sponsor's expense. He also remembered how road cars were purchased each season and sold off again to help tide the team through the winter months. He saw the tough times and the good times, but he never lost his affection or admiration for the man himself despite a series of incidents and escapades in his employment. One one occasion, Eddie asked Paul to represent him at a sale of Rolex watches. 'He wanted me to go to this sale and to buy watches he had identified in a catalogue,' he recalled. 'I had shown him the catalogue and he had put an asterisk by about 50 watches: "I want this", he said, "and this". So, I went and made bids for 50 watches and got them, or most of them, under the reserved price. I thought I had done a decent deal. Then I rang Eddie and told him I had got the watches and he went ballistic! He said I was an idiot and so on and I had to hold the phone away from my head. He had wanted them, but did not want to admit that he wanted to buy them. We had spent £58,000 to buy them, I think!' It is understood that many of the watches remain stored away awaiting a call to duty in the Jordan life.

'When Leyton House collapsed,' Paul recalled, introducing another anecdote, 'we bid for the whole lot: the motor homes, the trucks, the whole lot.' It was another story that led to hilarity as, this time, once the motor homes had been repainted into the colours of new sponsors for their expensive use, the former identity of the motor homes was unwittingly and unintentionally revealed when the awnings were unfolded at the opening race and, instead of declaring 'Barclay' in cream and brown (as expected and promised) they boasted the old Leyton House Racing across them. 'It was a blue awning – the wrong colour, with Leyton House Racing across the top – and all the BAT (British American Tobacco, owners of the Barclay brand) guys went ballistic. When we went to check inside the motor home, where they were with some guests, there were mushrooms growing in the microwave and it was dreadful! But Eddie arrived and he smooth-talked them and he said that they had not paid for the awning! He said it was an extra and if they wanted it they had to pay extra costs. And he got away with it! When you see him on form, at a sponsorship presentation, or something like that, he can do it! I remember, in 1997, we had F Oliver as a sponsorship clothing company and he told this guy that I was his younger brother and he had put me on the case personally to keep it in the family! Every time I went to Germany, I was treated like part of the family!'

Eddie's ingenuity and big heart impressed Paul Jordan as they have done everyone. 'I lost my parents when I was very young,' he said. 'But right from the first day, they (Eddie and Marie) really looked after me and virtually adopted me. He calls me "son" and I'd call him Dad. I've been with him off and on for so many years, working, that his support for me has become a very important part of my life. For me, he is amazing. He is so fantastic. He is so generous and warm. He is always the first person I call if I have a problem and he has always been there for me. I have worked for him so many times. Five times I have left and five times I've gone back. I love the guy dearly. He is a great guy to me.'

His life, under pressure, is still held together by the same foundations of Ireland, people, music and money. 'He's not a day-to-day factory type of person, but he is someone who, when he does come in, can remind everyone of what it was that allowed Jordan to survive and grow from the start,' said Ian Phillips. No, Eddie is certainly no ordinary man – as testified by that madcap signing session in a well-known Dublin bookstore. The shop had ordered four hundred copies of Maurice Hamilton's account of the Jordan team's season in 1998, thinking that would be more than enough. They sold out, and Jordan's fans were seen rushing to rival shops to return with copies for Eddie to sign. That kind of popularity and kinship is the reward for his many qualities. In July 2002, he was awarded an honorary doctorate for services to international sport by the University of Ulster (Duniv). Eddie attended the graduation ceremony held in the Waterfront Hall in Belfast, his degree presented to him by Professor John Wilson. 'The sound education I received in Dublin has stood me in good stead throughout my 35-year career in motor racing,' said Eddie in his acceptance speech. 'And to get the best out of education you need to set very clear targets and goals for yourself. Having worked with some of the sport's top drivers, I have learnt that to succeed with your targets, you need total belief in yourself. With education, clear goals and self-belief, you can achieve your ambitions in life.'

No one can argue that Eddie has not followed that philosophy himself. That is why, in the summer of 2002, he decided to 'put a few things straight' after growing tired of suggestions that because he had implemented some changes in management structure and staffing at Jordan Grand Prix, and because he had talked about the dangers of the downturn in the world economy, he and the team were in trouble. He saw it very differently. 'My job is, and always will be, to provide the financial resources necessary to compete in Formula One, and then to motivate the team, our sponsors and technical partners to achieve what it is I want most – and that is to win the world championship. Some say we'll never achieve it, and perhaps we won't, but as long as there is breath in my body I believe we can do it. I don't believe in failure.'

INDEX